Analogical Thinking

Analogical Thinking

Post-Enlightenment Understanding
in Language, Collaboration,
and Interpretation

Ronald Schleifer

Ann Arbor

THE UNIVERSITY OF MICHIGAN PRESS

J

Copyright © by the University of Michigan 2000
All rights reserved
Published in the United States of America by
The University of Michigan Press
Manufactured in the United States of America
♾ Printed on acid-free paper

2003   2002   2001   4   3   2   1

A CIP catalog record for this book is available from the British Library.

Library of Congress Cataloging-in-Publication Data

Schleifer, Ronald.
    Analogical thinking : post-Enlightenment understanding in language,
    collaboration, and interpretation / Ronald Schleifer.
        p.   cm.
    Includes bibliographical references (p.   ) and index.
    ISBN 0-472-11088-8 (alk. paper)
    1. English literature—20th century—History and criticism—Theory,
    etc.   2. Yeats, W. B. (William Butler), 1865–1939—Criticism and
    interpretation.   3. Dreiser, Theodore, 1871–1945—Criticism and
    interpretation.   4. American literature—20th century—History and
    criticism—Theory, etc.   5. Mailer, Norman—Criticism and
    interpretation.   6. Analogy—History—20th century.   7.
    Authorship—Collaboration.   8. Modernism (Literature).   I. Title.
    PR471 .S335 2000
    302.2—dc21   00-008326

for Nancy

Contents

Preface

As I will suggest in the introduction, *Analogical Thinking* grows out of my recent study of cultural modernism, *Modernism and Time: The Logic of Abundance in Literature, Science, and Culture 1880–1930,* in which I examine changing modes of explanation and representation in the context of the historical and cultural events of the second Industrial Revolution at the turn of the twentieth century. But this book grows out of many other things as well, and it might well be said that *Modernism and Time* is a product of the kinds of analogical thinking I have been exploring in semiotics, literary criticism, and different kinds of collaborative, institutional work I have been lucky enough to participate in for many years. Collaboration is the heart of our intellectual work—in our teaching, our research, and our work together to create institutions of knowledge that condition possibilities of understanding and insight—and, as I mention at the end of this preface, I have been particularly blessed with generous and insightful collaborators.

In chapter 4 I quote David Davidson's assertion that a central "theoretical" problem with interdisciplinary work is that, while "it is one thing for developments in one field to affect changes in a related field, [it is] . . . another thing for knowledge gained in one area to constitute knowledge of another" (1986:247). The contrast between the *affectiveness* of knowledge and the *equivalence* of different forms of knowledge across disciplines is inscribed in the heart of what I am calling analogies, and in the introduction I discuss this at some length. But here for a moment I want to discuss the ways the developments in the parts and chapters of this book "affect" one another so that I might spell out, as clearly as I can, the connections among the formalist, postformalist, and semantic understandings of analogy I pursue in these chapters. In part 1 I examine the science and methodology of semiotics and, in chapter 2, attempt to describe the powerful *formal* analogy between structural semiotics and poststructural deconstruction. The discussion throughout part 1 is *formal*: I take up the formal languages of linguistics and semiotics to present a way of understanding—of "semanticizing" to use a rather awkward neologism—more or less "formal" attempts to describe the

conditions of meaning in structuralist semiotics and to go beyond structuralism in the work of Jacques Derrida. I even considered presenting subtitles for
each of the parts of *Analogical Thinking.* The subtitle for part 1, "Language," could well be "The Work of the Negative in Analogical Meaning."

In part 2 I examine science more generally conceived, in the early
articulation of the sciences of economics and information—sciences of
value—in the eighteenth and twentieth centuries in chapter 3 and in the
laboratory science of chapter 4. The discussion in part 2 is what I call in
chapter 4 "postformalist": I attempt to articulate analogies between historical and disciplinary modes of explanation—between political economy and
information theory in chapter 3 and literary studies and laboratory science
in chapter 4—in order to explore the ways historically conditioned developments in one field might affect changes in a related field. If part 1 focuses on
more or less formal descriptions of analogical thinking, then part 2 focuses
on the collaborative element of "witnessing" contained in understanding
that is implicit in Bruno Latour's examination of the scientific revolution in
the seventeenth century examined in chapter 3 and explicit in my discussion
of literary theory in chapter 4. Such witnessing, I suggest, is part and parcel
of the verbal assertions of analogical thinking that situate themselves, as I
note in the introduction, on the border between language and the world.
The subtitle of part 2, "Collaborations," could well be "The Worldly Work
of Analogical Knowledge."

Part 3, which offers detailed examinations of literary works in relation
to their form, content, and the kinds of semantic collaborations that inhabit
the combination of syntax and semantics in discourse, further extends the
concept of analogical thinking. The discussion throughout part 3 is *interpretive:* each chapter pursues the postsemiotic definition of *interpretation* that
A. J. Greimas and Joseph Courtés had described to make sense of modes of
understanding in the early twentieth century. Moreover, in doing so, the
three interpretive chapters of part 3 retraverse the three modes of analogy
the book as a whole presents: the formal, postformalist, and interpretive
modes of analogical language, collaboration, and interpretation. The subtitle of part 3, "Interpretation," could well be "Between Semiosis and
Event: The Explanations of Analogical Comprehension." As this suggests,
the three parts of *Analogical Thinking* focus on analogical meaning, analogical knowledge, and analogical comprehensions.

The counterpoint to the presentation of modes of analogical thinking I
set forth here—a kind of drumbeat sounding almost everywhere in these
chapters or, to use an analogy I suggest in *Rhetoric and Death,* a kind of
overtone that makes the oboe sound so rich—is the opposition and analogy

between what I call Enlightenment and post-Enlightenment modes of apprehension. I take up these terms explicitly in the introduction, and I return to
them throughout the book in the repeated analogies I assert between criteria
for truth and understanding that found early, often hesitating, articulation in
the eighteenth century and those developed in our century. The analogy
between Enlightenment and post-Enlightenment modes of apprehension is
most explicitly pursued in the book's postscript, the examination of René
Descartes and Michel Foucault. In many ways Descartes's combination of
the individualism of a salvationist religiosity and his vision of a mechanical
universe can stand as a prototype of the combination of subjective idealism
and general semiotics I discuss in chapter 3, which I use, somewhat crypti-
cally perhaps, to define the outlines of the Enlightenment ethos.

Some friends and collaborators—notably Robert Markley and Daniel
Cottom—have suggested that the description of the Enlightenment and,
implicitly, Enlightenment reason I sometimes present in the following chapters is almost a skeletal straw man. And surely the rich historical accounts
of the turmoil of the seventeenth century in scholars like Stephen Toulmin
and Stephen Gaukroger (whom I quote in the postscript)—or the powerful
analogy I don't quite suggest between the culture of the Thirty Years' War
in the seventeenth century and that of our own thirty years' war in the first
half of the twentieth century—as well as Dan's and Bob's own work on the
science and culture of the seventeenth, eighteenth, and nineteenth centuries
might well make my Enlightenment seem somewhat rictus-like. But the
criteria for judging and measuring truth in the sciences that grew out of the
turmoil, contests, and confusions of the seventeenth and eighteenth centuries, which I occasionally claim embody a kind of "modern" secularism—
namely, the accuracy, generalizability, and simplicity I mention throughout
these chapters—do, I think, offer a powerful example of a mode of understanding and explanation based upon equivalences to the exclusion of
analogies, even if, as Markley argues, we shouldn't mistake the simplicity of
this retrospective and interested formulation for the confluence of politics,
theology, and simple confusion that conditioned what has come to be described as Enlightenment science (Markley 1990, 1993); and even if, as
Cottom argues, reason itself can be understood as "a rhetorical device, a
personification, used to give a seeming unity to all sorts of cultural objects,
forms, and practices that are ultimately incommensurable and irreducible to
a common spirit" (1991:15–16). The "Enlightenment" criteria I educe,
even if they have been retrospectively read into the Enlightenment, can
fruitfully be taken up to describe what I call a post-Enlightenment ethos, if
only in the manner of Freud's "deferred action" (*Nachtraglichkeit*), by

means of which, Freud argues, we are able to create the illusion of egoistic continuity and of the unity Cottom mentions (Freud 1963:232). Such a post-Enlightenment ethos, measuring itself against a "deferred" Enlightenment, among other things (as I argue in the postscript) supplements modes of apprehension associated with Descartes by adding similarity to equivalence in mathematical formalism, community and collaborators to the Cartesian individual, and the temporality and feedback of information conceived as interpretation to Cartesian mechanics.

The figure for these supplementations is, of course, analogy, which, I argue, does not quite erase the manner in which its insights are *witnessed* insofar as the verbal nature of its articulations is never quite effaced; and neither does it quite erase the fact that the connections it asserts between the formalities of language and the meanings of the world—its syntax and semantics—are never established once and for all but are repeated in time, feedback, and renewals of both knowledge and comprehension. Such renewals articulate themselves in interpretations, which find expression in the semantic formalism, the postformalist collaborations, and the self-conscious paraphrases of analogy. It is my hope that the chapters that follow—not only in their progression but also in the analogies that form and re-form among them—might give rise to a sense of analogical thinking, which I believe is at work in the much of the exciting intellectual work of our time.

Acknowledgments

As I mentioned, I have greatly benefited from the collaborations of friends, colleagues, and sometimes strangers. First of all I would like to thank Daniel Cottom, Robert Con Davis, and Robert Markley, all of whom read through the penultimate version of this book. Similarly, I thank the anonymous readers for the University of Michigan Press. The thoughtful and generous advice of these friends and strangers has made this book better than it might have been, though not, I'm sorry to say, as good as they wished and even, in their generous readings, as good as they apprehended. Still, many of the virtues of this final version of *Analogical Thinking* stem from their thoughtful responses. In addition, working with LeAnn Fields of the University of Michigan Press, who has been a friend for years, has deepened my sense of how well she serves our intellectual lives.

Others have read even earlier versions of this book with thoughtful and generous responses. Eve Bannet read through the introduction with great encouragement and insight; members of the Bible and Culture Collective generously responded to an early version of chapter 6; and the members of an interdisciplinary graduate seminar in scholarly writing from the English Department and the Department of History of Science at the University of Oklahoma—Professor Peter Barker, Gary Kroll, Maureen McCormick, Barbara Robbins, Gabriel Rupp, and Samantha Ward—all read the post-script with great care and insight. I owe a particular debts of gratitude to Nancy West, who helped me to understand Isak Dinesen; Hunter Cadzow, who helped me understand Foucault; and Ken Knoespel, who helped me understand Descartes. Mitchell Lewis compiled the index with great care.

Many of these chapters had their first tentative exposure to the community of scholars as papers and talks at various venues, where both friends and strangers helped clarify my thinking and expositions. I thank the faculties and staffs at the University of Hawaii at Manoa, the National Library of New Zealand in Wellington, colleagues at the annual convention of the Modern Language Association, friends at the Kansas State University Cultural Studies Conference and at the University of Kansas, and the organizers and participants of the Foucault and Culture Conference sponsored by the Humanities Center, at the University of Aberdeen, Scotland—especially George Rousseau and Hugh Crawford.

Parts and versions of several of these chapters have appeared elsewhere. A version of chapter 1 appeared in *Literary Criticism and Theory: The Greeks to the Present*, edited by Robert Con Davis and Laurie Finke (New York: Longman, 1989). Chapter 2 first appeared in different form in *College English* 49 (1987). Copyright © 1987 by the National Council of Teachers of English. Reprinted with permission. A version of chapter 4 appeared in *College English* 59 (April 1997). Copyright © 1997 by the National Council of Teachers of English. Reprinted with permission. Chapter 5 is a revision of "Yeats's Postmodern Rhetoric," which appeared in *Yeats and Postmodernism*, edited by Leonard Orr (Syracuse: Syracuse University Press, 1991), 16–34; chapter 6 is a revision of "Writhing Nets and Goodly Pearls: *The Postmodern Bible*, Collaboration, and Storytelling," *Centennial Review* 40 (1996): 385–99; and chapter 7 is a revision of "American Violence: Dreiser, Mailer, and the Nature of Intertextuality," which appeared in *Intertextuality and Contemporary American Fiction*, edited by Patrick O'Donnell and Robert Con Davis (Baltimore: Johns Hopkins University Press, 1989), 121–42. Copyright © 1989 by The Johns Hopkins University Press. I thank all the editors and publishers for their help on the original versions of these chapters and for their kind permission to reprint parts of them in this book.

The dedication of this book is to my wife, Nancy Mergler, with whom I launched myself into interdisciplinarity and collaboration in articles and a book we wrote together and many other things. Her patience and care has made completing this book configure itself neatly in activities in which the distinctions between work and leisure, contentment and concern, and understanding and comfort fade in the light of quotidian affection.

Introduction: Analogical Thinking

The basic argument of *Analogical Thinking* is that some time around the turn of the twentieth century a new mode of comprehension arose supplementing received Enlightenment ideas concerning the nature of understanding and explanation. Those ideas revolved around Descartes's conception of "clear and distinct ideas" and the larger assumption, central to Enlightenment science from Newton to Einstein, that the criteria for scientific explanation entailed three global concerns: accuracy, simplicity, and generalizability. These intellectual matters were and are closely tied to the politics of the Enlightenment, which entailed a curious combination of liberation, based upon remarkable notions—above all, *secular* notions—of individualism and equality; and domination, based, at best, upon an unreflective sense of the self-evidence of both Enlightenment truth and the criteria of Enlightenment truth and, at worst, upon ruthless power disguised as disinterested reason. Bruno Latour, in his powerful analysis of Enlightenment modernity, describes this as the great achievement of Enlightenment modernism, the "double task of domination and emancipation" (1993:10).

Both the intellectual and political assumptions governing Enlightenment values are founded upon modes of representation that take reduction and hierarchy to be the "methods" of science and wisdom. The great achievements of Enlightenment science can be seen in the representations of phenomena in terms of mathematical formalism: the reduction of experience to repeatable formula. This, after all, was Descartes's achievement in philosophy and Newton's achievement in natural philosophy at the beginning of Enlightenment modernity. Reduction—in mathematical formalism, in representative government, and in perspectival art—is governed by hierarchies of synecdoche, in which parts are taken to stand for the whole or, less usually, wholes are taken to stand for parts. Synecdoche isolates the "essence" of phenomena: in language it is the meaning of a sentence that is more than the sum of its parts; in science it is laws governing phenomena that transcend those phenomena themselves; in society it is the general will; in aesthetics it is the "aura" of a work of art. This is why Roman Jakobson asserts as he does that the nature of language is above all "synecdochic" (1987:459) and Paul de Man argues that in the synecdochic symbolism of Romanticism "the material substantiality dissolves and becomes a mere reflection of a more original unity that does not exists in the material world" (1969:177). The reductive hierarchies of Enlightenment science, politics, and art nicely parallel—they *analogically* parallel—the emancipation and domination of the Enlightenment altogether.

At the turn of the twentieth century the mode of explanation and understanding by means of reduction within hierarchies of principle and example or form and content came into question across the arts and sciences in Western culture. Descartes's clear and simple ideas and Leibniz's "necessary and sufficient truth" were confronted with modes of explanation such as the "overdeterminations" of psychological life Freud described and Picasso depicted, the "retrospective" analyses of quantum physics Niels Bohr and Werner Heisenberg articulated, the "constellations" of understanding that Walter Benjamin and Ludwig Wittgenstein discuss, and the very crisis of laissez-faire liberalism in Western societies. Recently, in *Modernism and Time: The Logic of Abundance in Literature, Science, and Culture, 1880–1930* I examined these modes of representation in relation to the explosion of consumer goods, intellectual ideas, and human populations at this moment of historical development in early-twentieth-century Western culture, what I describe as "post-Enlightenment" culture. In *Analogical Thinking* I examine these modes of representation in relation to the development of linguistics, structuralism, and semiotics in the early twentieth century.

Analogies of Meaning, Collaboration, and Interpretation

I am calling this new mode of explanation "analogical thinking"—I use a similar term in *Modernism and Time*—which supplemented without replacing the reductive hierarchies of Enlightenment explanation. In such analogical comprehension one item doesn't replace another in the sense of articulating its truth or its hidden meaning in the way, for instance, that a falling body is an instance of a universal law or that the seeming intentional actions of individuals are "really" instances of large social forces. Rather, in analogical thinking different articulations follow one another in metonymic series rather than synecdochical hierarchies—to use figures from rhetoric and discourse. This is what Benjamin means by "constellations": "ideas," he writes, "are to objects as constellations are to stars. This means, in the first place, that they are neither their concepts nor their laws. They do not contribute to the knowledge of phenomena, and in no way can the latter be criteria with which to judge the existence of ideas" (1977:34). Ideas for Benjamin—articulated in the analogical figure of constellations—are not a hierarchically superior principle under which particular phenomena can be placed as instances. Instead, ideas are "arrested" or apprehended configurations, to use a figure that Claude Lévi-Strauss uses (1984:167), grasped at a particular moment that, momentarily, gather together a meaning.

Such meanings are "momentary" precisely because they do not stand once and for all as the universalist truths of Enlightenment reduction stand, once and for all, for the phenomena they comprehend. Instead, they emerge and disappear, and the time of their validity, as I argue in *Modernism and Time,* is governed by the analogous existence of different temporal moments rather than the interchangeability of temporal moments, the self-consistent homogeneity of Newtonian conceptions of time based upon the universal equation of moment to moment. In important ways equation is the reductive opposite of analogy: it stresses, as Eve Tabor Bannet has argued, "resemblance over difference to make different entities more or less alike [by transforming] analogy into an equivalence" (1997:658). At the turn of the twentieth century Bertrand Russell pointed out the limited nature of equation in mathematics and philosophy: "the word 'equal,' " he wrote, "has many meanings, but if it is taken to mean what we have called 'similar,' there is no contradiction [in the mathematical infinitive, in which 'the part should be equal to the whole'], since an infinite collection can perfectly well have parts similar to itself. Those who regard this as impossible have, unconsciously as a rule, attributed to numbers in general properties which can only be proved by mathematical induction, and which only their familiarity makes us regard, mistakenly, as true beyond the region of the finite" (1993:80–81; see also Burrell 1973:10, for the relation of analogy to equation). Russell's example of the reductive conception of "equal" is the work of Leibniz (1993:80), in which induction—the "accuracy" and "simplicity" of Enlightenment science—takes an implicit precedence over "generalizability."

Generalizability, as Bannet suggests, is the realm of analogy precisely in the ways that analogical thinking participates in but is not finally reducible to the abstract formalisms of induction—precisely, that is, to the point that its generalization encompasses similarity *and* difference (rather than general identities). The generalizations of analogy are different from the general identities of the sciences precisely in that they do not create hierarchical equations, once and for all (see the discussions of general terms, universals, and paradigmatic sets in Burrell 1973; Anderson 1967; and Ross 1981); they are different because analogy never quite "forgets" its linguistic nature. "For Wittgenstein, and indeed for traditional rhetoricians," Bannet writes, "an analogy is not an identity; it is a figure which marks both the likeness and the difference in our application of words from case to case. The gaps, the discontinuities, and the differences are as important as the likeness because, Wittgenstein insists, we are always moving meaning from one situation to another which might not be quite the same" (1997:656). Meaning—which inhabits semiotics, collaboration, and (among other things) the interpretations of literary criticism examined in this book—cannot be reduced to the formal invariants of classical equation; as Charles Taylor argues in a passage I quote in chapter 4, meaning is not fully subject to the explanations of nomological science. Theodor Adorno calls this lack of a central—a basic or invariant—kernel of thought the "athematic" element in Benjamin's work and presents it, as Benjamin does his configuration of ideas, by means of an analogy. Thus, Adorno writes that "just as in its most uncompromising representatives modern music [i.e., the music of the early twentieth century] no longer tolerates any elaboration, any distinction between theme and development, but instead every musical idea, even every note, stands equally near the center, so too Benjamin's philosophy is 'athematic.' " (1992:229). By *athematic,* then, Adorno means nonhierarchic, nonsynecdochical: the juxtaposition or superimposition of analogical figures.

Linguistics and semiotics, as they developed in the early twentieth century—which I examine in the first section of this book—pursue such constellations of meaning in a mode of analogical thinking. They do so—as I do in this book—because, as I have suggested, *analogy* as a figure of speech has a special relationship in articulating the relationship between the self-conscious use or functioning of language and experience. "Analogical expressions," David Burrell has written,

> come into play precisely at those points where one wishes to speak of language itself or of the relation between language and the world, and yet realizes that one must have recourse to a language. At these points we need expressions that function within our language but whose serviceability is not restricted to their role within the language. They must function within the language so that we can get our bearings in using them; but they cannot be restricted to that intrasystematic function if we want to be able to use them in speaking of what we can do with the language as a whole. (1973:224)

Analogy stands between language (conceived as systematic semiotics) and the world (conceived in terms of more or less collaborative action). Analogy, as I will argue in a moment, traffics in constellations of wholeness.

Thus, it allows, as Burrell says, the self-conscious apprehension of language as a whole in relation to its work in the world—among other things, the work of collaboration and interpretations that I examine in the last two sections of this book. It is for this reason, I suspect, that analogy was such a forceful mode of relating understanding to the world and experience in pre-Enlightenment theology (see McInerny 1996; and Anderson 1967). Analogy, Burrell suggests, as *ana-logic,* has an affinity with logic: "the very word analogy suggests a 'super-logic' " (1973:243; see also Miller 1991:142, 144), which works beyond the self-contained "intrasystematic" functionings of both language (semantics) and logic (formalism) to include the future-oriented aims and purposes of the speaker as a *worldly* creature; its mode of functioning, as I describe it here and in *Modernism and Time,* is precisely its ability to create *semantic formalism.* Analogy, as I have said, pursues constellations of meaning that work purposefully in the world in an "unprovincial, interested manner" (1994:151), to allude to a passage from Edward Said I examine in chapter 3.[1]

One such pursuit is Ferdinand de Saussure's "synchronic," rather than historical, mode of analysis, which attempts to understand and comprehend language and meaning in terms of structural synchronic configurations. Within this analysis the conception of "levels" of analysis is of utmost importance. The concept of levels both embodies and transforms the hierarchic nature of comprehension. Levels embody hierarchy in its strict order; but they also transform hierarchy by making reduction and instantiation a problem: as in Russell's mathematics, "equality" expands to include similarity as opposed to strict identity. As A. J. Greimas notes in *Structural Semantics* (which is among the most rigorous and *systematic* expressions of linguistic structuralism), the "edifice" of language "appears like a construction without plan or clear aim" (1983:133). This is because "discourse, conceived as a hierarchy of units of communication fitting into one another, contains in itself the negation of that hierarchy by the fact that the units of communication with different dimensions can be at the same time recognized as equivalent" (1983:82). Words, for instance, are

---

1. What I have characterized as the function and aims of analogy are nicely gathered together in Stanley Tambiah's description of "standard dictionary glosses" of *analogy,* which "include the following features: a similarity of rates or proportions; resemblance in particulars between things otherwise unlike; agreement or resemblance in certain aspects as in form or function; similarity without identity" (1996:49). These glosses leave out the powerful aspect of analogy as a linguistic phenomenon, its activity of *naming* in its "application of words from case to case" (Bannet 1997:656): the self-conscious semantics of analogical thinking.

hierarchically subordinate to sentences; yet in language—because, of what Saussure calls the arbitrary nature of the sign (see chap. 2)—in always-possible cases, a sentence can be equal to a word (in an utterance like: " 'I like apples' is my favorite sentence"). What creates these possibilities are *purposes* (and "purport") of its users that exist on a level of abstraction that remains semantic even if it allows different (i.e., similar but not equal) *fields* of significance to confront and play against one another. In this way the semantic formalism of analogical thinking disrupts atemporal formalism with the timeliness of meaning (see Schleifer 2000: chap. 4).

Just as semiotics developed and elaborated modes of analogical thinking in relation to the generalizations of meaning, so the Enlightenment subjects of knowledge, conceived above all as the *individual* subject in Cartesian understandings equal to all other subjects in the secular liberalism of Enlightenment politics, was elaborated in the "socialization" of knowledge with the development of research universities at the end of the nineteenth century. Such reconfigurations of subjectivity—which I examine in the second section of this book—take the form of analogical descriptions of information theory and the possibility of analogies between the sharply contrasting sciences and humanities as they developed in the nineteenth century. Above all, these analogical descriptions are attested to and "witnessed" in a manner in which networking and collaboration articulate and authorize knowledge in contexts of its institutionalization within the classroom, scholarly disciplines, and research institutions.

Finally, the interpretations of literary criticism—the repeated re-thematization of literary works—are modes of analogical thinking insofar as they add (or "superimpose," to use a figure of Latour's repeatedly encountered in these chapters) other readings, new contexts, and transformed configurations onto texts. In the last section of this book I offer three such interpretations, corresponding to the semiotics, collaboration, and criticism of the book's larger structure: an examination of Yeats's high Modernist poetry comprehended in relation to the particular purposes governing the rhetoric and syntactics of his discourse that suggests a "postmodern" rhetoric analogous to the rhetoric of modernism; a reading of the Bible—a critical study entitled *The Postmodern Bible*—and a short story of Isak Dinesen comprehended in relation to intellectual collaboration; and an intertextual reading of Theodore Dreiser's novel *An American Tragedy* and Norman Mailer's *Executioner's Song* comprehended in relation to semiotic and social readings—corporate apprehensions—of narrative. The conception of intertextuality in the final chapter—like "the notion of *analogy* [which] stands as a kind of mean between simple conceptual identity and sheer notional heterogeneity" (Anderson 1967:2)—gathers together the linguistic and social concerns of the preceding chapters and the book as a whole.

Semiotics, collaborative disciplinarity, and the analogical thinking of literary criticism all emerge or reemerge in the early twentieth century—even the Bible, in its postmodern reading, is a book of our time—and together they suggest what this book as a whole attempts to suggest, that the analogical thinking it presents and demonstrates is a kind of comprehension, added to received conceptions of understanding and explanation, particular to our time. (In *Modernism and Time* I elaborate a historical argument, tied to the emergence of widespread abundances of the second Industrial Revolution of the turn of the twentieth century, that can be constellated and comprehended in relation to the kinds of analogical thinking presented here.) In fact, analogical thinking itself can be apprehended as analogous to modes of comprehension that preceded Enlightenment positivism, individualism, and aestheticism. The alternating levels, the plural subjects, and the purposeful, interested wholes of analogical thinking mark, in important ways, our post-Enlightenment culture.

Analogical Knowledge

During the past decade a great deal has been written about the phenomenon of twentieth-century modernism in Western culture. In *Modernism and Time* I argue that a constellation of events in the period between 1880 and 1930 helped to condition what Stephen Kern describes in his social history of this period, *The Culture of Time and Space: 1880–1920,* as major changes in the very "foundations of experience" in Western culture. These events transformed daily life for most people in the very "feel," or experience, of life itself. Such changes can be seen in the effects of the telephone or incandescent lighting, in revolutions in science and mathematics, and in the progressive abstraction of the visual and plastic arts. In broader terms they included the democratization of Europe, the transformation to large-scale economic production, huge increases in urban populations, reconfigurations of nation-states and the relations among classes, and enormous changes in literacy, education, and in the relations between men and women.

Part of the constellation of phenomena of modernism is the transformation—or really the supplementation—of modes of explanation. I call modernism a "constellation of phenomena" precisely because the explanatory mode of cause and effect—closely tied to the hierarchical paradigm in which an essence or invariant can be isolated from epiphenomena or variants of experience—came to be a problem and a site of crisis in the era of twentieth-century modernism. That crisis was conditioned, in large part, by the historical moment when the laws of necessary and sufficient truth, based upon parsimony, confronted the enormous explosion of goods, ideas, and peoples of the second Industrial Revolution—the transformation of industrial capital to finance capital—in the late nineteenth century. The institution of *structural* linguistics initiated by Ferdinand de Saussure in this period can stand as a defining instance of a new mode for articulating understanding and experience, and in part I of this book I closely examine Saussurean linguistics. In the *Course in General Linguistics* Saussure suggested that the historical (or "diachronic") study of language be replaced by a structural (or "synchronic") study, in which the relation between the parts and the whole, rather than cause and effect, is the object of intellectual inquiry. Such a mode of explanation, I believe, is part of the rise of phenomenology in philosophy and psychology at the end of the nineteenth century, and this development itself takes its place in the constellation (rather than hierarchic structure) of modernism.

A. J. Greimas and Joseph Courtés describe this phenomenon when they discuss a new form of "interpretation" that seemed to arise at the turn of the twentieth century. In *Semiotics and Language: An Analytical Dictionary* they associate this form of interpretation with Husserlian phenomenology, Saussurean linguistics, and Freudian psychoanalysis. In a mode of explanation shared by these movements, they argue, "interpretation is no longer a matter of attributing a given content to a form which would otherwise lack one; rather, it is a paraphrase which formulates in another fashion the equivalent content of a signifying element within a given semiotic system" (1982:159). In this "new" mode of interpretation form and content are not distinct. Instead, every "form" is, alternatively, a semantic "content" as well so that the criteria that govern judgments of precise, or "scientific," knowledge—simplicity, accuracy, and generalizability—seem mixed and confused. In this mode, interpretation offers an analogy or paraphrase of something that already has a meaning within another system of understanding. Instead of creating an interpretation by filling in an abstract form with a concrete content—instead of using *examples* of a particular content to instantiate abstract forms and make them "real"—this mode of interpretation offers *analogies* in which model and example are interchangeable.

Relativity and quantum physics participate in this wide-ranging shift that I am calling intellectual modernism. Perhaps the clearest example is the complementarity of the Copenhagen interpretation of quantum theory, but even Einstein's relativity theory, as Lewis Feuer (1974) and Bruno Latour (1988) have suggested, is Modernist in this way, as is Planck's lifelong attempt to reconcile quantum mechanics and traditional science. In *Physics and Philosophy* Werner Heisenberg presents a version of this analogical thinking by describing Bohr's contention that wave and particle descriptions of subatomic entities "complement" one another. The "two pictures," Heisenberg writes, "are of course mutually exclusive, because a certain thing cannot at the same time be a particle (i.e., substance confined to a very small volume) and a wave (i.e., a field spread out over a large space), but the two complement each other" (1958:49). The conception of complementarity, Heisenberg notes, encourages physicists "to apply alternatively different classical concepts which would lead to contradictions if used simultaneously" (1958:179). A chief feature of analogical thinking is its presentation of alternatives: it is the *temporal* element of its explanations and assertions, which do not posit themselves, as Enlightenment universals do, once and for all.

Closely related to this is a second feature of analogical thinking: its plurality and redundancy. Analogies do not satisfy themselves with single instances. For example, when Benjamin attempts to articulate his understanding of "ideas," he does not satisfy himself with the single analogy of astral constellations. He goes on to liken ideas to mothers within a family. Thus, he writes that "just as a mother is seen to begin to live in the fullness of her power only when the circle of her children, inspired by the feeling of her proximity, closes around her, so do ideas come to life only when extremes are assembled around them. Ideas . . . remain obscure so long as phenomena do not declare their faith to them and gather round them" (1977:34–35). Analogizing his apprehension of ideas, Benjamin needs more than one way of saying it. Here he uses figures that are both natural and cultural—stellar constellations and family constellations—just as Niels Bohr analogizes physical entities and biological life in describing complementarity. Burrell describes this feature of analogy as its "propensity of employment in diverse contexts in spite of the acknowledged differences in meaning" (1973:23).

A third feature of analogical thinking is its repeated, if momentary, apprehension of wholes. In *Atomic Physics and Human Knowledge* Bohr argues that "the features of wholeness" are central characteristics of his concept of complementarity (1958:2). In an analogy he repeats throughout that book he compares physics and biology to articulate his concept. "On the one hand," he writes,

the question of a limitation of physics in biology would lose any meaning if, instead of distinguishing between living organisms and inanimate bodies, we extended the idea of life to all natural phenomena. On the other hand, if, in accordance with common language, we were to reserve the word mechanics for the unambiguous causal description of natural phenomena, such a term as atomic mechanics would become meaningless. I shall not enter further into such purely terminological points but only add that the essence of the analogy being considered is the obvious exclusiveness between such typical aspects of life as the self-preservation and self-generation of individuals, on the one hand, and the subdivision necessary for any physical analysis on the other hand. Owing to this essential feature of complementarity, the concept of purpose, which is foreign to mechanical analysis, finds a certain field of application in biology. Indeed, in this sense, teleological argumentation may be regarded as a legitimate feature of physiological description which takes due regard to the characteristics of life in a way analogous to the recognition of the quantum of action in the correspondence argument of atomic physics. (1958:10)

In this passage Bohr is describing the self-contained wholeness of the elements of analogy in the "obvious exclusiveness" of those elements even while he points out their similarities. Moreover, the focus of the analogy between physics and biology, "purpose," is not altogether arbitrary. Rather, it comes to be central in Bohr's extended discussion. In a neat, if unconscious, analogy to Bohr's discussion of purpose, Louis Hjelmslev redefines meaning as "purport" in his logical systematicization of Saussurean linguistics (1961:50–55). Similarly, Keith Holyoak and Paul Thagard identify *purpose* as one of "the three basic kinds of constraints on analogical thinking": "analogy," they write, "is guided by the person's goals in using it, which provide the *purpose* for considering the analogy at all" (1995:5, 6; see also 34–37). (The other constraints they name are "structure" and "similarity," which are analogous to the linguistics and solidarity I examine in relation to semiotics and collaboration.) In both Hjelmslev's linguistics and in the examination of "creative thought" Holyoak and Thagard pursue, *purpose* suggests temporally conditioned wholes. Purpose contains a temporal element, a future orientation that is the opposite of the orientation toward origins of cause and effect. At the same time, however, the concept of purpose, as Bohr suggests, requires that phenomena be apprehended (or "arrested") as a whole rather than in parts. To use the words of Jakobson I quote in chapter 1, it conceives of phenomena not as a "mechanical agglomeration but as a structural whole" (1971:711).

The analogy between physics and biology that Bohr presents exemplifies the definition of interpretation that Greimas and Courtés articulate. Such analogical thinking can also be seen in Lévi-Strauss's analysis of the

opposition between structure and form, in Freud's concept of overdetermination, in Husserl's concept of intention, in T. S. Eliot's definition of the
"mythical method" in Joyce's writing, in Dewey's development of pragmatism, and in Russell's definition of equation as similarity beyond the region
of the finite. It even encompasses what Paul Klee described as modernism's
general quest to discover "the essential nature of the accidental."

Bringing together essence and accident characterizes the juxtapositions
of different scientific paradigms that Thomas Kuhn has examined. "Proponents of different theories," he argues, "are . . . like native speakers of different languages. Communication between them goes on by translation, and it
raises all translation's familiar difficulties." Moreover, even this analogy, he
says, is incomplete, because theories may use the same words with different
meanings. "Some words," he writes, "in the basic as well as in the theoretical
vocabularies of the two theories—words like 'star' and 'planet,' 'mixture'
and 'compound,' or 'force' and 'matter'—do function differently. These differences are unexpected and will be discovered and localized, if at all, only by
repeated experience of communication breakdown" (1977:338). Such break-
downs bring together accident and essence: as Freud suggests—but I could
add Eliot, Heisenberg, Picasso, Saussure, Schoenberg, Wittgenstein, Woolf,
and a host of others writing in the early twentieth century—"communication
breakdown" is not simply accidental but the very motor of psychoanalytic
understanding and analogical knowledge. It is marked in the breakdown of
the wholenesses of language, in incomprehensions of purport, in the lack of
connection between things—all of which are answered by the similarities
and differences of analogy. Analogy accomplishes what I describe later in this
chapter as the "work" of the negative.

Perhaps Paul Ricoeur gives the best definition of such analogical thinking in *Time and Narrative,* in which he describes it in terms of the ways that
narrative discourse encompasses Bohr's "features of wholeness" in story and
language. In that study Ricoeur analyzes the mimetic and cognitive functioning of narrative in terms of the "ideas of the Same, the Other, and the
Analogous" (1988:143). These ideas, in important ways, can be delineated
within the semiotic square Greimas developed within structural linguistics.
With the semiotic square Greimas attempted to discover the logics of binary
opposition that govern meaning by systematically organizing contrary and
contradictory oppositions in relation to apprehended meaning. By bringing
together the semiotic square and Ricoeur's description of narrative, one can
perceive the square as a kind of "narrative sketch" (see Schleifer, Con Davis,
and Mergler 1992:10–11, for an elaboration of this relationship). Take, for
example, a Greimassian semiotic analysis of the semantics of "old."

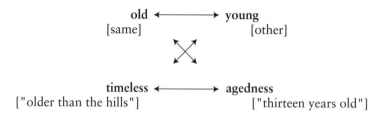

old ⟷ young
[same]   [other]

timeless ⟷ agedness
["older than the hills"]   ["thirteen years old"]

In a "narrative" analysis of the square the first corner begins with a semantic value /old/ that is seemingly simple and "self-same." Then, it suggests its contrary, or "other," /young/, to inhabit the second position on the square. The third position, the contradictory, on another "level" of the square, posits a broader category of /agedness/ of which /old/ and /young/ became "parts"—in this way species of the "same." Finally, the contrary to /agedness/, /ageless/, designates the fourth corner of the square. The concept /ageless/ is "analogous" to /old/—we say "older than the hills"—positing a similarity that is, finally, only an act of judgment, an analogy insofar as it presents a different way of articulating and judging experience. In this particular instance the fourth corner describes a mode of judgment by means of timeless, transcendent categories instead of temporally bound apprehension, but it describes such transcendental terms in the analogical vocabulary of temporality ("older than the hills"). The iteration of the same word in different contexts—in this case *old*—underlines Bannet's assertion that in Wittgenstein's understanding "we are always moving meaning from one situation to another which might not be quite the same" (1997:656); it underlines the timely transferences of analogical semantics. Most important, this "analogical" expression is more *abstract* than the initial term and offers in its abstraction what I describe in chapter 2 in this book—but also in *Modernism and Time*—as "semantic formalism."[2]

2. In *Modernism and Time* I discuss such abstraction in the context of Mikhail Bakhtin's conception of "answerability." "Answerability," I observe, "is a translation of the Russian word *otvetstvennost'* which, as Gary Saul Morson and Caryl Emerson note, can be rendered as *responsibility* or as *answerability*. By Bakhtin's work of the mid-1920s, they argue, 'a case could be made for either translation, ethical responsibility or addressive answerability (that is, the presence of response). There is an ethical component in answerability as well, of course, but it is more abstract and less tied to a specific act. One's obligation in answerability is to rescue the other from pure potential; reaching out to another consciousness makes the other coalesce, and turns the other's "mere potential" into space that is open to the living event' " (2000:21; the citation in Morson and Emerson 1990:76). It is precisely analogy's ability to be "more abstract" and "less tied" to the specific meaning of a self-identical verbal expression that allows it to combine formalism and semantics. In chapter 4 of *Modernism and Time* I

In this, as Greimas and Courtés say, we are presented with "a paraphrase which formulates in another fashion the equivalent content of a signifying element within a given semiotic system." We have, in other words, an analogy that uses a system of meaning to a purpose different from that which it was designed for and, in so doing, emphasizes the purposefulness of language and understanding. In Bohr's terms complementarity discovers analogies between parts and wholes, what he describes in his essay "Light and Life" as "the subdivision necessary for any physical analysis" (parts) and self-preserved and self-generated individuals (wholes). Narrative, Ricoeur argues, accomplishes analogical thinking—he calls it the "synthesis of the heterogeneous" (1984:ix)—by organizing a series of events "into an intelligible whole, of a sort such that we can always ask what is the 'thought' of this story" (1984:65). Latour describes this operation as the "superimpositions" of different modes of analysis, the "networking" of understanding (1986, 1988, 1987). For Ricoeur narrative seeks neither the simplicity of the same nor the multiplications of otherness, neither identity nor heterogeneity. Instead, narrative configures disparate elements by means of "the Analogous, which is," he says, "a resemblance between relations rather than between terms per se" (1988:151). (See also Leatherdale 1974:2, who quotes W. S. Jevons defining *analogy* as the "resemblance not between things, but between the relations of things.") The larger analogy discernible in the semiotic square is that between its "levels," which describe resemblance between relations rather than terms.

In describing narrative, Ricoeur examines all three of these modes of understanding, what he calls "theoretical," "categoreal," and "configurational" modes of comprehension. "According to the theoretical mode," he writes,

> objects are comprehended in terms of a case or as examples of a general theory. The ideal type of this mode is represented by Laplace's system. According to the categoreal mode, often confused with the preceding one, to comprehend an object is to determine what type of object we are dealing with, what system of a priori concepts organizes an experience that otherwise would remain chaotic. Plato aims at this categoreal comprehension, as do most systematic philosophers. The configurational mode puts its elements into a single, concrete complex of relations. It is

---

examine "semantic formalism" in relation to the "abstract formalism" of Russell's mathematics; in chapter 2 of the present book I examine it in relation to linguistic neutralization and philosophical deconstruction.

the type of comprehension that characterizes the narrative operation. All three modes do have a common aim, ... the act "of grasping together in a single mental act things which are not experienced together, or even capable of being so experienced, because they are separated by time, space, or logical kind." (1984:159; Ricoeur, citing Mink 1970:547)

For Ricoeur narrative configurations—the apprehension of temporal wholes and elemental events from serial and disparate phenomena or data—accomplish the complementarity of analogy Bohr and Heisenberg describe in quantum mechanics, Schoenberg enacts in serial music, France established when it abandoned the gold standard after World War I, and Woolf narrates in *Mrs. Dalloway.* Such analogical knowledge, like narrative itself, does not reduce difference to the same, nor does it satisfy itself with the contingency and accident of arbitrary likenesses. Like narrative in Ricoeur's description, it "unifies into one whole and complete action the miscellany" of "circumstances, ends and means, initiatives and interactions, the reversals of fortune, and all the unintended consequences" of action (1984:x) without reducing the elements of that miscellany—the congeries of circumstances and events enumerated—to simple, subordinate parts. Umberto Eco describes this process in terms of Peircean semiotics as the transformation of "a disconnected *series*" into "a coherent [textual] *sequence*" that allows us to recognize the " 'aboutness' of the text which establishes a coherent relationship between different and still disconnected textual data" (1983:213).

As these descriptions of language and narrative suggest, analogical knowledge is irreducibly complex. It traffics in similarity and difference that cannot be reduced one to the other. In one register Norbert Wiener describes such complex knowledge when he defines information theory, as we will see in chapter 3, as neither matter nor energy: "Information is information, not matter or energy," he writes in *Cybernetics.* "No materialism which does not admit this can survive at the present day" (1961:132). In a very different register Shoshana Felman describes analogical knowledge—what she calls the "referential knowledge of language"—as "not knowledge *about* reality (about a separate and distinct entity), but knowledge that *has to do with reality,* that acts within reality" (1983:77). Such "activity," like all *acts,* encompasses the complexities of alternatives, purport, and temporally conditioned wholeness. That is, as Donald Davidson suggests, the concept of event is irreducibly complex precisely because it can be analyzed globally (e.g., the queen killed the king) and atomistically (e.g., the queen moved her hand, poured the poison, and the poison killed the king a week later by affecting his nervous system in such and such a way [which itself can be analyzed in greater and greater detail]; see Davidson 1980:57–61; Ricoeur 1984:122–23; Schleifer, Con Davis, and Mergler 1992:18–21). The very apprehension of events, like the apprehension of phonemes and melodies, configure *changing* unities from a larger number of elements. "The way of judging about particular cases," Ricoeur notes, "does not consist in placing a case under a law but in gathering together scattered factors and weighing their respective importance in producing the final result" (1984:125).

Analogy gathers together scattered factors and, to one degree or another, judges the importance of its gathering. Such judgments, however, are provisional: they take place outside the imperative of choosing once and for all. That is, analogical knowledge, like narrative itself, suspends the law of the excluded middle. Instead, it offers versions of comprehension—configurations, analogies, wholes, that do not erase parts—that can, in fact, be superimposed upon one another precisely to create "middles." In Greimas's words it is "neither pure contiguity nor a logical implication" (1983:244). Greimas is describing narrative in this formulation, but he could well be describing history as well. Analogical thinking allows for certain kinds of historicism—one might call it a "new" historicism—that suspends the opposition between historical time and timeless truth that, to a large degree, governed Enlightenment thinking. Richard Rorty articulates one such historicism in Dewey's "historicist vision" in which "the arts, the sciences, the sense of right and wrong, and the institutions of society are not attempts to embody or formulate truth or goodness or beauty. They are attempts to solve problems" (1982:16). Like analogical thinking, problem solving is timely, purposeful, and local, even if one form that analogy takes, as in Derrida's "deconstruction" (examined in chap. 2), is to analogize the local and the global.

In any case analogy reconceives both the local and the global—both empiricism and idealism, or matter and energy—in terms of the complexity of activity and historical events. Such complexity is metonymic rather than hierarchic, eschewing the aestheticism of "simplicity," the reductiveness of "identity," and hierarchy of atemporal "generalization." It calls for a content of apprehended configurations and a method of multiplied narratives. But, of course, content and method defined in this way immediately suggest their own confusion. The way out of this confusion, I think, is to pursue the situated knowledge of analogies. Science specifically and understanding more generally progress by means of such *superimpositions* of different "settings" and understandings upon one another. In other words, analogical thinking—in Heisenberg and Bohr, in Eliot and Freud, in Hjelmslev and Greimas—is cultural knowledge that brings together complementary parts and wholes, individuals and collectives, moments and sequences, in order to make provisional sense and achieve constellations of ideas and what Donna Haraway calls "situated knowledges" (1991).

The Work of the Negative: Discourse, Paradigms, Conceptual Schemes

One set of ways of talking about analogies that developed in recent years can be seen in he disparate work of Michel Foucault, Thomas Kuhn, and Donald Davidson under the categories of discourse, paradigms, and conceptual schemes. These categories, I believe, offer analogical modes of apprehending the analogical thinking I am presenting here, and the very disparateness of Foucault's poststructuralist arguments, Kuhn's attempt to understand intellectual revolutions in disciplinary history, and Davidson's attempt to configure frameworks of understanding emphasize what is always implicit in analogical thinking, the importance of difference as well as similarity, the work of the negative. This might be clearer if I articulated these categories more fully as "the order of discourse," "disciplinary matrixes," and "the critique—or the very idea—of a conceptual scheme," an articulation that repeats, at least by analogy, the language, collaboration, and interpretation of the title and structure of *Analogical Thinking*. Even this rearticulation, however, doesn't make clear what the piling together—the "superimposition"—of these works might effect; what harmony or cacophony, what music or noise or mad pursuit, might result.

The work of the negative in analogical thinking points toward the global effect of understanding—the combination of Keats's music, noise, and mad pursuit—what Greimas calls the "still very vague, yet necessary concept of the *meaningful whole* [*totalité de signification*] set forth by a message" (1983:59). Greimas's semiotic square schematizes this work by emphasizing negative, oppositional relationships. But Burrell perhaps describes more fully the larger purport of analogical thinking when he distinguishes analogy from metaphor in terms of the "negative shift" analogy gives rise to (1973:260). Such a negative shift takes place in what Burrell describes as the double meaning of global understandings, "which can be read either collectively, to mean the sum total of all the parts, or distributively, to mean what all share in whether they be taken singly or all together" (1973:260; Burrell, citing Thomas Gilby). Collective meanings, inhabiting parts, are susceptible to the positive meanings of metaphor;

distributive meaning, however, sets forth a meaningful whole that only the *differences* inhabiting analogy can suggest. Burrell quotes Thomas Gilby's attempt to define the "common good" of political philosophy and marks the negative shift of analogy he is describing by italicizing particular phrases. (Such italicization is analogical insofar as it marks the similarities and differences inhabiting the same word.)[3]

> Distributively, the common good is a freer value [than the "majority value" of the common good collectively conceived], more versatile, and *not so easily imagined*. It is *not* an accumulation of particulars, but a whole that can be repeated again and again. As in the logic of predication so in the philosophy of society, a whole is formed which suffers *no* diminution or subtraction from the presence or absence of particular subjects. (Gilby, cited by Burrell 1973:261)

3. In chapter 2 I examine the similarity and differences inhabiting the "same" word in terms of the technical linguistic category of *marking*. Traditional study of analogy, beginning with Catejan's *De Nominum Analogia* (1498), distinguish analogies of proportion, attribution, and inequality. Analogies of inequality, as McInerny describes them (1996:7–8), are analogies conveyed by the same word bearing different kinds or nuances of meaning. In *Portraying Analogy* J. F. Ross pursues "a systematic account of the meaning relationships different tokens of the same word have to one another (*drop*/stitch, *drop*/friend, *drop*/hint)" (1981:1). One category of "same-word" analogy, which he calls "paradigmatic sets" of "co-applicable words" (1981:54), can be understood in terms of the technical analysis of linguistic marking. Thus, Ross writes that these analogies can be described as "same words, taken in pairs, that differ but are related in meaning. Some near synonyms (say 'picked up' and 'received' for 'collect', 'make' for 'create', and 'prove' for 'establish'), of the one instance are also near synonyms for the other. . . . [I]f we listed the near synonyms, the contraries, hyponyms, determinables, determinates, and the like, for each instance, they would differ, even though there would be a definite overlap of common words. I call such difference a 'predicative' difference" (1981:7). The words *old* and *aged(ness)* I mentioned earlier in relation to Greimas's semiotic square form one example of such near synonyms, and they are related through the complications of markedness I examine in chapter 2. The category of markedness in linguistics gives a *formal* way of understanding the vague sense of "meaningful whole" that Greimas is trying to describe, which, because it is fully inhabited by *semantics,* does not result in the reductive simplicities and atemporal generalities of an *abstractly* formal account. Rather, precisely because of the irreducible negativity inhabiting "marking," it combines the alternatives and local generality of analogical thinking.

Ross's "predicative" difference is closely related to the modalities of language, which I examine in relation to linguistic markedness in chapter 5 of *Modernism and Time,* "Analogy and Example: Heisenberg, Linguistic Negation, and the Language of Quantum Physics." That chapter most closely links *Analogical Thinking* to *Modernism and Time.*

This description of social value, like Russell's description of the mathematical infinite—like the word *infinite* itself—suggests meaning by means of negation. Such a description presents itself as the metonymic play of what Derrida calls "seriality without paradigm," a series whose elements are "at once analogous (hence the series) and utterly different, offering no guarantee of analogy" (1979:130). Derrida's figure for this, like Latour's, is the "superimprinting" of texts (1979:137), and it replaces (but not altogether) the synecdochic hierarchies of clear and distinct ideas with metonymies of analogy.

A more positive description of the analogical thinking that is implicit in such superimposition is the *conceptual negativity* of its activity. The "activity" of negative apprehensions I am trying to describe can be figured as an optical illusion in which some vision of truth arises not in the positive "facts" of empirical evidence or the analytical statements of logical implication or even the invariants of phenomena discovered among their variety but in the negative "facts" of patterns of background and foreground. The optical illusion superimposes the negative space of its own background on the positive space of its foreground so that another picture, a new vision, springs forth to be grasped, a rabbit appearing in place of a duck, talking faces where a simple vase had been, a woman young and old.

Such superimprinted figures coexist serially but not simultaneously; they arise negatively in the interplay "of differences, distances, substitutions, transformations" (1972:37) that Foucault argues is the basis of "disciplinary unity" in histories of medicine, economics, or grammar. One could add other disciplines besides these Foucault examines or the "same" disciplines existing across time that Kuhn explores in terms of "scientific revolutions" or the larger conceptual schemes of apprehension of Davidson as well. The differences among these approaches to understanding are differences of level of analysis, forms of attention, which, taking the purpose and purport of analysis and attention into account, might well define, in the negativity of juxtaposition, what we mean by disciplines altogether.

In the *Archaeology of Knowledge* Foucault describes the history of ideas as uncertain and unstable, yet he also describes it as constituting "a style of analysis, a putting into perspective" that crosses "the boundaries of existing disciplines" (1972:137). In this sense the history of ideas, like history itself, is thoroughly interdisciplinary. As soon as this is said, however, the further question arises of whether Enlightenment canons of knowledge—disinterested understanding that is generalizing, accurate, and simple—are congruent with the nature of interdisciplinary studies. Are studies interdisciplinary simply by marshaling the vocabularies or modes of inquiry of different intellectual "fields," interfacing different *epistemes* as Foucault might say, the different *paradigms* of Kuhn's history of science, the different *conceptual schemes* Willard Quine describes and Davidson takes up? Or is interdisciplinarity the activity of "marshaling" itself, what Latour describes as the "mobilization" and "networking" of allies and arguments that constitutes knowledge conceived now *institutionally* rather than epistemologically?

Samuel Johnson, whose Enlightenment struggle with mobilization forms the very theme of Boswell's biography when it is read in a particular way, may help to clarify these questions, if not their answers. Let's look at the beginning of *The Vanity of Human Wishes*.

Let observation, with extensive view,
Survey mankind, from China to Peru,
Remark each anxious toil, each eager strife,
And watch the busy scenes of crowded life;
Then say how hope and fear, desire and hate,
O'er spread with snares the clouded maze of fate.

In these lines Johnson reduces busyness to simplicity: he offers four terms for seeing—observation's view surveying and remarking mankind without any hint of the verbal "witnessing" of seeing I describe in chapter 4—and, like the Enlightenment more generally, assumes that hope and fear, desire and hate, are everywhere equivalent. The simple universality of the "knowledge" presented here in the accumulation of the sum total of parts leaves out *analogical* knowledge between people, things, and activities that do not completely erase their differences.

One way to acknowledge those differences is in terms of the form of what Foucault calls *episteme*. "The episteme," he writes in *The Archaeology of Knowledge*, "is not a form of knowledge or a type of rationality which, crossing the boundaries of the most varied sciences, manifests the sovereign unity of a subject, a spirit, or a period; it is the totality of relations that can be discovered, for a given period, between the sciences when one analyzes them at the level of discursive regularities" (1972:191). The term *level*, as I have already mentioned, is a linguistic term that describes a hierarchical system by which distinct elements of one level combine to create elements of the next level. The discursive regularities that Johnson participates in posit the positive objects of language and of the world, in which it is imaginable, as the scientists of Laputa thought, for language to be replaced by a satchel of things carried about by servants. Each such object, Foucault argues, does not "await in limbo the order that will free it and enable it to become embodied in a visible and prolix objectivity" (1972:45). Yet the discursive regularity of Johnson's prolix scene produces precisely this sense of "objectivity," Johnson's famous simple-minded empiricism. That is, his discourse effects what Quine describes as the "multiplicity of identifiable and discriminable objects." "We talk so inveterately of objects," Quine says, "not because our objectifying pattern is an invariable trait of human nature, but because we are bound to adapt any alien pattern to our own in the very process of understanding or translating the alien sentences" (cited by Davidson 1974:13).

Quine's description of what he calls the *conceptual scheme* of a particular way of knowing seems parallel to Foucault's description of *episteme* and his description of discursive regularities. This is especially notable when Quine describes "physical objects" as "cultural posits" (1961:44–45). Still, he differs from Foucault when he describes a second mode of the interfacing of interdisciplinarity in terms of translation. If Foucault, in this early work, wants to uncover general but temporally conditioned *regularities*, translation offers the possibility of accounting for the breadth of Johnson's vision by trafficking in *analogies*. Here the model is not the discursive regularities of linguistics but the analogical translations of psychoanalysis and desire or of speech-act theory and intentionality. Johnson renders Juvenal's verb *dinoscere* as "survey," "remark," "watch," and "say," but more precisely it means "to recognize as different, to distinguish." Saying the difference between the particularities of toil and strife and the generalities of desire and hate attempts an accuracy of statement by transforming, analogically, performative to constative language.

Richard Rorty describes this as a global transformation in the history of philosophy, which he situates in the person of Descartes, who helped effect what he calls "the triumph of the quest for certainty over the quest for wisdom" so that "science, rather than living, became the philosopher's subject, and epistemology its center" (1979:61). This "transformation" is translation with a vengeance, which creates what Kuhn calls "different worlds." "The proponents of competing [scientific] paradigms," he writes in *The Structure of Scientific Revolutions,*

> practice their trades in different worlds. One contains constrained bodies that fall slowly, the other pendulums that repeat their motions again and again. In one solutions are compounds, in the other mixtures. . . . Practicing in different worlds, the two groups of scientists see different things when they look from the same point in the same direction.

Again, that is not to say that they can see anything they please. (1970:150)

Kuhn, as we have seen, suggests, negatively, by means of analogy that "proponents of different [scientific] theories are like native speakers of different languages," which often results in "communication breakdown" (1977:338). Such "breakdown," however, is not *simply* negative but, rather, does the work of the negative, which is to suggest that the logic of opposition—the same versus the other—does not exhaust possibilities of experience and comprehension.

That is, the negative suggests that the self-evident and commonsensical might not be universal and timeless. In both Quine's and Kuhn's descriptions of scientific disciplines the operative concept is that of "conceptual scheme." Such schemes, Davidson says,

> are ways of organizing experience; they are systems of categories that give form to the data of sensation; they are points of view from which individuals, cultures, or periods survey the passing scene. There may be no translating from one scheme to another, in which case the beliefs, desires, hopes and bits of knowledge that characterize one person have no true counterparts for the subscriber to another scheme. . . . what counts as real in one system may not in another. (1974:5)

Here again we can hear Johnson's simple (or simple-minded) survey, but we hear that survey negatively conceived as precisely the snares and maze of the accidents of "fate" determining the conceptual scheme we inhabit.

Are Foucault's "discursive regularities" a version of "conceptual schemes"? Is there a homology between his work and that of Quine, Kuhn, Davidson, and Rorty? In one sense the answer is clearly no. Unlike the conceptual schemes and paradigms and disciplinary matrixes, for Foucault

> a discursive formation is not . . . an ideal, continuous, smooth text that runs beneath the multiplicity of contradictions, and resolves them in the calm unity of coherent thought; nor is it the surface in which, in a thousand different aspects, a contradiction is reflected that is always in retreat, but everywhere dominant. It is rather a space of multiple dissensions; a set of different oppositions whose levels and roles must be described. Archaeological analysis, then, erects the primacy of a contradiction that has its model in the simultaneous affirmation and negation of a single proposition. (1972:155)

The primacy of contradiction is the work of the negative; it underlines the *nonreductive* nature of analogical thinking so that homologies cannot be definitively asserted. Yet, in another sense, in its simultaneous opposition to both the "deep" coherence of thought and the "surface" incoherence of the "everywhere" of reality, Foucault's discursive formations *function* in relation to the "two competing conceptual schemes" that Quine posits and explores, "a phenomenalistic one and a physicalistic one" (1961:17). Kuhn examines the relation between these schemes, willy-nilly, in his history of science that doubles in the word *world* fact and experience, and Davidson and Rorty, like Foucault, explore the very opposition of fact and experience in attempts to describe wisdom as opposed to knowledge, in which the "antics of familiar objects," as Davidson says, "make our sentences and opinions true and false" (1974:20).

In piling these descriptions together—discourse, paradigms, and conceptual schemes—I am trying to enact the negativity of discursive formations Foucault describes. Like the "information theory" that Wiener adds to "matter" and "energy" (1961:132) as something that is not simply reducible to one or the other, the negativity I am describing confuses the opposition between mode and content that schemes of discourse, translation, and the opposition between reality and phenomena maintain. That is, the very opposition of mode and content—the opposition of background and foreground—is a recurrent object of critique in Quine and Kuhn, Davidson and Rorty, as it is in Foucault. The vehicle of this critique is the marshaling of methods I am pursuing, the superimpositions or super-imprintings I am following, what I might call, using the figure from Keats, the "mad pursuit" of analogical thinking. Latour develops his figure of superimposition in a remarkable essay, "Visualization and Cognition: Thinking with Eyes and Hands" (discussed in chap. 3), in which he argues for a *parsimonious* explanation of understanding that "takes writing and imaging craftsmanship into account" (1986:3). This explanation focuses on the very visualization governing Johnson's survey and the etymology of *theory* discussed in chapter 4, but it does so neither to account for objects of knowledge nor, as in Kuhn, to articulate a world of experience. Instead, Latour's visualization—his "writing"—is, like the witnessing of theory itself, a form of *semantics* that attempts to describe the social networking of knowledge that extends across time as well as space in the semiotics of a host of local encounters. In such an explanation Johnson's "mankind" is neither the hypostatized masculine rational material species that Johnson imagined nor simply an element in an entirely homogeneous theoretical vocabulary that Kuhn describes. Rather, it is the abstraction of moveable meaning gathered in a word so that the visualization Johnson engages in—which Quine asserts is built into the conceptual scheme of our process of understanding and Rorty argues is simply an accident of history—allows for the superimposition of frames of understanding that, for Latour, are neither strict hierarchical levels nor arbitrary juxtapositions. Visualization, Latour says, allows for *simplification* when it makes perception *"less confusing"* (1986:13). He also asserts, however, that simplification is only the beginning of knowledge—not its end, as the Enlightenment often assumed. For Latour knowledge, like the "series" of history, never fully ends. Knowing, he says, "is not a disinterested cognitive activity" (1986:16).

In his figure for narration Greimas describes Latour's sumperimposition, Foucault's discursive formations, and the analogies of observations I am pursuing: narrative, he says, "is neither pure contiguity nor a logical implication" (1983:244); it is neither pure accident nor pure system. In the same way, analogical understanding is neither the pure contiguity of accidental objects nor the logical implication of conceptual phenomenology. Rather, it is knowledge conceived as event. Foucault, in fact, posits a definition of *event*—I pursue this at greater length in relation to Descartes in the book's postscript—that is close to the work of the negative in Greimas's "neither . . . nor." "The event," he writes,

> is neither substance nor accident, neither quality nor process; the event is not of the order of bodies. And yet it is not something immaterial either; it is always at the level of materiality that it takes effect, that it is effect; it has its locus and it consists in the relation, the coexistence, the dispersion, the overlapping, the accumulation, and the selection of material elements. (1981:69)

Like the superimpositions of this chapter, like the complex relationships embodied in analogy, *event* here embodies the serial work of the negative. In fact, analogies set forth linguistic events, that "function within our language but whose serviceability is not restricted to their role within language" (Burrell 1973:24). That "service" is to do the work of the negative within the world. "Discrepancies proliferate," Latour says, not in the immediate phenomenal experience of reality, "not by looking at the sky, but by carefully superimposing columns of angles and azimuths. No contradiction," he continues, "no counterpredictions, could even have been made visible. Contradiction . . . is neither a property of the mind, nor of the scientific method, but is a property of reading letters and signs inside new settings" (1986:20). Contradiction, he might have said, is a property of analogical thinking.

Obtaining new settings, Latour argues, is the activity of ethnography, going farther and farther out of the usual ways of knowledge and also coming back, to contest understandings by analogically multiplying and superimposing their simplicities. Clifford Geertz calls such superimpositions the thick descriptions of ethnography. In these terms Johnson's survey is very thin indeed, like the South Sea Bubble of his youth. Still, Johnson's survey can be marshaled as one among other simplicities within the history—the analogical seriality—of ideas to offer the event or repeated events of understanding. Like Geertz's ethnographic surveys of politics and cockfights or my slighter survey of Foucault, Davidson, Kuhn, and others—like history itself—such events of understanding, as Geertz says, are "intrinsically incomplete" (1973:29), a series without paradigm, analogical thinking without the stability of a base to which the analogues can be reduced, floating instead, like stars in the sky or an optical illusion, to be repeatedly, momentarily, anchored.

Analogical thinking, as I describe it throughout this book in the methods of semiotics, in collaborative knowledges, and in interpretation, brings different objects or levels or orders together in order to illuminate particular aspects of each momentarily. As Wittgenstein says, analogical thinking begins to "light up an aspect" of what it examines that was not perceived before (cited in Bannet 1997:666). That is, analogical thinking is not reductive, or at least not reductive once and for all. Instead, it presents momentary or emergent insights by noting similarities, rather than identities, that suggest trajectories to pursue rather than resting places to inhabit. This is another sense of what I mean by the work of the negative. Analogies do not present or assert positive entities, invariants, essences. Instead, they offer insight and frameworks of understanding born of relationships that can always be apprehended as provisional, the source of beginning rather than ending. The work of the negative, like the action of analogy, is to start over, again and again.

The Plan of the Book

Analogical Thinking attempts to create such frameworks of understanding within its three sections and across them. As I have mentioned, the parts of the book—language, collaboration, and interpretation—traverse the similarities and differences of the order of discourse, of disciplinary matrixes, and of critique of conceptual schemes I have followed in Foucault, Kuhn, and Davidson. Part 1 examines the *scientific* project of semiotics by setting forth its governing principles, examining the confrontation of its attempt at the hierarchic formalism of nomological science with the "negation of that hierarchy," as Greimas describes it (1983:82), in both "neutralization" and "deconstruction" (two terms and procedures that form a complex analogy with each other). In doing so, it sets forth an understanding of analogy as a species of *semantic formalism* that is located at the juncture of the formality of language and the phenomenality of the world. Moreover, it pursues *analogical meaning* by means of what I have called in this introduction "the work of the negative."

Part 2 sets forth another way of apprehending analogy, what I call *postformalist* understanding, which attends to the positive and unique nature of analogies by emphasizing the repeated and temporal quality of their meaning that precludes the precisions of formal manipulation. To this end the chapters of part 2 offer extended analogies between intellectual practices and intellectual disciplines: chapter 3 sets forth Latour's conception—his "disciplinary matrix"—of superimposition as the form, I suggest, of *postformalist* analogy in the cheerful Enlightenment science of the political economy of Adam Smith and the contested post-Enlightenment science of twentieth-century information theory; and chapter 4 pursues the analysis of disciplinary matrices across disciplines, following the analogy of the conjunction of semantics and syntactics with the conjunction of the humanities and the sciences. Chapter 3 pursues postformalist analogies across history, while chapter 4 pursues them across disciplines. In the course of its discussion the former chapter suggests that information theory has a particular purchase on historical understanding because of its combination of Enlightenment and post-Enlightenment apprehensions. Similarly, the latter chapter suggests that the humanities—disciplines of language study—has a particular purchase on cross-disciplinary understandings because of the conjunction it presents of phenomenal seeing and verbal witnessing in the collaborative understanding of theory. Part 2 situates *analogical knowledge* in the context of what Edward Said calls "worldliness."

Finally, part 3 examines the analogy between "modern" and "postmodern" modes of apprehension in pursuing the paraphrases of "interpretation" Greimas and Courtés set forth in readings of Yeats, the Bible, and the relationship between Dreiser and Mailer in which the sense of modernism I have suggested here is related to contemporary conceptions of postmodernism. The chapters of this section pursue a critique of the "conceptual scheme" of modernity—both Enlightenment modernity and what I take to

be its crisis articulated in twentieth-century modernism—simply by constel-
lating the three-part framework of *Analogical Thinking* together, as alternating ways of making sense of interpretation and experience. It creates
possibilities of *analogical comprehension* in the operation of analogy as
both meaning and event.

The postscript examines Foucault in relation to the initiation of Enlightenment values and methods in Descartes in order to circumscribe what
I am calling a post-Enlightenment ethos. The book concludes with a postscript in order to underline the linguistic, temporal, interpretive, aspects of
analogy: the fact that analogy traffics in language or—as I mention in the
postscript—the "naming" of phenomena; the fact that analogical compari-
sons take place and are repeated in time; and the fact that even something
as self-evident as an event entails the language and collaborative witnessing
of interpretation. The *post* of postscript takes its place among the poststructuralism of part 1, the postformalist knowledge of part 2, and the postmodernism of part 3. The end of *Analogical Thinking* is not the "conclusion" of
Enlightenment thought but, I hope, an occasion for something more to be
said—the "variety of retellings" by which Benjamin describes the power
and generosity of storytelling (1969:93)—of the post-Enlightenment ethos
found throughout this book.

In any case, the three parts of the book, taken together, enact the
features of analogical thinking I have described in this chapter, the presentation of alternatives (embodied in semantic formalism), its pluralization and
redundancy (embodied in postformalist witnessing), and its momentary and
purposeful apprehensions of wholeness (embodied in interpretation). The
plan of the book I am describing somewhat schematically, however, might
better be apprehended in terms of the family resemblances that Wittgenstein describes—which I have already likened to Benjamin's constellation—
in which resemblance and similarity cannot be defined formally, once and
for all, as one-to-one correspondences between features but analogically, in
terms of wholes apprehended repeatedly within alternating orders of discourse, disciplinary matrices, and conceptual frameworks. This is why the
discussion of scientific semiotics in chapter 1 focuses on literary interpretation, the discussion of disciplines in chapter 4 focuses on syntax and semantics, and the reading of the postmodern Bible and Isak Dinesen's modernism
in chapter 6 focuses on the collaborative element within narrative conceived
as an institution.

There is a kind of generosity in Benjamin's description of ideas as constellations of objects in the world and family relationships within the world: in
Benjamin's understanding of ideas cultural and intellectual work passes on

apprehensions of meaning as something to be reworked and revalorized by people who come later—the kind of free-floating purport Greimas describes in what he takes to be the revolution in Modernist linguistics, its conception of itself as "a linguistics of perception and not of expression" (cited in Schleifer 1987:xix). Analogical thinking calls for such later perceptions, the handing on of meanings and values for others to take up and reconfigure; at its best it passes on the kind of generosity that inhabits so much of Benjamin's work. It is my hope that the configured chapters of *Analogical Thinking* participate in such generosity so that, in the analogies they present, they lend themselves to new understandings and renewed value that might allow their progression, as Yeats said in another context, to take fire "in someone's head and [become] virtue or freedom" (1962:336).

Part I

Language

Chapter 1

Scientific Semiotics and Interpretation

The two chapters of this section trace the scientific project of semiotics and its relationship to the poststructuralist project of deconstruction. In these chapters—especially in chapter 2—analogy is described as embodying "semantic formalism," which conjoins the formality of language with what Jacques Derrida calls the "phenomenality" of meaning (1981:30). In this conjunction the semantic formalism of analogy comes into play to articulate what David Burrell calls "the relation between language and the world" (1973:224). Still, in this focus on the formal structures of language, part 1 is loosely opposed to the phenomenal, disciplinary analogies—the "post-formalist" analogies—of part 2. An important aspect of my point, both here and throughout this book, however, is that analogical thinking supplements the abstract formalism of strict parallels even while it uses the apprehension of similarities—of "parallels"—as its starting point. That is, analogical thinking *begins* with similarities, even if it never quite apprehends similarities as strict equations. In this chapter, then, I examine the similarity of semiotics to the project of Enlightenment science—its attempt, formally, to articulate truth in terms of its simplicity, accuracy, and atemporal generalizability. The following chapter focuses on the differences between the semantic project of semiotics and its modeling itself on mechanical science, while the chapters of part 2 attempt to examine these similarities and differences in terms of the historical occasions of these models, the analogical resemblance, as Ricoeur says, "between relations rather than between terms per se" (1988:151).

The World of Signs

In the third voyage of *Gulliver's Travels* Gulliver visits the School of Languages at the Grand Academy of Lagado, where he encounters a strange scheme for the abolition of all words in order to preserve the health of our lungs. Instead of using words, people would simply carry around with them "such *Things* as were necessary to express the particular Business they are to discourse on" (1961:158). This scheme, Gulliver noted, "hath only this Inconvenience attending it; that if a Man's Business be very great, and of various Kinds, he must be obliged in Proportion to carry a great Bundle of *Things* upon his Back, unless he can afford one or two strong Servants to attend him" (1961:158). Such a scheme, as Swift well knew, is impracticable and wrongheaded: not only would such discoursers sink "under the Weight of their Packs, like Pedlars among us" (1961:158); more strikingly, as Swift demonstrates in the next voyage of *Gulliver's Travels,* such a conception of the nature of language as "only Names for *Things*" does not allow for one of the most powerful aspects of language, the ability of language to say "*the Thing which was not*" (1961:206): to make promises, to imagine and define worlds different from our own (like those of *Gulliver's Travels*), to describe the future, to lie, to articulate values, to create communities, to do the work of the negative—all things that cannot fit in the packs people would have to carry with them to replace language.

In this negative example Swift is describing the great convenience of language, the power it affords us to represent or "signify" absent entities. The science of such signification—which studies language more carefully, I think, than the scholars of Lagado—is semiotics. The term *semiotics* comes from the Greek word *semeion,* which means "sign," and semiotics is the study—or the science—of the functioning of signs. Signs function all around us every time we use one entity to *signify* or *represent* another. For instance, the sounds that constitute the word *tree* in English signifies the physical object of a tree; and the graphic mark *tree* signifies the sound *tree,* etc. Signification takes place all the time, even when we are not intentionally attending to some discursive business or another: this is part of Swift's mockery of the single-minded nearsightedness of the scholars of Lagado. But signification does more than allow us to signify absent entities in thought or speech or other modes of communication; it saves us from more than the heavy bundle of things Swift's scholars carry. More complexly than a simple conception of representation, signification helps determine experience and perception: the fact that English has a sign *tree*—especially in relation to the sign *shrub,* for instance—contributes to the determination of experience and perception so that the world takes on an orderly shape, communities are possible, and things gain both value and a future.

This is perhaps clearer in my second example, in which the seeming precise sound of the word *tree* is designated by a graphic sign (or a combination of graphic signs, t-r-e-e). Even though most of the pronunciations of the sound of the word *tree,* spoken by old men and young women, children, people with accents from different parts of the country, screams and whispers, are measurably different in terms of the physical properties of sound, we experience or perceive these manifestations of the word as the same. In fact, some variations of the sound *tree* are far more different from one another than the difference between *tree* and *three* just as scrub oaks and palm trees are far more different from each other than scrub oaks and woody shrubs, yet the designation—the sign *tree*—helps us delimit the "object" the sign represents. This conception of signification does not assume that signs represent *preexisting* entities (which we could carry around in a sack). Rather, it sees the process of signification as one in which signs designate "mental images" or "thoughts" or "ideas" but in such a way that such ideas or thoughts do not preexist the process of signification but, rather, gain their definition by means of signification. In this conception a sign does not "re-present" some entity or thought but, rather, the process of signification gives definition to an idea—it *realizes* it—when that idea, like a promised future, was only a vague, indefinite possibility before.

In this conception the ways signs *refer* to objects (including mental objects) in the world is less important than the generative capacities of signification, the ways that signs create the possibility of definition and intelligibility. In fact, Claude Lévi-Strauss, studying the nature and functions of myths in human culture—that is to say, of the meanings or significations of communal narratives—describes the function of signs as the expression of "intelligible" meaning by means of "tangible" physical entities. When we think about it, the fact that intelligibility—the apparently private experience of understanding—can be expressed and communicated by means of things that can be tangibly *perceived* is remarkable. Yet, as I shall argue, semiotics teaches us that this seeming private process of understanding is socially determined in such a way that we must rethink not only the ordinary conceptions of what meaning and understanding are but even rethink the apparently simply oppositions between meaning and fact, principle and example. If signification helps determine the entities it seemingly represents, then private understanding may not preexist its public communication: signification becomes less an activity we engage in, like taking things out of a sack, than a world we inhabit.

In any case the complex relationship between perception and meaning—between the tangible and the intelligible—is woven closely into everything we do. A striking part of being human is the ability to discern meaning—to apprehend signs—wherever we look: not only in stories we hear or experiences we remember but in things as subtle as the tone of voice of people close to us, facial expressions, the accidental ways light might strike a tree, color of cloths, sequences of sounds. Literature, of course, teaches us to apprehend such signs better than we might—it does so, I believe, by making "accident" an unacceptable mode of explaining the perceptions it presents to us—and, if this is so, then semiotics, the science of signs, can teach us *how* literature achieves its ends. Later in this chapter I will examine how semiotics can help us to read and understand literary texts more fully (and how literature can help us understand semiotics), and still later I hope to describe the sea change that semiotics suggests in our understanding of what takes place when we "understand" or "comprehend" anything—the analogical thinking I described in the introduction and which I examine more closely in subsequent chapters. But here I want to emphasize that semiotics does not aim to discover *particular* meanings in its objects of study. Rather, semiotics seeks to understand the *conditions* of meaning, to isolate and describe those conditions under which signification can take place. (In the following chapter I will suggest the ways that semiotics presents a mode of analogical thinking by examining it in relation to deconstruction.) The great questions of semiotics are: how is meaning possible? what is its nature? how does it work? how is it possible to represent something that is absent? what is the nature of intelligibility and its relationship to representation and signification? and what, finally, is the relationship between signification and what I call the "collaborations" of community?

Humanities and the Human Sciences

A striking fact about the history of science is the ways in which the great revolutionary figures in the development of science—Newton, Darwin, Einstein, perhaps Freud—gained their insights by asking questions where most people had seen simple self-evident truths. For instance, Darwin asked, why are there so many species? Marx asked whether belief systems do more than articulate general truths, and, if so, what particular social ends do they serve? Einstein asked, what is the significance of the nature of light for understanding the relationship between time and space? In each case—and, of course, they could be significantly multiplied—science is asserting there is a question to be asked concerning the human situation and experience that is so close to everyday life that no one ever stopped to notice it *was* a question. In each case, as Northrop Frye says in "The Function of Criticism at the Present Time," science transforms itself from the condition of "naive induction," which attempts to classify the immediate sensations of experience, into more sophisticated questioning, which attempts to explain the very phenomena it examines "in terms of a conceptual framework different in shape" from that phenomena itself (1994:39).

The same is true of semiotics. Just as scientific physics was impossible for the ancients, as Frye argues, because they did not imagine that the different elements so close to human life—earth, fire, air, and water—could be understood beyond the simple recounting of their existence, so the semiotic science of the signifying process is a late development among the sciences because it could not be formulated as a science until basic questions about the nature of meaning that focused on seeming self-evident truths could be asked. One such question (which I have already touched upon) examines the concept of the sameness of different entities or events, the question of the difference between similarity and identity, that I suggested in the introduction analogical thinking raises. What makes two sounds or two concepts or two experiences the same? Such a question—which became more and more pressing to philosophers in the course of the nineteenth century in the work of precursors of semiotics such as Marx, Durkheim, Nietzsche, and Freud—is basic to larger questions of: *how* is it that signification is possible? what takes place when one entity "stands for," or signifies, another? And, finally, how is it possible for such signification to be *interpersonal* communication? Roman Jakobson, the great linguist and semiotician, defines meaning itself as the "translation" of one set of signs into another set of signs, a definition of meaning that, raising these questions, is closely tied to the conception of the same.

The science of semiotics attempts to create a conceptual framework in which such questions about language, signification, and communication can be rigorously addressed and answered. As Lévi-Strauss has argued, at the heart of signification is the process of analogical translation:

> I have tried to transcend the contrast between the tangible and the intelligible by operating from the outset at the sign level. The function of signs, is, precisely, to express the one by means of the other. Even when very restricted in number, they lend themselves to rigorously organized combinations which can translate even the finest shades of the whole range of sense experience. We can thus hope to reach a plane where logical properties, as attributes of things, will be manifested as directly as flavors or perfumes; perfumes are unmistakably identifiable, yet we know that they result from combinations of elements which, if subjected to a different selection and organization, would have created awareness of a different perfume. (1975:14)

In this passage Lévi-Strauss is articulating the great ambition of semiotics: to be a *science* of signs that can account for the myriad meanings of signification—the "phenomenal," or "felt," sense of meaning that experience continuously presents to us—with the same rigor as the articulation of the laws accounting for our experience and perception of chemical compounds and their activity that chemistry has achieved. Just as the smell of perfume is a phenomenal effect of chemical combinations whose *invariant* elements and active properties can be formulated, recorded, and predicted to behave in certain ways in certain situations, so, Lévi-Strauss hopes, meaning is also a phenomenal effect that can be accounted for and predicted by the scientific isolation and discovery of invariant elements and processes of signification.

In other words, Lévi-Strauss assumes that the "intelligible" effects of meaning are in no way "mysterious" or "spiritual" or "intangible" or "unique." Rather, he assumes they are recurrent *phenomena* that, like other phenomena science studies, can be understood in terms of what Frye calls the "conceptual framework different in shape from them" of science. Science begins by assuming that phenomena are more than a collection of unique events; it assumes that they are related to one another and can be explained within a framework that articulates the relationships—the repetition of the same invariant elements—across seeming unique events. In the same way Lévi-Strauss assumes that different meanings are related to one another as palpable effects on human perception that can be accounted for in the same way that the effect of smell is accountable in relation to the general laws of chemical combinations—the rigorous scientific analysis of chemistry. How else, Lévi-Strauss implies, could meanings present so many seeming invariables (such as the word *tree*)? How else could meaning be *shared*? How else could the ability to speak and understand an almost infinite number of sentences be learned in the first three years of life?

For this reason A. J. Greimas, who was an important follower of Lévi-Strauss, notes that the science of semiotics assumes that the phenomenon of meaning can be understood in the same ways other phenomena are understood. In *Structural Semantics* (1966) he says:

> It may be—it is a philosophic and not linguistic question—that the phenomenon of language as such is mysterious, but there are no mysteries in language.
>
> The "piece of wax" of Descartes is no less mysterious than the symbol of the moon. It is simply that chemistry has succeeded in giving an account of its elementary composition. It is toward an analysis of the same type that structural semantics must proceed. It is true the *effects of meaning* do hold good in both cases, but the new analytic

plane of reality—whether it is in chemistry or semiology—is not less legitimate. (1983:65)

The "piece of wax" Greimas is talking about is the fact that Descartes notes in his *Meditations* that wax manifests itself variously—changing its qualities when he brings it close to a fire—so that, while each of the qualities that "came under taste, smell, sight, touch, or hearing, has altered—yet the wax remains" (1984:20). Since Descartes's time chemistry has developed as a science insofar as it can reduce a large number of phenomena such as the perceived different qualities of wax Descartes describes to *variations* governed by *invariant* chemical laws and substances. Greimas hopes that semiotics can achieve the same scientific simplicity, coherence, and scope for the science of meaning and signification: that it can account for the effects of meaning such as the "symbolic" meanings associated with the moon with the same kind of abstract *formal* description that chemistry accounts for the phenomenal effects that chemical compounds produce.

Behind this assumption—as it is behind those of Lévi-Strauss and Frye—is a significant reconception of the nature of those areas of knowledge that have traditionally examined the nature of meaning in human affairs, the "humanities." The humanities—whether it studied literary texts, musical compositions, philosophical treatises, works of art—have always assumed that each object of study was a unique and unrepeatable event. After all, Shakespeare only wrote *Hamlet* once; Descartes meditated on the nature of the human mind once at a particular moment in the history of ideas; Mozart's *Hunt* quartet is an unrepeatable event in the history of music, just as Darwin's *Origin of the Species* is a unique event in the development of science. But, since the humanities have always understood the objects of its attention to be unique events, they have always limited themselves as a body of knowledge to description and paraphrase. Thus, literary criticism has interpreted literary works by paraphrasing its meanings in other words, or it has described literary works in terms of its unique elements.

As the linguist, Louis Hjelmslev has noted, according to this traditional view "humanistic, as opposed to natural, phenomena are nonrecurrent and for that very reason cannot, like natural phenomena, be subjected to exact and generalizing treatment. . . . In the field of the humanities," he continues, "consequently, there would have to be a different method [from that of science]—namely, mere description, which would be nearer to poetry than to exact science—or, at any event, a method that restricts itself to a discursive form of presentation in which the phenomena pass by, one by one, without being interpreted through a system" (1961:8–9). This "method," Hjelmslev suggests, is "history" in its most chronological manifestation. Since the objects of humanistic study are unique, they can be catalogued only in chronological order. For this reason the humanities have traditionally been "historical" studies: the history of philosophy, the history of art, history itself, the history of science, literary history, and so forth. Frye says a similar thing in "The Function of Criticism": "literature as yet being unorganized by criticism, it still appears as a huge aggregate or miscellaneous pile of creative efforts. The only organizing principle so far discovered in it is chronology" (1994:44).

Implicit in Frye and Hjelmslev is the basic assumption of scientific semiotics: that the humanities can reorient themselves and adopt a scientific model in their study. Instead of pursuing the "naive induction" of cataloguing unique events, they can, as Hjelmslev says, attempt "to rise above the level of mere primitive description to that of a systematic, exact, and generalizing science, in the theory of which all events (possible combinations of elements) are foreseen and the conditions for their realization established" (1961:9). Such a discipline could examine signification from a host of different points of view. It could examine the elements that combine to create the "meaning-effects" Greimas describes; it could study the recurrent elements of myth and narrative Lévi-Strauss examines; it could explore the ways in which signification takes place in language as Saussure and Hjelmslev do; it could even account for the collaborations of communal meaning-formations in the sciences or in the Bible. In more particularly literary examples it could study the systematic nature of "literature" itself, such as the general theory of genre Frye suggests and Tzvetan Todorov pursues in relation to the genre of the fantastic; it could examine the systematic relationship among the objects of humanistic study conceived in terms of linguistic syntax or the "textuality" and "intertextuality" that Roland Barthes has described and that I examine in the relationship between Norman Mailer and Theodore Dreiser in chapter 7; it could study the genesis or genealogy of intellectual disciplines and organs of knowledge; or it could examine the relationship among the assumptions that govern particular modes of interpretation, as I do later in this chapter in relation to analogical thinking.

In these ways what has traditionally been called the humanities can reconceive themselves as the "human sciences." In such a conception, as Frye notes, literary criticism would take its place among the social sciences rather than the natural sciences. Saussure as well as Frye called for the understanding of semiotic science as a "social" science, and one of the aims of this book is to open up the sense of the sociality of meaning implied in semiotics and criticism by examining strategies of collaboration. In any case the very opposition between "humanities" and "human sciences" can be seen in the social sciences themselves. For instance, Saussure himself notes in *The Course in General Linguistics* the difference between two methods of studying economics—economic history and the "synchronic" study of the economic *system* at any particular moment. Most of the social sciences are divided in this way: psychology, for instance, encompasses the analysis of unique case histories of "clinical" psychology and "experimental" psychology that attempts to articulate the "general" functioning of mental activity. Anthropology encompasses both the study of unique cultures and, as in Lévi-Strauss's work, the "general" functioning of aspects of culture. Even history, the seeming model of humanistic study of unique and unrepeatable events, is sometimes taken to be a social science in whose conceptual framework, as Frye says, "there is nothing that cannot be considered historically" (1994:42).

In this way literary study also can be seen to offer two "methods" of study—in Frye's terms, literary history and more or less systematizing criticism. What allows the systematization of criticism, however, is the common and most "recurrent" element of traditional humanistic study, the fact that, as Hjelmslev notes, all the humanities deal in the study of language and discourse—in the study of signification. In other words, if the humanities all participate in areas of the social sciences, they do so because the *foundation* of society are the signifying systems that allow for intelligible social intercourse. From this vantage the overarching social science is semiotics: it studies the functioning of signs as an always *social* functioning basic to psychology, sociology, history, economics, and the other social sciences. In this framework literary criticism would take its place among the social and, more broadly speaking, the human sciences: its study of the signifying forms of literature would be a special case of the study of signification altogether, the study of semiotics. Such a human science would attempt to describe what distinguishes literature from other signifying practices and what literature shares with them. It would attempt, as many have already attempted, to situate literary practice within other cultural practices (including linguistics, teaching, politics, psychology, history, philosophy, ideology, sociology, and so forth). It would study literary works not as special cases but as *representative* cases, as possessing and presenting the forms of signification that can help us to understanding the nature and generation of meaning in general.

Structural Linguistics

Lévi-Strauss, Greimas, and Hjelmslev base their understanding of signification on the studies of the great linguists of the twentieth century and especially the work of Continental (as opposed to Anglo-American) linguistics.
At the head of this tradition is the Swiss linguist Ferdinand de Saussure,
whom I've already mentioned in passing. In fact, Saussure called for a
science of "semiology" in the several courses in general linguistics he offered at the University of Geneva in 1907–11. Almost simultaneously in the
first decade of the twentieth century the American philosopher and logician
Charles Sanders Peirce used the term *semeiotic* to describe the general
science of the functioning of signs in various sciences—what Jonathan
Culler describes as the "science of sciences" (1981:23). (In the 1970s the
International Association for Semiotic Studies opted for Peirce's term *semiotics*.) Peirce saw semiotics in relation to logic and developed elaborate
taxonomies of types of signs. Saussure, on the other hand, has exerted much
greater influence by calling for semiotics to model itself as a discipline in
relation to linguistics (even if, as some recent writers have noted, this modeling has produced a narrow definition of the sign based upon the special
properties of linguistic signs [Culler 1981:23; Blonsky 1985:xvii]).

In any case the coincidental articulation of a neologism to describe a
science that did not exist but which, as Saussure said, had "a right to exist"
(1959:16) is one of the remarkable events in the history of ideas, comparable to the coincidental development of calculus by Isaac Newton and
G. W. Leibniz at the turn of the eighteenth century. Moreover, like the
introduction of calculus, which allowed Newton to calculate and predict in
a short time the elaborate measurements of planetary motion that Johann
Kepler had recorded over the course of more than twenty years, and like the
linguistic science Saussure developed and the discovery of "the truth about
the general reference of symbols to their objects" that Peirce was pursuing
(1958:403), semiotics is an attempt to reduce the myriad of facts about
signification—that is, about meaning in human affairs—to a manageable
number of propositions about the functioning of the signifying process in
human life within a rigorous conceptual framework.

Saussure defined semiology as the science "*that studies the life of
signs within society,*" which "would be part of social psychology and
consequently of general psychology." "Semiology," he goes on, "would
show what constitutes signs, what laws govern them. . . . Linguistics is
only a part of the general science of semiology; the laws discovered by
semiology will be applicable to linguistics, and the latter will circumscribe

a well-defined area within the mass of anthropological facts" (1959:16). Whether linguistics is "part" of semiotics, as Saussure contends here, or whether semiotics is modeled upon linguistics is a debate that has received a good deal of attention in the last three decades. At the other extreme from Saussure's position is Roland Barthes's contention that *all* semiotics systems—including the "natural semiotics" of animal sign and signal languages, the "connotations" (as opposed to the "denotations") of human linguistic systems, and nonverbal semiotic systems such as music and painting—can be understood as species of what Umberto Eco has called "translinguistics" examining "all sign systems with reference to linguistic laws" (Eco 1976:30). It is Barthes's position that linguistic science, rather than psychology, has developed the conceptual framework in which to understand signification in general.

Whether scholars assume semiotics simply *extends* linguistics beyond the sentence or that it *subsumes* linguistics in its understanding of the functioning of signs in general, it is clear to all that linguistics has offered the most rigorous examination of the process of signification of all the "branches" of semiotic science. I believe this is because the object of linguistics is more rigorously defined than other semiotic systems (see Schleifer 1987:169–72). Moreover, despite Saussure's description of semiology's inclusion within general psychology, the rigor of structural linguistics and semiotics has established itself, as we shall see, in their avoidance of psychological and cognitive explanations—*causal* explanations—in defining the linguistic (and semiotic) sign. It is precisely this avoidance that situates semiotics as a species of analogical thinking, despite its aim at making itself a "nomological" science governed by a small number of rigorous and universal laws. The definition of the linguistic sign begins with Saussure's reorientation of linguistics in the *Course of General Linguistics* from the historical study of language—and especially etymology—to the "systemic" study of language that he inaugurated in his work. Saussure's reexamination of language is based upon three assumptions. The first of these, which I have already touched upon, is the assumption that the scientific study of language needs to develop and study the *system* rather than the history of linguistic phenomena. In Saussure's terms he distinguishes between the particular occurrences of language—its particular "speech-events," which he designates as *parole;* and the proper object of linguistics, the system that governs those events—its "code," which he designates as *langue*. Moreover, he argues for the "synchronic" study of the relationship among the elements of language at a particular instant rather than the "diachronic" study of the development of language through history.

This assumption gave rise to what Jakobson came to call "structuralism" in 1929: "Were we to comprise the leading idea of present-day science in its most various manifestations," he wrote,

> we could hardly find a more appropriate designation that *structuralism*. Any set of phenomena examined by contemporary science is treated not as a mechanical agglomeration but as a structural whole, and the basic task is to reveal the inner . . . laws of this system. What appears to be the focus of scientific preoccupations is no longer the outer stimulus, but the internal premises of the development: now the mechanical conception of processes yields to the question of their function. (1971:711)

In this dense passage Jakobson is articulating the scientific aim of linguistics I have described more generally as the aim of semiotics. But, more than this, he is also describing the second foundational assumption in Saussurean— we can now call it "structural"—linguistics. The second assumption is that the basic elements of language, and of signification more generally, can only be studied in relation to their *function* rather than their *cause*. Instead of studying particular and unique events and entities, those "events" and "entities" have to be *situated* within a systemic framework in which they are related to other so-called events and entities. This is a radical reorientation in conceiving of the world, one whose importance the philosophy Ernst Cassirer has compared "to the new science of Galileo which in the seventeenth century changed our whole concept of the physical world" (cited in Culler 1981:24).

I have already touched upon this matter when I attempted to define *sign* at the beginning of this chapter. Saussure describes the nature of the linguistic sign as the union of "a concept and a sound image," which he called "*signified [signifié]* and *signifier [signifiant]*" (1959:66–67). But the nature of their "combination" is what makes this conception functional: for Saussure neither the signified nor the signifier is the "cause" of the other. Rather, they exist within the linguistic sign in what Greimas calls a relationship of "reciprocal presupposition": the signifier presupposes the signified that, after all, it signifies; but at the same time the signified presupposes the signifier: otherwise it couldn't be "signified [by something]." Such reciprocal presupposition governs the relationship between the elements of analogies as well: to assert that my love is like a rose connects love and roses in a way that doesn't allow either the love or the rose to so overwhelm and absorb its analogue that one is reduced to the other. Similarly, Saussure defines the basic element of language, the sign, *analogically* and *relationally*. Such a relational definition allows him to explain the problem of the *identity* of units of language and signification I mentioned at the beginning of this chapter: the reason we can recognize different pronunciations of the word *tree* as the same word is that the word is not defined by inherent qualities—it is not a "mechanical agglomeration" of such qualities—but, rather, it is defined in relation to other elements in a system, a "structural whole," of the English language. In the context of a positivism that assumes irreducible, positive qualities of entities, such a relational mode of understanding is "negative," a product of the work of the negative.

For Saussure this relational definition of an entity—it is sometimes also called a "diacritical" definition—governs the conception of all the elements of signification. This is clearest in the most impressive achievement of Saussurean linguistics, the development of the concepts of the phonemes and "distinctive features" of language. Phonemes are the smallest articulated and signifying units of a language. They are opposed to "phones," which are the actual sounds that a language utilizes. Phonemes are not the sounds that occur in language but the sounds that are phenomenally apprehended as conveying meaning: for instance, in English the letter *t* can be pronounced with an aspiration (a slight *h* sound seemingly added to it) as in an emphatic pronunciation of the word *take* [*t'*]; or it can be pronounced unaspirated, as in *steak*. But in both cases an English speaker will recognize it as variations (or "allophones") of a /t/ phoneme so that someone speaking with an accent that aspirates all /t/s could still be understood. In some languages what are variations of a single phoneme in one language constitute distinct phonemes: thus, English, unlike Chinese, distinguishes between /l/ and /r/, and native Chinese speakers have great trouble with the distinction between these English phonemes precisely because in their native language they are simply variations of the same sound. In every natural language the vast number of possible words is a combination of a small number of phonemes. English, for instance, possesses less than forty phonemes that combine to form over a million different words and the vast number of *different* pronunciations these words are susceptible to.

The phonemes of language, however, are themselves systematically organized. In the 1920s and 1930s, following the lead of Saussure, Jakobson and the great Russian phonologist, N. S. Trubetzkoy isolated the distinctive features of phonemes. These features are based upon the physiological structure of the speech organs—tongue, teeth, vocal chords, etc.—and they combine in "bundles" to form phonemes. No distinctive feature can exist outside of combination with others within a phonemic articulation (one cannot engage the vocal chords without doing other things to produce a sound), and this fact has led some "positivist" thinkers to assert that distinctive features are simply heuristic devices that do not "really" exist. What is more striking, however, is that distinctive features organize and *define* themselves through a logic of binary opposition in terms of their presence and absence. For instance, in English the difference between /t/ and /d/ is the presence or absence of "voice" (the engagement of the vocal chords), and on the level of voicing these phonemes reciprocally define one another; the difference between /p/ and /t/ is that the former possesses the feature of "labiality" (i.e., it is produced by the lips) while the latter is "dental," and again they are defined in relation to one another. In this way phonology is a specific example of a general rule of language Saussure describes:

> in language there are only differences. Even more important: a difference generally implies positive terms between which the difference is set up; but in language there are only differences *without positive terms*. Whether we take the signified or the signifier, language has neither ideas nor sound that existed before the linguistic system, but only conceptual and phonic differences that have issued from the system. The idea or phonic substance that a sign contains is of less importance than the other signs that surround it. (1959:120)

In this framework "positive" identities—what constitutes sameness and, finally, meaning itself—is determined not by inherent qualities but by systemic, structural, relationships.

This conception of the elements of signification being diacritically determined through a system suggests a third assumption governing Saussurean linguistics and semiotics, what Saussure calls "the arbitrary nature of the sign." By this he means that the relationship between the signifier and signified in language is never necessary (or "motivated"): one could just as easily find the sound signifier *arbre* as the signifier *tree* to unite with the concept of "tree." But, more than this, it means that the signified is arbitrary as well: one could as easily define the concept "tree" by its woody quality (which would exclude palm trees) as by its size (which excludes the "low woody plants" we call shrubs). This relationship is not necessary because it is not based upon *inherent* qualities of signifier or signified: the nature of the sign—and of signifiers and signifieds—is governed by systematic diacritical relationships. Moreover, this should make clear that the numbering of assumptions I have been making is not an order of priority:

each assumption—the systemic nature of signification (best apprehended by studying language synchronically), the relational, or "diacritical," nature of the elements of signification, the arbitrary nature of signs—is in relationships of reciprocal presupposition with the others.

In this we can see that the science of signification, like the science of chemistry, is governed by a conceptual framework that understands the phenomena it studies in overarching relationships of *contrast* and *combination*. The elements of language are defined on any particular "level" of understanding in terms of the ways in which they contrast with other elements on that level (just as the periodic table offers the chemical elements in a *systematic* framework of contrasts); while they combine with elements from their own level to create the elements of the next linguistic level (just as chemical elements combine in a systematic fashion determined by their contrasting qualities). Thus, distinctive features combine to form phonemes, and phonemes combine to form morphemes (the smallest units of meaning such as prefixes, suffixes, etc.), and morphemes combine to form words, and words combine to form sentences. In each instance the "whole" of an element is greater than the sum of its parts (just as water, H_2O, is, in Saussure's example, more than the mechanical agglomeration of hydrogen and oxygen).

The great difference, however, between a semiotic (or human) science such as linguistics and a natural science such as chemistry is Saussure's third assumption: the arbitrary nature of the sign. In chemistry the elements of the framework of understanding—particles, chemical elements, molecules—do not present themselves as "arbitrary" but, rather, seem inherent and necessary within the object of study. In studying meaning, on the other hand, the elements present themselves *as* arbitrary: signification can use *any* phenomena to signify. In this aspect of signification we can see the both the basis and manifestation of analogy. Analogues do not seem motivated the way in which the systematic analyses of chemistry do. Rather, analogues, in the very multiplicity, seem arbitrary and capricious. That is, the particular cases of analogy are not in the same relation to the science of meaning that the particular cases of chemical compounds are in relation to the science of chemistry. As Charles Taylor notes in a passage I quote in chapter 4, an analogue is "not a mere example, nor is it a particular case of a regularity" (1991:176). Instead, it is an orientation or an orienting feature that points in a particular direction of developing thought. The clearest example of the difference of the arbitrariness of language and discourse from the seeming motivations of chemistry can be seen, I think, in those instances in which language uses the *absence* of some feature as part of its signifying system, when, as Saussure says, "a material sign is not necessary for the expression of an idea; language is satisfied with the opposition between something and nothing" (1959:86). In chemistry material is always necessary, and the absence of oxygen, say, is simply its absence. But in language—in signification—the negative *works* so that an absence, such as that of "voicing," is more than the simple absence of the sound produced by air rushing across vocal chords. Such absence also produces a signification that, in English, can be perceived in the difference between *site* and *side, dew* and *two*. Absence here is not simple; as Jacques Derrida says in another context, it—and signification in general—is "irreducibly nonsimple" (1982:13).

Such an understanding of the arbitrary nature of the sign leads some to assert the great difference between the natural sciences and the human sciences. Thus, Emile Benveniste has argued that one should draw a fundamental distinction between two orders of phenomena:

> on the one side the physiological and biological data, which present a "simple" nature (no matter what their complexity may be) because they hold entirely within the field in which they appear . . . ; on the other side, the phenomena belonging to the interhuman milieu, which have the characteristic that they can never be taken as simple data or defined in the order of their own nature but must always be understood as double from the fact that they are connected to something else, whatever their "referent" may be. A fact of culture is such only insofar as it refers to something else. (1971:38–39)

The connection to something else that Benveniste describes is a nonreductive *analogical* connection. Moreover, the fundamental distinction he asserts is, I think, better conceived as a distinction in the *level* of analysis, since even the simplicity of physiological and biological data can be taken up, arbitrarily, as signs within systems of signification and thus can be apprehended as nonsimple. Still, Benveniste is correct in asserting that the overriding fact of culture is signification, the fact that phenomena— whatever we can "perceive"—always means something, always signifies. Semiotics studies such signifying cultural phenomena—the phenomenon of signification itself—in as exact and generalizing a way as the natural sciences study physical and biological phenomena, even if, as the poststructuralist critique of semiotics suggests, the irreducible "nonsimplicity" of signifying interhuman phenomena undermines, in significant ways, this scientific project.

Semiotics and Interpretation

It is in the remarkable and revolutionary assumptions about meaning and about the kinds of explanation the phenomenon of signification in language called for, developed by structural linguistics, that led Cassirer to claim that it changed our whole concept of the world. "For this to happen," Culler says of this claim, linguistics "would have to become a model for thinking about social and cultural activities in general . . . [so that we would] come to think about our social and cultural world as a series of sign systems comparable with languages" (1981:25). In other words, because of the linguistic concepts of the arbitrary nature of sign and the relational nature of the elements of signification, semiotics can study signifying phenomena beyond the limits of the sentence—the usual limit of linguistic analysis— within a conceptual framework similar to, if not identical with, that of structural linguistics. Thus, in *Elements of Semiology* Barthes argues that the connotations of language arise systematically when language takes up the accidental variants of its elements and uses them, arbitrarily, within a relational system of signification: "the rolled *r* is a mere combinative variant at the denotative level," he writes, "but in the speech of the theatre, for instance, it signals a country accent and therefore is part of a code, without which the message of 'ruralness' could not be either emitted or perceived" (1968:20). In the same way discourse can take up a whole sign—*wine* in French culture, for example—and have it, as the union of its signifier and signified ("an alcoholic drink made from grapes") function, connotatively, to signify, as Barthes argues, the French nation itself (1973:58–61).

Besides such more or less linguistic phenomena, semiotics studies various social forms that function in the manner of a language: Barthes's work on the *Mythologies* of culture is an example in which he describes the significance of such nonverbal phenomena as wrestling, wine, or Greta Garbo's face as signifiers in culture. In a similar way Lévi-Strauss analyzes the *Elementary Structures of Kinship* in so-called primitive cultures in a manner analogous to that in which Saussure and Jakobson analyze the elementary structures of language. In this analysis Lévi-Strauss sees the women exchanged between men of different tribes as governed by underlying structures of binary oppositions that produce its significance. In later studies he pursues this "structuralist" analysis in cultural myths, but he is less interested in myth as linguistic phenomena than as semiotic, cultural phenomena that serve social ends. Thus, he argues that myths are structured like a language on a level that is higher than linguistic analysis—on the level of the narrative discourse as a whole—in analyses that define "a 'universe of the tale,' analyzable in pairs of opposition interlocked within each character who—far from constituting a single entity—forms a bundle of distinctive features like the phoneme in Roman Jakobson's theory" (Lévi-Strauss 1984:182). In one example he notes that "in a tale a 'king' is not only a king and a 'shepherdess' not only a shepherdess; these words and what they signify become recognizable means of constructing a system formed by the oppositions *male/female* (with regard to *nature*) and *high/low* (with regard to *culture*), as well as permutations among the six terms" (1984:187).

In this, as Culler says of Cassirer, Lévi-Strauss is creating a model for thinking about social and cultural activities by raising the largest questions about the relationship of nature and culture in a conceptual framework that is coherent and systematic. In this way semiotics has examined phenomena as different as the general semiotics of the natural world and the special semiotics of the legal system. In *A Theory of Semiotics* Eco describes the range of semiotics from the study of the "the communicative behavior of non-human . . . communities" in *Zoosemiotics* through *olfactory signs, tactile communication, codes of taste, visual communication,* to specific cultural codes like those of *medicine, music, writing, text theory, aesthetic texts,* and *mass communication* (see Culler 1981 for this taxonomy). Some of the most important work in semiotics is being done in film studies. But, more than this, semiotics can also examine social and political phenomena: it can help us understand racism and sexism as functioning signifying systems. All these areas of study clearly indicate the arbitrary nature of signs: signification (or, the broader sense of signification, "semiosis"), as I have said, can and will use anything at hand—sound, color, gender, skin color— for the sake of its meanings, its process of signification.

In this we can see that literary criticism has a central, and perhaps a leading, role in semiotics insofar as criticism pursues, more or less systematically, interpretation. Moreover, it should be equally clear that the semiotic study of literary texts as signifying systems has an important role in literary studies. Literature is important to semiotics because the nature of literary texts underlines the central importance of semiosis in human life. In fact, many literary texts make the processes of signification their very theme. I am thinking not only of more or less "experimental" texts, like *Tristram Shandy* or *Ulysses* or *Pale Fire,* but even more "traditional" texts such as *Moby-Dick* or *Mansfield Park* or *The Prelude.* Literature makes the process of finding meaning in the world—of signifying—something to be examined, so that when the life of Fanny Price is described in *Mansfield Park* it is described as the narrative of her learning how things signify in a social class different from her own. This is the object of Norman Mailer's criticism of Edith Wharton, which I discuss in chapter 7, in whose work he discerns an upper middle class looking for "a refinement of itself to prepare a shift to the aristocratic" (1966:96) by means of a particular mode of interpretation of experience.

Moreover, literature forces us to attend to the process of signification itself. When Augustine distinguishes between things and signs in *On Christian Doctrine,* he defines a thing as "that which is not used to signify something else," much as Benveniste does. Augustine's theological semiotics requires such a distinction as part of its faith that "doctrine"—that is, Christian significations—is more than one sign system among others. (Benveniste does so to assert that *his* doctrine, linguistics, is more than one systematic treatment of meaning among others.) But nothing (no *thing*) in a literary text is not used to signify something else—each literary text is simply a sign system (or subsystem) among others—so that, as I mentioned already, literature cannot be satisfactorily explained by "accident" or by saying that its representations are simply the way things are. In literature, then—as in analogical thinking more generally—the *things* a literary text presents and which constitute it are apprehended, analogously, as *events* in the world. (I pursue this relationship between things and events in the postscript.) Literature—and the interpretations of literary criticism—need to account for everything literary texts contain in terms of their *function,* what sense they make. In this, literature lends itself, perhaps more strikingly than other signifying phenomena, to demonstrating semiosis.

But, more than this, the study of literature, with its self-conscious use of figurative language and its constant foregrounding not only of the "contents" of meaning but the "process" of their presentation can help to *situate* semiotics and the human sciences—to locate semiotics within culture. For instance, in a novel like *An American Tragedy,* or even *Gulliver's Travels,* the ways in which the narrator understands the world is as important to the text as the worlds these books present. And this doubling—always present in literature precisely because literature, as Culler says, "is cut off from the immediate pragmatic purposes which simplify other sign situations" so that in it "the potential complexities of signifying processes work freely" (1981:35)—not only reiterates Benveniste's distinction between natural and human science; it also marks the limits of semiotics. As Derrida (among others) demonstrates in his "poststructuralist" critique—I examine this in the following chapter—the scientific aim of semiotics is undermined by the doubleness of signification. If all things signify—if, as Derrida says, *logos* has a "father" to which it is "connected" within the human milieu—neither that father nor that signification is "in any 'real' sense prior to or outside all relation to language. . . . In other words, it is precisely *logos* that enables us to perceive and investigate something like paternity" (1981a:80). In the same way, signification allows us to investigate semiotics: as I argue in the following chapter, the arbitrary nature of the sign means that signs can signify their own meaninglessness; that, if signification is everywhere, it is also nowhere. Thus, if semiotics teaches us that literature can be studied scientifically, then literature teaches us that science—and especially semiotic science—can be understood as unique *rhetorical* events that also can be situated within *historical* frameworks. This double movement is one of the ways analogies work: the connections they make are altogether nonreductive so that traffic backward and forward is always possible.

Still, if literary interpretation has a central role in semiotics, then semiotics can help us reconceive and understand more fully the nature and functioning of literary texts. Frye is perhaps most clear about this in his essay calling for the scientific study of literature, and his book *Anatomy of Criticism* is a sustained argument for the systematization of literary studies in ways that would produce knowledge comparable to the discoveries of knowledge that physics and chemistry—and linguistics, for that matter—have achieved. That is, semiotics can raise important new questions about the nature of literature and the nature of the meanings and meaning-effects it achieves from the minute particulars of the functioning of its metaphors and rhetoric through the ordering of its common modes and genres to the largest questions, such as I raise in relation to biblical studies in chapter 6, about its social functions: how it helps to create desire and social roles (e.g., sexual, class, religious, and racial roles) and to carry the "burden" of cultural values in general that Matthew Arnold described as the function of literature. The study of signs in culture has been one of the ways people have attempted to understand what Locke calls "human understanding" and Augustine describes as more than human understanding from the beginnings of our culture in the West. Such understanding has consistently focused on language and literature. Semiotics is attempting to systematize that understanding so that we can know how literature functions to affect us individually and socially.

Chapter 2

Deconstruction and Linguistic Analysis

"However the topic is considered," Jacques Derrida begins *Of Grammatology,* "the *problem of language* has never been simply one problem among others" (1976:6). This is because, as he says elsewhere in describing Husserl's phenomenology, "all experience is the experience of meaning *(Sinn)*. Everything that appears to consciousness, everything that is for consciousness in general, is *meaning.* Meaning is the phenomenality of phenomenon" (1981:30). Nevertheless, the problem of language—the science of linguistics—has always hovered on the margins of literary studies (if not philosophy), as if the "meaning" Derrida talks of were somehow outside the language that manifests it, as if language were simply the means to the end of meaning. For Derrida, however, this is precisely the "problem" of language: the complex relationship, whose existence linguistics forces us to acknowledge, between meaning and communication. Moreover, for Derrida this complex relationship is not one "marginal" problem among many; it is a "central" problem, representative, founding, titular. For this reason he argues that in recent times linguistics has taken a special place in the study of what has come to be called the "human sciences." "The very modernity of linguistic science," Derrida asserts, can be reconceived in the formulation of "modernity *as* linguistic science, since so many other 'human sciences' refer to linguistics as their titular model" (1982:139). Derrida is "modern" in this way as well, using the "semiology" of Ferdinand de Saussure as a model of sorts for his own "grammatology" (1981:26–27).

His use of Saussure's model, however, is problematic; it is what some would call an abuse rather than a use but which more precisely is a mode of analogical thinking. It is a *deconstructive* rather than a *destructive* use of Saussure. There is, as I argue here, a direct relationship between Derrida's procedures of deconstruction and the methods of linguistic analysis. But that relationship does the work of the negative, of negation or denial; it is a negative relationship that Derrida himself calls an "explosion": deconstruction "explodes" or "exceeds" the logic of linguistic science. Such a negative relationship, however, does not simply negate its object by effacing or erasing it; rather, it "denies" it, to use a term translated from the French *dénégation* of A. J. Greimas, or puts it "under erasure," to use Derrida's own early expression (see *Grammatology*), so that what is denied is destroyed and exploded but not reductively taken up within the simple unity of another mode of apprehension. What is denied (negated) is also susceptible to excess; although exploded, Saussure's semiology *remains* enough of a model to be exceeded. Poststructuralist deconstruction remains connected to the scientific structural linguistics, the scientific semiotics, it explodes.

The Linguistic Model

Saussurean linguistics can be a model for modern thought because it offers what Derrida calls "an entire theory of language: a functional, systematic, and structural theory" that attempts to comprehend the phenomena of signification (1982:144) in the manner described in the preceding chapter. In a way—perhaps as always—Derrida is redundant in his description of the entirety of theory: for linguistics *functional, systematic,* and *structural* all refer to the same perception about the nature of language and to the same assumptions necessary for its scientific study. "We can say," Saussure notes, "that what is natural to mankind is not oral speech but the faculty of constructing a language; i.e. a system of distinct signs corresponding to distinct ideas" (1959:10). Such a definition of language seems a truism, but there have been several schools of linguistics in the twentieth century that attempted to study language without regard to meaning, or "ideas."[1] Nevertheless, Saussure defined meaning as the *function* of language that could not be bracketed in the science of linguistics, and in doing so he implied that linguistics needs to be functional, systematic, and structural.

As we have seen in the preceding chapter, the systematic and structural aspects of modern linguistics—and the methods in various "human sciences" they have spawned—are closely connected to its scientific aim.

---

1. Such attempts, I should add, are not as absurd as this may sound. They are a gesture of American linguistics usually associated with the name of Leonard Bloomfield. An overriding influence on American linguistics has been the existence, and progressive extinction, of hundreds of unrecorded languages of Native American speakers. Early in the twentieth century linguistics in America was faced with the urgent necessity of describing hundreds of American Indian languages in the process of dying out. "In these circumstances," John Lyons notes, "it is not surprising that American linguists have given considerable attention to the development of what are called 'field methods'—techniques for the recording and analysis of languages that the linguist himself could not speak and that had not been previously committed to writing" (1977:21).

The systematic aspect of language, what Saussure calls *la langue* and Roman Jakobson calls the "code," Saussure describes as "a self-contained whole and a principle of classification," which, as soon as it is given "first place among the facts of language," introduces "a natural order into a mass that lends itself to no other classification" (1959:9) in which, we have seen, the structures of language determine its elements solely in relationships of what Greimas calls "reciprocal presupposition" (1983:8). In this conception the elements of language inhabit a systematic structure and are purely relational and negative (without positive poles). Thus, Saussure inscribes in his theory of language the distinction Roman Jakobson makes, which I cited in the preceding chapter, between mechanical agglomeration and structural whole. "To consider a term as simply the union of a certain sound with a certain concept," Saussure asserted, "is grossly misleading. To define it in this way would isolate the term from its system; it would mean assuming that one can start from the terms and construct the system by adding them together when, on the contrary, it is from the interdependent whole that one must start and through analysis obtain its elements" (1959:113). Echoing Benveniste's assertion of the necessary "connections" within semiotics systems (what I am describing as *analogical* connections), Saussure wrote elsewhere that

> the absolutely final law of language is, we dare say, that there is nothing which can ever reside in one term, as a direct consequence of the fact that linguistic symbols are unrelated to what they should designate, so that *a* is powerless to designate anything without the aid of *b,* and the same thing is true of *b* without the aid of *a,* or that both have no value except through their reciprocal difference, or that neither has any value, even through a certain part of itself (I suppose "the root," etc.) other than through this same plexus of eternally negative differences. (Cited in Benveniste 1971:36)

Implicit here is that two related concepts govern structure and system: the arbitrary nature of the sign (or "linguistic symbols") and the negativity of Saussure's definition of the elements of language.

It stands to reason, beginning with Saussure's conceptions of system and structure, that the goal and function of language—what I will call meaning and communication—must be inscribed in linguistics. If one cannot begin with isolated terms but only with a system, while at the same time the system is only manifested in terms themselves defined relationally (i.e., negatively), then one must reorient oneself toward functions and goals rather than toward causes. Such conceptions—as Derrida is at great pains to demonstrate—eliminate *origin* as an explanation; they replace origin with a nonoriginary play of differences and thus make *function* rather than *cause* the criterion for understanding.

Still, inscribed here, at the heart of structural linguistics, is the *problem* of language. That problem is the doubleness of linguistic "function" as both a means and an end, as both a communicating and signifying structure. Thus, Thomas Sebeok noted that the subject matter of semiotics "is communication, message exchanges of every conceivable variety, although it is also centrally concerned with the study of signification" (1986:14). That is, *function* is not a simple concept: it signifies both function and goal. The function of language is what Benveniste calls "intersubjective communication" (1971:219), but that "functioning" entails, "is concerned with," *meaning:* distinct signs corresponding to distinct ideas. Language, functionally conceived, establishes meaning in general and the particular meanings of communication. And the *nonreductive* analogical relationship between the level of global meaning and the particular meanings of communication is the central *problem,* as Derrida says, of language.

This problem is most clearly delineated in the great achievement of structural linguistics, its virtual invention and development of phonology between 1929 and 1939 by the Prague School of Linguistics along Saussurean lines. Linguistics, Derrida notes in the *Grammatology,* "wishes to be the science of language," and "the scientificity of that science is often acknowledged because of its *phonological* foundations. Phonology, it is often said today, communicates its scientificity to linguistics, which in turn serves as the epistemological model for all the sciences of man" (1976:29). Prague phonology, as opposed to phonetics, studies the sound patterns of language insofar as they are functional in the sense of *communicating* meaning. It studies the discriminating function of the physical sounds of language. Its unit is the phoneme, which, not meaningful itself, nevertheless distinguishes *differences of meaning* in language. Such distinctions, as Saussure says, are purely "negative."

Phonetics studies the occurrences of sound in language, all the differences, signifying or not, in pronunciation. In English, for instance, phonetics might examine the difference between the aspirated *t* in *ton* as opposed to the unaspirated *t* in *stun*. While such a difference is a physiological datum of English, it is not a "distinctive" difference, since in English it never *functions* to communicate different meanings; it never discriminates between two significations. In English the *phonetic* unit, the aspirated [t'], never creates a signifying difference in contrast to the unaspirated *t* in the way the *phonological* unit /t/ is distinct from /d/ producing the difference in meaning between *two* and *dew*, to repeat an example from the preceding chapter. (In some languages other than English aspiration is a distinctive feature.)

In phonology, then, as Jakobson wrote in 1932, "the basic linguistic function of sound differences is the distinction of meanings" (1962:231). Moreover, every phoneme can be analyzed as a collection of immanent features—"ultimate linguistic constituents," which Jakobson calls "distinctive features" (1962:422)—which, as we saw, are never realized independently but only in combinations within particular phonemes. Distinctive features create *signifying* differences in contrast with their binary opposites in the combination (or bundle) of features of different phonemes. Thus, the forty-two phonemes of Russian can be described by combining some or all of only eleven distinctive features in terms of their presence or absence (Jakobson 1962:450–51). Such distinctive features—voiced versus unvoiced in the opposition of /d/ versus /t/ in English, in a simple instance I have already noted—exist only in a structure of negative differences. By systematically establishing the differential nature of linguistic elements, phonology has most convincingly confirmed Saussure's theory of language. Phonology systematically substantiates Saussure's contention that "a material sign is not necessary for the expression of an idea; language is satisfied with the opposition between something and nothing" (1959:86): the absence of voicing in this instance is just as signifying as its presence. It was this systematic aspect of Prague phonology, more than anything else, that became the "model" of the human sciences. It led Lévi-Strauss in his structural anthropology, for example, to liken the characters of folktales and myth to the "bundle of distinctive features like the phoneme in Roman Jakobson's theory" (1984:182).

Such a conception of phonology emphasizes the scientific aspect of linguistics I examined in the preceding chapter by emphasizing the "physiological" rather than the significative aspect of language in the abstract formalism of nomological science. It separates and emphasizes the *communicative function* of language, achieved by the construction of differences, from its articulations of *meaning*. That is, this conception of phonology separates what Louis Hjelmslev calls the planes of "content" and "expression"; it separates what André Martinet calls the "semantic content" from the "phonic shape" of language. It assumes that language is "biplanar" and thus leads to what Martinet describes as the "double articulation" of language, the separation of the articulation of meaning from the negative articulation of phonological differences as such. Following Saussure, Martinet argues that the "first articulation" of language constructs a system of distinct signs corresponding to distinct ideas, that it creates its signifying values by means of the reciprocal differences of its elements. The "second articulation," however, constitutes the minimum meaningful units more "simply," solely by means of abstract formalism, the presence or absence of physical properties. Thus, Martinet offers this functional definition of language: "A language is a medium of communication according to which human experience is analysed, differently in each community, into units (monemes) with a semantic content and a phonic shape. This phonic shape, in its turn, is articulated in distinctive and successive units (phonemes)" (1962:26). The second articulation functions *negatively* in terms of the "marked" presence and absence of its elements (such as the presence and absence of voicing). Thus, phonemes, Martinet argues, unlike the other elements of language, can be established by distributional analysis "listing all the phonemes that appear in a given context" (1962:41).

The significant distinctions of the first articulation, even though they are constituted diacritically, are "additive," while those of the second articulation are "destructive." Thus, the diacritical opposition, presence versus absence, functions differently on two planes of articulation. The presence of a phoneme, Martinet writes,

> signalizes that any inference, as to the meaning of the utterance, which might be drawn from the context considered without it is wrong: if, to the statement *it is good,* I add *very,* I am just adding some additional information without deleting what was previously there, but if to the statement *it is a roe* I add a /d/ phoneme, the statement becomes *it is a road;* one element of information *roe* is deleted and replaced by another one. (1962:36)

The second articulation of "sounds" (or really the "sound images" of phonemes, as Saussure calls them) is simple in comparison to the first articulation of meaning. The "addition" of information functions in the manner analogy functions, to thicken and complicate meaning.

Such a conception of language as a system of the combination of elements, not meaningful in themselves, that produces meaning governs the *semiological* analyses of Lévi-Strauss and Roland Barthes. But with this difference: the elements of the second articulation in language are articulated solely (and "simply") for the purpose of the functioning of language in both senses of *functioning;* the elements of the second articulation of other semiological systems—myth, fashion, food—are found at hand, a kind of *bricolage.*² As Barthes says, "in opposition to human language, in which the phonic substance is immediately significant, and only significant, most semiological systems probably involve a matter which has another function beside that of being significant (bread is used to nourish, garments to protect)" (1967:68). In semiology, as opposed to linguistics, the second articulation does not exist as such.

While language seems to differentiate more clearly between the communicative functioning and the signifying goal than other semiotic systems and thereby achieves, more "immediately," as Barthes says, the immediacy of purpose and functioning—the immediacy of "significance"—there are moments in language when the differentiation breaks down. One such moment occurs in what N. S. Trubetzkoy described as phonological *neutralization.* While the binary oppositions of some phonemes can be "constant"—that is, the opposition distinguishes significations "in all conceivable positions" (1969:77)—other phonological oppositions no longer function to distinguish meanings in particular positions or contexts. Thus, Trubetzkoy argues, "in German the bilateral opposition *d-t* is neutralized in final position [of words]. The [phoneme] which occurs in the position of neutralization, from a phonological point of view is neither a voiced stop nor a voiceless stop" (1969:79). Trubetzkoy calls such neutralized phonemes "archiphonemes," by which, he notes, "we understand the sum of distinctive properties that two phonemes have in common" (1969:79).

An example from English will make this clear. The "significant" distinction between *two* and *dew* is a function of the phonological distinction between /t/ and /d/ based upon the presence and absence of the distinctive feature voicing: /t/ does not engage the vocal chords, while /d/ does. In the context of /s/, however, in *stew* for instance, the phonological opposition between /t/ and /d/ no longer distinguishes meaning. "It's due" and "it's stew" are indistinguishable; *stew* could just as well be written as **sdew.* Instead, in place of the /t/ of *two* in this context we pronounce an archiphoneme that has all the characteristics of /t/ except that it is not opposed to /d/. Here, then, the phoneme /t/ is analogous to the "bread" in Barthes's description of semiology: designed for some other purpose, it is

2. *Bricolage* is a term Lévi-Strauss coined in *The Savage Mind* (1966:17ff.) to signify material *already at hand* to do the work of signification. Thus, *bricolage* signifies the second articulation conceived as nonsystematic, that is, nonarticulated. Derrida addresses Lévi-Strauss's concept in the *Grammatology* (1976:138–39) and argues that the opposition between engineer and *bricoleur* is one founded upon a "technotheological significance"—a significance that inhabits linguistics (especially phonology) conceived of as "scientific."

appropriated by language to serve *its* purposes (in this instance to create a phoneme that is not a part of the English phonological system, the neutralized archiphoneme).

The neutralized archiphoneme, as Trubetzkoy conceives it, manifests itself as the *unmarked* phoneme, in this example as /t/ (in which voicing is unmarked, absent). Here we can explore the wide-ranging significance of the *unmarked* feature in language. In phonology the term *unmarked* is quite literal: what is unmarked does not possess the feature in question. Thus, an unmarked term conveys less information than a marked term. But the absence of a feature is not "simple": an unmarked term exists both as the *restricted* opposite of a marked term (unvoiced as opposed to voiced) and as the manifestation of the *general* neutralization of the oppositional category altogether, as the neutralized archiphoneme. That is, the unmarked term is a complex structure, and its complexity is marked, precisely, by analogical understandings that cannot be reduced one to the other.

Jakobson argues that the opposition between marked and unmarked terms and its possible neutralization exist on the morphological and semantic levels of language—the plane of the first articulation—as well as on the phonological level. (On the plane of the first articulation, however, the unmarked sign is not simply the "absence" of a particular signification the way it is in the second articulation. It is this difference that distinguishes the strict difference between the planes of language Martinet perceives and the strict identity of structures Jakobson sees.) In both phonological and semantic analyses of language the unmarked term conveys less information than the marked term and articulates the neutralization of the opposition. That is, the unmarked element articulates both a general term and a restricted term in relation to the marked term. In the phonological example I am using, *restrictedly* /t/ is /unvoiced/ in relation to /d/, and *generally* it displaces the category of voicing as a distinctive feature of English in the contexts in which it articulates the neutralized archiphoneme. In semantics an unmarked term, *old* for instance, is opposed to *young;* but in the context of a sentence such as "Benjamin is fifteen years old" the opposition is neutralized so that *old* simply signifies /agedness/. "In comparison to the unmarked term," Elmar Holenstein writes,

> the marked term provides more information. This is best illustrated by the example of polar adjectives and nouns. The statement "Peter is as young as Paul" is more informative than the statement "Peter is as old as Paul." Someone unfamiliar with Paul's age knows, after the first statement, that he is relatively young while the second statement reveals

nothing about his age. *Young* is the marked term, *old* the unmarked term. Two oppositions overlap in the relation marked/unmarked—the opposition between a positive and a negative term and between an indefinite and a definite one. (1976:131)

An "indefinite" signification is still an *existing* signification, but its lack of definitiveness is precisely the absence of a "marking."

Moreover, the unmarked semantic term is an instance of what I have called *semantic formalism,* in which formal properties—in this case the formal binarity of marked versus unmarked—generate meaning. Thus, Gary Saul Morson and Caryl Emerson distinguish between *responsibility* and Mikhail Bakhtin's conception of *answerability* and note that answerability "is more abstract and less tied to a specific act" (1990:76) in the same way, analogically, that *old* is no longer tied to its polar opposite, *young,* but signifies the more abstract "agedness." In Bakhtin's neologism they are presenting the semantics of a formally unmarked term. But, when they go on to assert that one's responsibility or obligation "in answerability is to rescue the other from pure potential; reaching out to another consciousness makes the other coalesce, and turns the other's 'mere potential' into space that is open to the living event" (1990:76), the "coalescence" they describe takes place *formally* on another level of meaning. In this way the "answerability" Bakhtin describes—or, more generally, the "semantic formalism" I am describing—imports and superimposes, as analogy does, one level of meaning onto another. In this context we can even see, as they do not, that coalescence describes the realization of an archiphoneme—or, rather, an "archi-sememe"—of abstract, unmarked meaning. This, I am arguing, is the *semantic* work of analogy and analogical thinking: analogies coalesce the potential abstractions of unmarked meaning into the living fabric of signification. To assert the analogical relationships between disciplines of arts and sciences, as I do in part 2, or between modernism and postmodernism, as I do in part 3—or even the analogical relationship between Descartes and Foucault, which is the purport of the postscript—allows for the *realization* of meaning from the negative work of logical contradiction. "Contradiction," as Bruno Latour asserts in a characterization that could also describe analogy, "is a property of reading letters and signs inside new settings" (1986: 20). (In chap. 4 I describe such "realization" as the "notation of knowledge" to get a sense of the combination of the recognition of meaning and the formal depiction of writing, between seeing and witnessing.) The *semantic formalism* of such "reading" neutralizes the opposition between the formality of letters and the phenomenality of the world.

Still, the unmarked term that Holenstein describes *allows for* the formal reductions—the *abstract formalism*—of nomological science, the subsumption of the particular case in the general case rather than (or along with) the momentary semantic realizations and notations of analogical thinking. Such subsumption erases the particularities of local meaning in the "timeless" universals of general meanings. But, given the arbitrary nature of the sign, such an operation can always be apprehended as a sign of meaning, a coalescence of meaning *analogous* to politics, for instance—which is to say "interested," "conflictual," and "violent"—even if *this* politics functions by rendering its position "self-evident" and seemingly disinterestedly, abstractly "true." Thus, an example of the coalescence of meaning within a seemingly "formal" neutralization—one that pronounces the always-present political implications of this analysis—can be seen in the opposition between *man* and *woman*. The neutralization occurs in contexts such as *chairman* in which -*man* signifies /person/, in which the absence of the morpheme /wə/ no longer signifies. And it occurs in the context of the opposition between unmarked *he* and the marked *she* (marked by the phoneme /š/), which is neutralized as the general *he*. A similar "politics" can be seen in the opposition between *old* and *young* that Holenstein presents and I presented in the introduction insofar as the unmarked term, *old*, defines itself as standard and normal. It can also be seen in the opposition between *responsibility* and *answerability* in Bakhtin insofar as the unmarked term, *responsibility*, seems to make the interpersonal relationship of self and other simply one relationship among others.

The semantic formalism of neutralization, I am arguing, allows for the *effect* of abstract formalism even while it brings together different levels of meaning. In doing so, it creates a possible relationship between logic and semantics—logical understanding and analogical understanding—by allowing the apprehension of the formal, seemingly abstract term to coalesce into meaning. In the Greimassian square I presented in the introduction, the seeming abstraction of /agedness/—"possessing any age at all," "existing in time," etc.—presents itself as an unmarked archi-sememe. Yet in the context of *its* opposite, /timelessness/, it is rendered a marked term on another level of meaning, in which the politics of the normal, unmarked meaning of *old* can be read. Thus, its formal neutralization of the opposition of old versus young generates another signifying opposition in its apprehension as similar to, but not identical with, the opposition it neutralizes. Such semantic formalism, like analogies themselves, can be endlessly repeated as a nonsemantic operation becomes a sign, in the same manner as, in Bannet's description of Wittgenstein's understanding, "we are always moving meaning from one situation to another which might not be quite the same" (1997:656). I believe that this description accounts for the operation of analogy—the ways that it prevents similarity from being too quickly absorbed into identity—in terms of formal, structural linguistics.

Deconstruction and Neutralization

I have spent so much time here on an exposition of concepts inhabiting classical Continental linguistics—and especially the terms of linguists (Saussure, Jakobson, Martinet, Benveniste, Hjelmslev) that Derrida repeatedly refers to and analyzes—because there is, as I have said, a direct relationship between the development of deconstruction and the methods of linguistic analysis. This relationship is analogical in a way that underlines the extreme of analogy, its *negative* functioning. To state this relationship succinctly: deconstruction is the contrary—the negation or denial—of linguistic neutralization. It emphasizes the work of the negative in signification that coalesces, absently, in the negativity of the *unmarked* term.

Inscribed in neutralization is the marking and unmarking of elements of language *and* the conception of language as inhabiting different hierarchical levels. That is, inscribed in neutralization is Saussure's central conception of language, what Jonathan Culler has called "the basic structural principle, that items are defined by their contrasts with other items and their ability to combine to form higher-level items" (1976:50). At the same time neutralization encompasses a "plexus of eternally negative differences," a double negation of opposition and its neutralization (Benveniste 1971:36). Thus, in *Margins of Philosophy*—in fact, on *its* margin, in the "preface" to that volume—Derrida describes "philosophical power" in terms that also describe neutralization: "philosophical power," he writes, combines "a *hierarchy*" analogous to the hierarchy of the opposition of unmarked versus marked terms and "an *envelopment*" in which "the whole is implied . . . in each part" (1982:xix, xx).

Throughout his work Derrida is anxious to note that deconstruction is not neutralization. "What . . . I am attempting to pursue," he says in *Positions,* is "a kind of *general strategy of deconstruction*. The latter is to avoid both simply *neutralizing* the binary oppositions of metaphysics and simply *residing* within the closed field of these oppositions, thereby confirming it" (1981:41). Derrida himself goes on to define *deconstruction* succinctly: deconstruction, he says, proceeds by the reversal, or "overturning," of classical binary oppositions, in which "one of the two terms governs the other" in a "violent hierarchy" (1981:41)—the hierarchy of what I am calling unmarked and marked semantic terms. Deconstruction then displaces the difference in a kind of neutralization that is no neutralization at all but, rather, *negates* ("explodes") neutralization, "resisting and disorganizing it," as Derrida says, "*without ever* constituting a third term, without ever leaving room for a solution in the form of speculative dialectics" (1981:43). Deconstruction does not "rest" in its "neutralizing" term. Hence, it is not neutralizing; rather, it is transformational, inextricably bound to a particular semiotic field, explosive: "the force and form of its disruption," Derrida says, "*explode* the semantic horizon" (1981:45).

Let me make this clear in the semantic opposition between "speech" and "writing," *to say* as opposed to *to write*. In this opposition *to say* is the unmarked term: the sentence "Derrida says so and so" indiscriminately can mean that he "says" so in an oral interview (such as *Positions*) and in a written text (such as *Margins*); the neutralized sense of *to say* is /to assert/. On the other hand, "writing" is the marked term: the sentence "Derrida writes so and so" can only mean in a text or book. In English "to say" (in the sense of "to assert") neutralizes the opposition between saying (speech) and writing. Deconstruction, then, would "overturn" this opposition, this hierarchy, and assert that speech, in fact, is a species of writing, that writing is the originary term of which speech is the special case: language itself, Derrida asserts in *Grammatology*, is "a species *of* writing" (1976:52). Such an overturning, or reversal, however, simply resides in the closed field of this opposition; it reinscribes the old hierarchy in a negative form. In order to *displace* this hierarchy, deconstruction presents a *deconstructive* term in the position of the neutralizing term in such a way that it resists and disorganizes the hierarchy. It accomplishes this by *analogy:* "displacement" is a strong description of the work of analogical thinking. Such thinking, in Derrida's "deconstruction," *positions* the marked term as if it were unmarked; it replaces hierarchy with analogy. In the opposition between speech and writing Derrida coins the term *arche-writing* not only to conceive of speech as a species of writing but to displace our "received" sense of language. His term is analogous to Trubetzkoy's term *archiphoneme*.

This is not, as we say, simply a matter of "semantics," simply the trivial case of different words for the same meanings. Rather, the radical analogy of deconstruction reorients us in relation to the seemingly "natural" and "self-evident" meanings that inhabit our language. This disruptive reorientation is perhaps more audible in the use of the pronoun *she* in contexts that call for the neutralized general term *he*. For instance, in the "Translator's Preface" to *Grammatology* Gayatri Spivak notes that "as she deconstructs, all protestations to the contrary, the critic necessarily assumes that she at least, and for the time being, means what she says" (1976:lxxvii). In such contexts we cannot but *hear* the attempt at, and the failure of, neutralization, the denial and negation of neutralization, in the same way we cannot help but note the semantic oddity of referring to someone as "ninety years young." *She* conveys more information than simply "a critic," the general critic, the critic as person: we are presented with a "female critic," and that greater information makes the "third term" impossible, "irreducibly non-simple" (1982:13). The deconstructive term *she* conveys what Derrida calls the violence inscribed in the seemingly natural and self-evident use of *he* to mean "person" or *man* to mean "humanity" or *old* to mean "possessing any age at all." The deconstructive term is neither second nor third.

Derrida occasionally calls such a marked unmarked term a "graft," the mark within the unmarked position the "trace." Such a "third term" is deconstructive rather than neutralizing: it is never quite constituted as a third term precisely because it is constituted as a hyphenated, "grafted" term. "Arche-writing" is one example, but "grammatology" is a defining example because it defines the graft itself: *grammatology* grafts together *gram*, the word for the "mark" of writing, and *logos*, the word for speech. In this way it is "irreducibly nonsimple." In the example I am using, what marks the graft—the nonassimilation of significances, the non-neutralization of meanings, which is the work of analogy—is precisely the fact that it uses a semantically marked term, *she*, to articulate the neutralization, and the marked term carries with it the semantic trace of its opposite (woman as a marked man, a species of man; young as a species of old). Such a trace, as we shall see, does not have to be meaningful; it can be "communicated" by the second articulation of language. But, of course, what is communicated is more than *difference of meaning* (though as a trace it is not clear how much more it is); it is also *the meaning of difference*: a particular meaning—or, rather, "explosion" of meaning—in a particular context.

Perhaps the most explicit articulation of deconstruction in Derrida's writing (as opposed to the spoken interview of *Positions*) occurs on the last page of *Margins of Philosophy*, the other margin from its preface.

> Very schematically: an opposition of metaphysical concepts (for example, speech/writing, presence/absence, etc.) is never the face-to-face of two terms, but a hierarchy and an order of subordination. Deconstruction cannot limit itself or proceed immediately to a neutralization; it must, by means of a double gesture, a double science, a double writing, practice an *overturning* of the classical opposition

and a general *displacement* of the system. . . . Deconstruction does not consist in passing from one concept to another, but in overturning and displacing a conceptual order, as well as the nonconceptual order with which the conceptual order is articulated. For example, writing, as a classical concept, carries with it predicates which have been subordinated, excluded, or held in reserve by forces and according to necessities to be analyzed. It is these predicates (I have mentioned some) whose force of generality, generalization, and generativity find themselves liberated, grafted onto a "new" concept of writing which also corresponds to whatever always has *resisted* the former organization of forces, which always has constituted the *remainder* irreducible to the dominant force which organized the—to say it quickly—logocentric hierarchy. To leave this new concept the old name of writing is to maintain the structure of the graft, the transition and indispensable adherence to an effective *intervention* in the constituted historic field. And it is also to give their chance and their force, their power of *communication,* to everything played out in the operations of deconstruction. (1982:329–30)

The "old name" is the marked term, and deconstruction functions by the analogical *displacement* of marking. Here again Derrida asserts that the subordination of writing to speech is *necessary* to the "former organization of forces" in the Saussurean sense that it *articulated* that order—assertions, mankind, agedness—in which the organization of forces came to rest. But that generalization itself is diacritically established in relation to what resists it, to what is, as Derrida says, a "*remainder* irreducible to the dominant force." If speech serves to communicate intentional meaning, then writing, conceived as Derrida conceives of it as the play of differences, as noncommunicative, as a "dead letter," is "irreducible" to the dominant force. Thus, if the neutralizing term creates this explosion: by using a marked term—*woman, writing, white, mark* itself—deconstruction conveys more information than neutralization permits. In this way it accomplishes an analogical thinking in which similarity isn't immediately assimilated to the same.

In this passage Derrida distinguishes between the "conceptual" and "nonconceptual" orders displaced by deconstruction, and this opposition precisely describes the first and second articulations of language. The conceptual order of deconstruction focuses on what Derrida calls the "logocentric hierarchy." This order is most clearly delineated in Hegel (whom Derrida takes to be the epitome of philosophy in general), and throughout his work Derrida describes deconstruction as the contrary to the *restricted* economy of Hegelian dialectics, which he says appropriates *everything* to *meaning*. Rather, deconstruction is a *general* economy that acknowledges what cannot be included, what Derrida calls "nothingness and pure nonsense" (1978:130). In Hegelian dialectics, Derrida writes,

> negativity is always the underside and accomplice of positivity. Negativity cannot be spoken of, nor has it ever been except in this fabric of meaning. Now, the sovereign operation, the *point of nonreserve*, is neither positive nor negative. It cannot be inscribed in discourse, except by crossing out predicates or by practicing a contradictory superimpression that then exceeds the logic of philosophy. (1978:259)

Shoshana Felman describes this "radical negativity" as "fundamentally fecund and affirmative, and yet without positive reference, [it] is above all *that which escapes the negative/positive alternative*" (1983:141), and Julia Kristeva calls it "the fourth 'term' " of Hegel's dialectic, "what remains heterogeneous to logic even while producing it through a movement of separation or rejection" (1984:112). Here we can see why deconstruction—and analogical thinking more generally—is not a "method," even though what I am describing here seems so methodical and formal: deconstruction is not a "procedure" that precedes or antedates the "material" it acts upon. Rather, *as a procedure* it proceeds *from* that material, *from* precisely the "particularities" for which Hegel says "philosophy provides no grounds" (1982:ix); it is only articulated "by crossing out predicates or by practicing a contradictory superimpression that exceeds the logic of philosophy" (1978:259).

The "nonconceptual order with which the conceptual order is articulated" that Derrida mentions in his description of deconstructive practice (1982:330), unlike Hegel's conceptual order, is at the margins of philosophy; it is linguistics conceived as a science. In deconstructing the opposition between speech and writing, or, more generally, between sign and mark, Derrida positions deconstruction in relation to the semantic formalism of linguistic neutralization and linguistics in general. He does so, as we have seen, with the "old name"—the *marked* name—of writing, now conceived as arche-writing and with that other name, neither old nor new, the name for the graft itself, grammatology. That is, deconstruction explodes and "exceeds" the classical logic of linguistic as well as philosophical neutralization by means of its grafting of marked and unmarked terms together. In this explosion it creates an *analogical* discourse beyond the *logical* discourse of classical thought. In language, deconstruction asserts, nothing is unmarked. Nothing, not even the binary oppositions of phonology, not the zero sign, not neutralized distinctive features, are the "pure" absence of "eternally negative differences." Yet nothing—no meaning—is not traced or marked by such negativity, such absence.

While Derrida uses semantically marked terms in the classical unmarked position, he also used unmarked terms as a mark, in order to mark. A chief example is Derrida's most famous "new name," *différance* (spelled with an *a*), a French neologism he defines at the beginning of *Margins of Philosophy* as "neither a word nor a concept" (1982:3). *Différance* is the most abstract term Derrida develops in his deconstructive practice; it is the least tied to the particularities of textual context. Instead of crossing out predicates, it adds them—causes them to coalesce—by supplementing the spatial significance of *différence* (spelled with an *e*), the English sense of *difference,* with the temporal and polemical sense of "deferring" and "differing" (1982:8). But it does so by means of a *phonological neutralization,* by the fact that in French in the position preceding /n/ the phonological opposition between /a/ and /e/ is neutralized. In *Dissemination* Derrida utilizes the same neutralization to describe "white on white," "a false true blank sense [*sens blanc*], without a blank [*sans blanc*]" (1981a:260), and Gayatri Spivak also uses it in the "Translator's Preface" to *Grammatology* to describe the book as "an entire text where 'penser' (to think) carries within itself and points at 'panser' (to dress a wound)" (1976:lxxxvi). In his essay "Différance" Derrida says that

> this in itself—the silence that functions within only a so-called phonetic writing—quite opportunely conveys or reminds us that, contrary to a very widespread prejudice, there is no phonetic writing. . . . And an examination of the structure and necessity of these nonphonetic signs quickly reveals that they can barely tolerate the concept of the sign itself. Better, the play of difference, which, as Saussure reminded us, is the condition for the possibility and functioning of every sign, is in itself a silent play. Inaudible is the difference between two phonemes which alone permits them to be and to operate as such. . . . If there is no purely phonetic writing, it is that there is no purely phonetic *phōnē.* The difference which establishes phonemes and lets them be heard remains in and of itself inaudible, in every sense of the word. (1982:4–5)

Such "inaudibility" includes the "sense" "non-sense"—the nothing, as Wallace Stevens says, that is there—and beyond that, "nothingness and pure nonsense," the nothing that is not. The silence is the silence of neutralization, the zero sign that communicates meaning through absence and the absence itself upon which meaning is inscribed. In the deconstructive neutralization of *différance* the opposition between the first and second articulations is deconstructed: phonological neutralization is negated and denied— or, as Felman says, it is fecundly affirmed—as a *semantic* mark, a mark that, manifested in neutralization, is unmarked, no mark, neither meaningful nor nonsensical. That it functions, as Derrida says here, "quite opportunely" underlines the seeming arbitrariness of analogy, which is to say that it functions always as a marked term, never suggesting a unmarked transcendental universal condition.

Linguistic Displacements

The relationship between deconstructive practice and linguistic analysis— what has made linguistics a "model" for deconstruction that Derrida both follows and dismantles—can be seen in Saussure's inaugurating insight of the arbitrary and differential nature of the sign. From this follows the defining character of language (as opposed to other semiological systems)— namely, its double structuration in relation to its double articulation: its hierarchic structure. Other semiotic systems—of gesture, for instance, or dress, or even the structure of literature into literary genres—are structured by a single articulation, by the articulation of signification by means of what Lévi-Strauss calls *bricolage,* by means of arbitrarily chosen elements that function to communicate in a diacritical but *nonsystematic* manner. There is no closed system of (or analogous to) the phonological plane of language in other semiotic systems. This is why structural linguistics distinguishes between the *planes* of language that, as Hjelmslev says, "are structured in quite analogous fashions" (1961:60). It is the very *form* of analogy—what Martinet and Greimas describe as the *isomorphism* of the planes of language—within the double articulation of language that allows for the systematic hierarchy of language. Thus, systematic neutralization— neutralization in its *restricted* linguistic sense—does not take place in semiology (generally conceived). In these terms linguistics, as Saussure asserted, would, in fact, be a special case of semiology, a case marked by double articulation, hierarchy, and neutralization (1959:16). Here linguistics, and especially the scientific phonological model inscribed in its double articulation, is a marked version of general semiology.

But the arbitrary nature of the sign in language also allows for another striking feature of language: namely, the fact that *any* element of the hierarchical linguistic structure may function as any other, what Derrida calls "the always open possibility of its extraction and grafting" (1982:317). In such cases, Greimas says, the "edifice" of language "appears like a construction without plan or clear aim" in which, for instance, "syntactic 'functions' transform grammatical cases by making them play roles for which they are not appropriate; entire propositions are reduced and described as if they behaved like simple adverbs," and so forth (1983:133), as I noted in the introduction. Greimas summarizes this situation, we saw there, by asserting that "discourse, conceived as a hierarchy of units of communication fitting into one another, contains in itself the negation of that hierarchy by the fact that the units of communication with different dimensions can be at the same time recognized as equivalent" (1983:82). Thus, while Martinet correctly defines the phoneme as possessing "a phonic shape, but no meaning" (1962:40), there are contexts in which phonemes are signifying units, what he calls "monemes." I do not mean the "biplanar" case of the phoneme /ay/ constituting the moneme *I*. I mean cases like that of *différance* in which a phoneme *as phoneme* signifies. Or cases in which grammatical morphemes and units, such as the word *between,* come to signify (Derrida 1981a:221). Or cases in which agrammatical strings, such as "the green is or," come to signify (1982:320). Or cases in which signifying elements of language, such as the dative case, are emptied of signification and function *communicatively* and not *meaningfully* (1978:95). These are cases of neutralization as such—"general" or "deconstructive" neutralization—in which the hierarchical structure of linguistics and language is displaced. Moreover, as the seemingly "marginal" category of phonological neutralization suggests, this *constantly* takes place and is the *condition* of "language" and "linguistics"—its seemingly *first* condition—now conceived of as including the special case of semiology (see Barthes 1967:11). In this conception "language" appropriates *everything* (including semiology) to its meanings: as Derrida says, "all experience is the experience of meaning" (1981:30).

The cases I have just cited are all examples of deconstruction, and what they show is that the "procedure" of deconstruction deconstructs, *first of all,* the opposition between the planes and articulations of language; it deconstructs, *first of all,* the opposition between phonology and semiology. If the neutralization of the opposition between semiology and phonology is language conceived as a double articulation, then the negation of language would be the nonopposition between phonology and semiology. That negation would be the "science" that marks the unmarked term, the science of markedness itself: grammatology. Yet such a science eschews the basic assumptions of science, the assumption of "neutral," unmarked data to be examined and lawfully (nomologically) organized—within the *simplicity* of data, the *accuracy* of examination, and the *generalizability* of law. Rather, grammatology asserts that *nothing* is unmarked and that the hierarchy established by the unmarked over the marked—the general hierarchy of positive science—is itself a kind of marking susceptible to the "overturning" neutralization of deconstruction. Analogical thinking makes the same assumption: that reductive hierarchy of the unmarked over the marked—the subsumption of the example in the principle, the similar in the same—is never fully achieved, once and for all.

I began this chapter by claiming, quoting, that Derrida believes meaning was "everywhere." But Derrida also believes—I have been quoting this too—that nonmeaning is everywhere as well. Or, rather, that meaning is "nowhere," without a place, displaced. In a restricted sense Derrida is describing the appropriating power of language that can use, as Saussure says, even absence as a meaningful zero sign; but in a general sense he is describing the place where language opens to nonlanguage—not in terms of Hegelian, philosophical "unities" of preexistent, prelinguistic referents (1982:183) to which language secondarily points but to the linguistic void of nonlanguage: nothingness and pure non-sense. Such a "place" could be called a **displace* (noun) in an analogy with the semantic morphological neutralization of the opposition *interest* versus *uninterest* manifested as *disinterest* (a negative that is affirmative and fecund). In any case such deconstructive displacement finally is *linguistic* but linguistics not *scientifically* conceived (by means of abstract formalism) but *rhetorically* conceived (by means of semantic formalism), under the baggy category of analogy. It is the displacement of meaning *by* linguistics and the linguistic model—the "scientific" concepts of "eternally negative differences," two articulations, and the isomorphism of the planes of language. And it is the displacement *of* linguistics as a model for the human sciences—the displacement of linguistic neutralization by analogical thinking and deconstructive practice. Here is the scandal of deconstruction, its nonsynthesizing contradiction, its difficult discursive functioning. "How to interpret," Derrida asks at the (marginal) beginning of *Margins of Philosophy,*

> the strange and unique property of a discourse that organizes the *economy* of its representation, the law of its proper weave, such that *its* outside is never its *outside,* never surprises it, such that the logic of its heteronomy still reasons from within the vault of its autism?
>
> . . . Can one then *pass* the singular limit which is not a limit, which no more separates the inside from the outside than it assures their permeable and transparent continuity? What form could this play of

limit/passage have, this logos which posits and negates itself in permitting its own voice to well up? (1982:xvi)

Linguistic science attempts to account for such limits and passage in discourse, its meaning and communication, in its seemingly marginal category of phonological neutralization. The explosion of neutralization in deconstruction and *its* discourse, such as this passage from Derrida, foregrounds the problem of language, its strange and unique properties, welling up— exploding—in its marked voice and multiplying analogies.

Part II

Collaborations

Chapter 3

Enlightenment Knowledge and Postmodern Information

If the seventeenth and early eighteenth centuries are the age of
clocks, and the later eighteenth and the nineteenth centuries
constitute the age of steam engines, the present time is the age
of communication and control.
—Norbert Wiener, *Cybernetics*

We have to rethink the definition of modernity, interpret the
symptom of postmodernity, and understand why we are no
longer committed heart and soul to the double task of
domination and emancipation.
—Bruno Latour, *We Have Never Been Modern*

If the chapters of part 1 examine the work of the negative in analogy in
relation to the semantic formalism of language and semiotics—in relation
to *meaning*—then the chapters of part 2 examine what I described in the
introduction as the "movement" of analogy and its "momentary" nature—
the fact that analogy never becomes a resting place of meaning once and for
all—in relation to historical and disciplinary formations of *knowledge*. In
chapter 4, discussing the more or less formal nature of disciplinary knowledge, I describe this as a "postformalist" mode of apprehension but in both
of the chapters of part 2 I emphasize the collaborations implicit in analogical knowledges: collaborations between past and present phenomena,
single and corporate subjects of knowledge, and complementary modes of
interpretation. Such an emphasis focuses on the *worldly* work of analogy, as
I describe it, following a figure from Edward Said, later in this chapter. In
fact, the two epigraphs to this chapter—as well as its double focus on
economics and information (similar to the double focus on economics and
analogy in the postscript)—encompass the breadth and value of temporal
and disciplinary worldliness.

More specifically, this chapter offers a discussion of Enlightenment
knowledge in an examination of the emerging science of economics in Adam
Smith's eighteenth-century masterpiece, *The Wealth of Nations,* and an

equally momentous intellectual achievement two centuries later, the development of information theory after World War II in relation to both the semiotics of part 1 and the interpretations of part 3. Smith's achievement is a remarkable consolidation of Enlightenment thinking in its amalgamation of what I call subjective idealism and general semiotics. The general semiotics of Enlightenment thinking is its assumption of the systematic working of phenomena, what Claude Lévi-Strauss in his discussion of structuralism describes as "Kantism without the transcendental subject" (1975:11). (Lévi-Strauss is quoting Paul Ricoeur.) It pursues the thoroughly *secular* idea of a natural order of goodness and progress that Smith describes as the "invisible hand" (1937:423) governing economic life. Such an idea of natural order is at the same time thoroughly humanist in its secularity: it assumes that the proper subject of experience is the individual human being. The link between these assumptions is the *equality*—the interchangeability—of all humans, whose gender, race, spatial and temporal location, beliefs, etc., are all assumed to be simply accidental. In this framework the "general individual" takes the unmarked names of "man" or "he." Finally, such a natural order combines empiricism, simplicity, and generalizability as its criteria for truth. As Ernst Cassirer argues in *The Philosophy of Enlightenment,* the "method of formulation of scientific conceptions [that was developed by the Enlightenment] is both analytical and synthetic" (1951:10); it was the "method of reason" that "consists in starting with solid facts based on observation, but not in remaining within the bounds of bare facts" (1951:21). Instead, it both analyzed those facts into simple elements and organized them into a general universal order.

The second moment I examine in this chapter is the development of information theory after World War II. This development was plural rather than individual: it consisted of a large number of people dealing with the felt problem that the assumption of a simple and general "natural order" that governed Smith's sense of the world no longer seemed adequate to twentieth-century experience. The abstract binary oppositions governing Smith's comprehension of the world—nature/artifice, matter/energy, private/public, world/mind, worldliness/atemporality, etc.—no longer provided satisfying explanations for experience that seemed chaotically abundant. The two moments I am examining, the articulation of classical economics and the development of information theory, stand at the beginning and the ending of a era—the most fruitful in Western history—characterized by the mode of thinking that privileges identity over similarity and logic over analogy. In examining these moments, we can see the ways in which a post-Enlightenment semiotics can recover analogical thinking for understanding and comprehend timely, apprehensible truth.

Adam Smith and Long-Distance Trade

In his critique of the mercantile system in *The Wealth of Nations* Adam Smith criticizes the mercantile restraint of trade, the goal of which is to accumulate gold and silver in a favorable balance of trade, by noting that it favors production and producers over consumers. "Consumption," Smith writes,

> is the sole end and purpose of all production; and the interest of the producer ought to be attended to, only so far as it may be necessary for promoting that of the consumer. The maxim is so perfectly self-evident, that it would be absurd to attempt to prove it. But in the mercantile system, the interest of the consumer is almost constantly sacrificed to that of the producer; and it seems to consider production, and not consumption, as the ultimate end and object of all industry and commerce. (1937:625)

This seems an odd argument for Smith, whose position throughout *The Wealth of Nations* is oriented toward the accumulation of capital rather than the consumption of wealth. Thus, in the famous distinction between productive and nonproductive labor Smith described the productive labor of a manufacturer that "fixes and realizes itself in some particular subject or vendible commodity, which [is] . . . a certain quantity of labour stocked and stored up to be employed, if necessary, upon some other occasion." Unproductive labors, on the other hand, "generally perish in the very instant of their performance, and seldom leave any trace or value behind them" (1937:314–15).

In this chapter I explore this seeming paradox in Adam Smith in relation to the mercantile system that he explicitly opposes in *The Wealth of Nations* and to a conception of semiotics he outlines in his distinction between money and capital. Of necessity this will be a complicated argument. The parts of this argument are threefold. In relation to Smith I examine mercantilism, labor, and money, which Jean Baudrillard describes in a very different context as "the three orders of production, consumption, and signification" (1975:30). In fact, Baudrillard aptly notes that "with the concept of labor, Adam Smith attacked the Physiocrats and the exchangists [mercantilists]" (1975:23). In relation to the larger historical category of what I call "long-distance" trade, I examine what Bruno Latour calls systems of "mind," "signs," and "mobilization" (1986:26). Finally, I examine both of these semiotic systems in the context of the assertion Norbert Wiener made in 1948, tutored by the second rather than the first Industrial

Revolution, that "information is information, not matter or energy. No materialism which does not admit this can survive at the present day" (1961:132).

The overall aim of this discussion is to describe the larger paradox of the Enlightenment in the example of Adam Smith's argument with the long-distance trade of mercantilism. My contention is that Enlightenment thinking successfully combines the local and the general in a series of equivalences rather than analogies: Robinson Crusoe, for instance, as the universal economic man (and the universal human); the particular discomforts of work as universal labor; daily consumption as universal need; individual motives as the realization of natural progress. Enlightenment thinking reduces the other to the same. *The Wealth of Nations* performs this reduction in terms of labor, talent, need, power, and so forth, and it does so by reducing difference and distance to the equation of the local and the general.

When Adam Smith asserts that "consumption is the sole end and purpose of all production," he reminds me of an important assertion of A. J. Greimas, perhaps the most scientifically "rigorous" of the French structuralists in the 1960s, to which I have already alluded. Structural linguistics began, Greimas noted early in his career, as "a linguistics of perception and not expression" (cited in Schleifer 1987:xix). Both Greimas and Smith share a sense that analysis should seek the ends and not the causes of phenomena, what Roland Barthes calls their "destiny" rather than their "origin" (1977:148). In this, Smith is opposing himself to the received ideas of mercantilism in his day. Mercantilism aimed at economic surplus over consumption, and this surplus takes the form of moneyed "treasure." For mercantilism, Mark Blaug argues, "money was falsely equated with capital, and the favourable balance of trade with the annual balance of income over consumption. This was the gist of Adam Smith's critique of mercantilism" (1985:11).

For Smith, then, the problem of mercantilism—besides the self-interest and greed that he repeatedly attributes to merchants—is its misunderstanding of value. For Smith, as for Ricardo and Marx after him, it is necessary to understand the twofold nature of both labor and money in relation to value. In an "early and rude state of society which precedes both the accumulation of stock and the appropriation of land" (1937:47), Smith writes, labor affords the only measure of value. Such a "state of society," as both Ricardo and Marx note (see Marx 1967:76 and n. 1), is best represented by Robinson Crusoe. Citing Marx and alluding to Ricardo, Baudrillard notes that "the Crusoe myth describes, in a 'transparent' isolation . . . , the ideality of bourgeois relations: individual autonomy, to each according to his labor and his needs, moral consciousness bound to nature—and, if possible, some Man Friday, some aboriginal servant" (1981:141). It is important to contrast Crusoe's shipwrecked state to the mobility of La Pérouse in his sixteenth-century travels for Louis XVI, which Latour uses as his initial example of the relationships among mind, signs, and mobilization I will cite later in this chapter: it is precisely the "distances" of Latour's conception of the mobilization of information that the local generalizations of the Enlightenment deny or render simply accidental. Such distances and the differences they imply can help us to answer the question Baudrillard poses after describing the ideality of bourgeois relations embodied in Crusoe: "if Crusoe's relations to his labor and his wealth are so 'clear,' as Marx insists," he asks, "what on earth has Friday got to do with this setup?" (1981:141).

Smith opposes precisely this bourgeois myth of generalizable individual autonomy to the regulated trade of mercantilism and its support of a *caste* of merchants. Smith's conception of the "invisible hand"—Blaug calls this "the central theme that inspires the *Wealth of Nations*" (1985:60)—is part of this myth, and it opposes the regulations of mercantilism insofar as they rely on private original purpose rather than the general order of "natural" goodness. Such a natural order is an "end" rather than a "cause": as Smith notes, every private individual within a system of political economy "neither intends to promote the public interest, nor knows how much he is promoting it." Rather, "by directing [his] industry in such a manner as its produce may be of the greatest value, he intends only his own gain, and he is in this, as in many other cases, led by an invisible hand to promote an end which was not part of his intention" (1937:423). In this classic statement Smith is joining the local and individual with the general and common. For Smith this is simply the "nature" of things, just as for his contemporary Enlightenment thinker Immanuel Kant there must be a "subjective principle of common sense," a "good nature" that allows for the harmony of human faculties and the harmony between the (universal) human and Nature (see Deleuze 1984:22–23; Davis and Schleifer 1991:12–15).

In positing, semiotically, the ends of natural order, Smith emphasizes the overwhelmingly *local* nature of individualism and consumption. "At the same time and place," he writes, "the real and the nominal price of all commodities are exactly in proportion to one another." Such proportion does not exist "at distant places," Smith says, and "the merchant who carries goods from the one to the other has nothing to consider but their money price" (1937:37). In this Smith locates and localizes money—now conceived as "capital," and, more tellingly, as both "fixed" and "circulating" capital—

as a store of value as well as a medium of exchange, and he describes *both* as modes of consumption. (Such a conception is directly analogous to the conception of the goal and function of language I described in the preceding chapter as meaning and communication.) In this argument mercantilist exchange across distances is a form of "production," leading to the accumulation of treasure; capitalist exchange within the nation is a form of "consumption." In this formulation the "wealth" of mercantilism becomes simply private wealth rather than the wealth of the nation. The mercantilist, that is, emphasized the relationship between money and trade rather than between wealth and goods.

For Smith wealth, labor, consumption—even the concrete manifestation of all of these in "money"—is at once particular and general. Friday, like the black clerks with starched collars in *Heart of Darkness*, is both English and other, a citizen and a servant. The "nation" itself, in *The Wealth of Nations*, is both local and the general aggregate of unique but interchangeable individuals and the aggregate of abstract, Newtonian "spaces." This is why Smith defines use value not in terms of particular consumption but in terms of generalized need: he thinks of "utility," Blaug argues, "not as the power to satisfy a particular want . . . but as the power to satisfy a generalized biological or social need" (Blaug 1985:40). With such generalization the "local" nature of consumption is also always general and universal, and wealth is always "national" in this particular combination of local and general. These assumptions, as I will note in a moment, leads Smith to argue against colonialism—this is the burden of the final pages of *The Wealth of Nations*—and it leads him to posit, absolutely, the categories of "mind" and "signs," the citizens and system of political economy that Latour describes dynamically in the struggle between different people under his figure of "mobilization."

Mercantilism, above all, is based upon precisely the differences—of distance, of caste, of peoples—that Smith, and the Enlightenment more generally, erased within its posited harmonies and natural goodnesses. For the mercantilists "the goal of state building can be achieved just as well, if not better, by weakening the economic powers of neighbors as by strengthening one's own" (Blaug 1985:14). Mercantilism itself, like the beginnings of financial capitalism in the eighteenth century, which Larry Neal describes, is above all based upon the development of "new financial techniques in order to exploit the opportunities of long-distance trade" (1990:4). These "techniques" include the development of joint-stock companies, the development of "secondary markets" in stocks themselves, information networks, double-entry bookkeeping, and the licensing of mercantilist companies to finance state debts (see Neal 1990:13, 52). Moreover, as John Maynard Keynes notes in his defense of mercantilism against Smith and classical economics more generally, mercantile policies created low interest rates and encouraged capital investment rather than saving (Blaug 1985:13–16). For Keynes, unlike Marx and Smith, unemployment is not an aberration, simply the result of ignorance or the temporary lack of goodness; it is not the faltering of the invisible hand leading us, despite ourselves, toward what Smith calls "the natural progress of things towards improvement" (1937:326). Rather, it is precisely the mark of the difference between human necessity and the "natural" order, the difference between the local and the general. This is why Smith could not see that, as another economist, Charles Wilson, has argued, "the desire for hard money in the mercantilist era had merits under the then prevailing circumstances that it later lost: the conditions of British trade with the Baltics and the East Indies were such as to make it necessary to achieve international liquidity through the acquisition of stocks of precious metals" (Blaug 1985:16–17).

The mention of these distances brings me to a second aspect of my discussion of Smith's Enlightenment knowledge: the place of language and semiotics within its development. In an important article discussing the origins of modern science in the Renaissance, Bruno Latour argues that neither the local humanism of individualism nor the semiotics of unconscious progress can explain the rise of Enlightenment science in the Renaissance. Rather, he says, one should focus upon the ways "writing and imaging craftsmanship" depend upon and de-emphasize movement—distances in time and space—in order to make sense of the great achievements, in science especially, of the Enlightenment (1986:3). Latour argues that such craftsmanship allows for the creation of "immutable mobiles"—unchanging traces or signs that can be superimposed, combined, and transported great distances, without distortion. His two examples of this craftsmanship are the South Sea travels of La Pérouse—"who travels," Latour says, "through the Pacific for Louis XVI with the explicit mission of bringing *back* a better map" (1986:5)—and, more generally, the circulation of money.[1]

---

1. The great general example of "immutable mobiles" is the "matter" of Cartesian mechanics I examine in the postscript in relation to Foucault. Stephen Gaukroger, in his powerful study of Descartes, describes the importance of craftsmanship to Descartes's career, especially, during his apprenticeship, "the ingenuity with which he is able to devise and manipulate various forms of compass" and "in his quite unprecedented attempt to provide the workings of the compass . . . [in] its apparent indifference as to whether a problem is arithmetical or geometrical" (1995:94). In his work with compasses—as in his mathematics more generally—Descartes was seeking "something that would

In short, Latour argues that the creation of signs and traces of information that can maintain their integrity across great distances is the best framework in which to comprehend Enlightenment science and, more generally, to understand why the Enlightenment combination of the local and the general seemed so self-evidently "natural" to Smith and his contemporaries. "Commercial interest, capitalist spirit, imperialism, thirst for knowledge," Latour writes,

> are empty terms as long as one does not take into account Mercator's projection, marine clocks and their markers, copper engraving of maps, ratters, the keeping of "log books," and the many printed editions of Cook's voyages that La Pérouse carries with him. . . . But, on the other hand, no innovation in the way longitude and latitudes are calculated, clocks are built, log books are compiled, copper plates are printed would make any difference whatsoever if they did not help to muster, align, and win over new and unexpected allies, far away, in Versailles. The practices I am interested in would be pointless if they did not bear on certain controversies and force dissenters into believing new facts and behaving in new ways. This is where an exclusive interest in visualization and writing falls short. . . . To maintain only the second line of argument would offer a mystical view of the powers provided by semiotic material—as did Derrida (1967); to maintain only the first would be to offer an idealist explanation. (1986:6)

The two lines of argument Latour mentions are those of semiotics and idealism. In this essay he is arguing that neither the "general" semiotics of political economy nor the "local" genius of subjective idealism can erase distances without distortion, and consequently their "harmonious" identification with one another always leaves something out—such as Crusoe's man Friday. With the example of South Sea exploration, he contends that what he calls these visualization processes of writing and image are the historical sites of knowledge and understanding. These sites are the locus of *particular* struggles between different people and different ideologies that manifest themselves in the mobilization across distances. Such processes are ignored, he says, in two ways: "one is to grant to the [concept of 'mind'] . . . what should be granted to the . . . [concept of 'signs']; the other is to focus exclusively on the signs *qua* signs, without considering

---

comprise a level of abstraction, dealing with magnitudes in general, that went beyond specific arithmetical and geometrical content" (1995:100).

the mobilization of which they are but the fine edge" (1986:26). Latour's three-part distinction among mind, signs, and mobilization corresponds to Wiener's distinction among materialism, energy, and information, which I mentioned earlier.

It is the last category, as Wiener says and Latour implies, that situates understanding outside both subjective idealism and general semiotics. "One interesting change that has taken place" in science, Wiener writes, "is that . . . we no longer deal with quantities and statements which concern a specific real universe as a whole but ask instead questions which may find their answers in a large number of similar universes" (1967:18–19). Such "similar universes" are the loci of analogy: Wiener is describing the *multiplication* of phenomena—the necessity of redundancies I will discuss in a moment—that allows cognition to take place. Moreover, it is here, in other "similar universes," that Friday comes into this setup: he comes in as the likelihood of otherness within the regime of the same.

In these terms we can see that Latour's "immutable mobiles" function literally in the manner of analogy, transporting meaning across different situations: as Eve Bannet argues, "for Wittgenstein, 'meaning *moves*' from case to case by means of analogies." "For Wittgenstein, and indeed for traditional rhetoricians," she continues,

> an analogy is not an identity; it is a figure which marks both the likeness and the difference in our application of words from case to case. The gaps, the discontinuities, and the differences are as important as the likeness because, Wittgenstein insists, we are always moving meaning from one situation to another which might not be quite the same. . . . Analogical reasoning has everything to do with how we "go on" because both in our disciplines and in our everyday uses of language, we are always using analogies to translate familiar terms, concepts, and images from one place to another place. (1997:656)

Latour, in his argument, situates his "immutable mobiles" precisely in relation to the subjective idealism and general semiotics of the Enlightenment. The Enlightenment, in what I call its great paradox, *identifies* these disparate categories by simultaneously localizing and generalizing the subjects and the objects of experience and understanding. The characteristic power of Enlightenment apprehensions of experience—its individualism, its humanism, the universalizing "methods" of its understanding of the world, and, above all, its translation of a conception of *sacred* eternity fully separate from the world into a conception of *secular* atemporality discoverable within the world as the "truth" of phenomena—all follow from this remark-able identification of subjective idealism and general semiotics (see Schleifer 2000: chap. 1, for elaboration of this argument). This identification, as I argue later in this chapter, transforms "experience" into "information." Latour's "mobiles," like Wittgenstein and Derrida, draw "our attention to the analogics underlying fixed and universal taxonomies, logics, and laws" (Bannet 1997:657). But, more important, such self-conscious analogy al-lows us to apprehend the differences that are obscured within the identifica-tion of local idealism and general semiotics; it allows us to apprehend the understanding of experience as information and, in so doing, to recognize the interests, politics, and history inhabiting "disinterested" knowledge.

The identification of subjective idealism and general semiotics consti-tutes Smith's critique of mercantilism. *The Wealth of Nations* makes the individual subjects of experience general and universal by defining use-value in terms of general and transcendental human "needs." By making the subjects of economic experience general "citizens" whose economic sphere is necessarily (if abstractly) local, Smith refutes the special licenses of mer-cantile trade. In this we can see that what Latour calls "mind" in the individualist-humanist tradition of the Enlightenment is the general subject of experience. Moreover, Smith makes the objects of experience and knowledge—labor, capital, the unconscious invisible hand of political econ-omy in general—comprehensible in terms of a general semiotics of "in-visible" binary oppositions: productive/nonproductive, exchange/storage, private/public, and, above all, the equation of nature and human goodness as opposed to the aberrations of artifice and division. By making the objects of economic experience signs that are best understood in an unconscious system of relationships, Smith refutes the positive and positivist nature of value that mercantilism implies. This is why, I think, *Robinson Crusoe* is such a good figure for Smith's bourgeois economics (though Ricardo and not Smith uses it): the novel combines the isolated individual as the subject of experience and economic calculations as the object of experience.

What it leaves out, as I have suggested, is real space and historical time: it leaves out Friday. Latour ends his discussion of immutable mobiles with a discussion of money. "As soon as money starts to circulate through different cultures," he writes,

> it develops a few clear-cut characteristics: it is mobile (once in small pieces), it is immutable (once in metal), it is countable (once it is coined), combinable, and can circulate from the things valued to the center that evaluates and back. . . . Money is used to code all states of affairs in

exactly the way that . . . in his log book La Pérouse registered both the places on the map and the values of each good as if it were to be sold in some other place. . . . Money is neither more nor less "material" than map making, engineering, drawing or statistics. (1986:30–31)

Here, then, I think, we can see the reasons why Smith not only wanted to refute mercantile theory but wanted to abolish colonial trade. The long-distance trade of mercantilism traffics in differences: between the licensed and unlicensed, between money and goods, between the different times and spaces entailed by trade. Like the *once*s in the passage from Latour I just quoted, mercantilism emphasizes and uses the differences of time and space in its very trade, its nonproductive labor.

Against this reading the Enlightenment economics of *The Wealth of Nations* reduces time and space to homogeneous containers and abstract universals—to secular atemporality and utopias—in its repeated attempt to understand economic experience in the light of the future: like twentieth-century semiotics, it seeks to discover ends, not causes, in a world of citizens, not political subjects. The distances of mercantile trade, on the other hand, encountered the "past": the otherness of so-called primitive non-Europeans, whom Smith takes great pains to describe as "accidentally" inferior to their European counterparts; the otherness of the traditional caste system of parliament and land; the otherness of "marginal" rather than universal value (as in the marginal economics of Keynes's teacher Alfred Marshall). In his argument Smith uses mind and signs against the privileged economics of mercantile trade, but he can do this only by reducing distance and movement to the abstract universals of Enlightenment science. The gain of his procedure is enormous: it provides us, as the Enlightenment did more generally, with the equality of citizens within the polity, the fraternity of social labor within the workplace, and liberty as a social good within a political economy. But reading Smith against mercantilism and Latour makes the cost of these positive values equally clear. That cost is the erasure of differences and distances in a regime of the same whose tyrannies operate by means of the invisible hands of silence, forgetfulness, and the confusion of local values and general truths.

Information, Wisdom, and the Postmodern

The relationship between local values and general truth is one of the great themes of Walter Benjamin, writing more than one hundred and fifty years after Adam Smith at the end rather than the beginning of Enlightenment culture, and the title of this chapter owes something to his distinction between "information" and "wisdom" in his remarkable essay "The Story-teller." In that essay Benjamin notes that there has been a powerful transformation in his lifetime—the time of the second Industrial Revolution—during which, he says,

> experience has fallen in value. And it looks as if it is continuing to fall into bottomlessness. . . . For never has experience been contradicted more thoroughly than strategic experience by tactical warfare, economic experience by inflation, bodily experience by mechanical warfare, moral experience by those in power. A generation that had gone to school on a horse-drawn streetcar now stood under the open sky in a countryside in which nothing remained unchanged but the clouds, and beneath these clouds, in a field of force of destructive torrents and explosions, was the tiny, fragile human body. (1969:83–84)

In this essay Benjamin designates the alternative to experience as information, what he describes as the stuff of newspapers. For Benjamin information is, above all, nonthematic, disjointed, unanchored; it is "shot through with explanation" (1969:89) that resonates only for a moment. George Steiner, in his extended attack on the postmodern in *Real Presences,* makes a point similar to Benjamin's: the genius of our age, he argues, is a "metaphysics" of journalism. "Journalistic presentation," he writes, "generates a temporality of equivalent instantaneity. . . . The journalistic vision sharpens to the point of maximum impact every event, every individual and social configuration; but the honing is uniform. Political enormity and the circus, the leaps of science and those of the athlete, apocalypse and indigestion, are given the same edge" (1989:26–27).

I am juxtaposing Benjamin and Steiner—I could also have added Nietzsche's description in the 1880s of the ways in which newspapers had replaced daily prayers (1968:44)—because, even though they do not offer us the definition of *information* that is missing from Smith's Enlightenment reading of value (the definition that was developed with information theory in the years after World War II), nevertheless their senses of *information* and the ways in which they distinguish it from received ideas of "wisdom," "experience," and even "real" presences can help us to comprehend the relationships between information theory, Smith's Enlightenment conceptions of knowledge, and the postmodern. It is for this reason, I think, that William Paulson begins his book, *The Noise of Culture,* by distinguishing, as I am doing here, between information and knowledge (1988:vii). Knowledge, he argues, was traditionally textual and bound to the authority of the individual authors of those texts. With the rise of experimental science in the Enlightenment this conception of knowledge was challenged by a different paradigmatic framework of understanding. "Knowledge," he writes,

> was presumed to reside in the written works of those authors who, by their writings, had originated the arts and whom the institutions of learning thus recognized as authorities. The function of the author was to guarantee the authority, the truth, of what was written. This is the opposite of modern scientific culture, which ostensibly claims that knowledge resides in a kind of statement whose truth depends not on authorship but on the procedures by which it is made. A valid scientific experiment can be, in principle, duplicated by anyone. (1988:6)

The new "knowledge" Paulson is describing is the knowledge of the Enlightenment, Adam Smith's knowledge, whose subject remains the individual subject of knowledge but strangely impersonal and timeless—"anyone," Paulson says—the transcendental subject of Descartes and Kant. (In "What Is an Author?" which I discuss in the following chapter, Michel Foucault offers another version of Paulson's intellectual history.)

The factual and positivist information of newspapers Benjamin describes at the time of World War I—nonthematic, repetitious, impersonal, whose chief quality, he says, is its "verifiability" (1969:89)—and the information of "information theory" developed after World War II both realized and challenged these Enlightenment ideals in related but opposite ways. Benjamin's information, like Steiner's, does it by *effacing* the subject of knowledge almost completely and, with that subject, the apprehended themes, traditions, and communities that Benjamin describes with such nostalgic passion. For Benjamin—and, I would add, for twentieth-century modernism more generally—the "subject" of the "transcendental subject" of the Enlightenment becomes a problem. After World War II information theory, willy-nilly, challenges the notion of knowledge by *pluralizing* the subjects of knowledge and the (temporal) situations of knowledge so that the "transcendental" of the transcendental subject becomes a problem. Thus, the information that Benjamin and Steiner resist is the information of journalism and of secular, fragmented positivism more generally: both Benjamin and Steiner inhabit the position of pre-Enlightenment religiosity. On the other hand, the post–World War II information of information theory is different, a kind of post-Enlightenment pragmatism. "In its pure form," as Jeremy Campbell writes, information theory "was an engineer's discovery"

(1982:16), whose goal was the practical solutions to particular problems occurring at particular times. It is for this reason, Wiener writes, that "the matter of time is essential in all estimates of the value of information" (1967:168). Such temporality essentially pluralizes information not reductively but explosively. The quality of disjointedness that troubles Benjamin remains a phenomenal quality of information after World War II, yet it does so not through the reductions of positivism but through multiplications and pluralizations, since information, as Wiener says, never deals in singularities (see 1967:172).

Thus, information theory (of the post–World War II kind) both participates in Enlightenment canons of transcendental truth and disrupts those canons in repeated ways. On the one hand, as Katherine Hayles notes, "information theory as [Claude] Shannon developed it has only to do with the efficient transmission of messages through communication channels, not with what messages mean." "For Shannon," she adds, "defining information was a strategic choice that enabled him to bracket semantics" (1994:448). Such bracketing—it is an "abstract" rather than a "semantic" formalism—universalizes information. In Hayles's terms it is "a concept of information that privileges exactness over meaning" (1994:457), the great Enlightenment project, in Richard Rorty's words, of "the Cartesian . . . triumph of the quest for certainty over the quest for wisdom" (1979:61). Such a definition subjects information to the "objectification" of scientific formulations and allows Shannon to develop the abstract "laws" of information comparable to Newton's laws of mechanics. "Just as Newton's laws of motion are not restricted to particular sorts of motion," Campbell writes, "Shannon's laws of information are universal, and in this way compel scientists and other thinkers to confront the fact that information itself is universal" (1982:17).

This concept allows Wiener to assert, as we have seen, that "information is information, not matter or energy" (1961:132). Campbell elaborates Wiener's assertion in important ways. "Evidently," he writes, "nature can no longer be seen as matter and energy alone. . . . To the powerful theories of chemistry and physics must be added a late arrival: a theory of information. Nature must be interpreted as matter, energy, and information" (1982:16). In a similar fashion Latour structures an important aspect of his argument in *We Have Never Been Modern* in terms that comport with this description when he divides up knowledge into the categories of "facts," "power," and "discourse." The Modernist problematic of power and knowledge, from Yeats (who asks, "Did she put on his knowledge with his power / Before the indifferent beak could let her drop?") to Foucault, precisely attends to the issues arising in information theory without attending to the tripartite constellation, to use Benjamin's phrase, that Wiener and others articulate. Instead, twentieth-century modernism, like the earlier Enlightenment modernity of Smith's eighteenth-century apprehensions, divides experience between the poles of matter and energy, the individual and the semiotic system, the empirical instance and the universal law.

The "universality" of information that Campbell asserts as central to Shannon's work, however, is not simply another "law" of nature—if it were, both Benjamin and Steiner would be much less distressed—and information theory is a problem for as well as an example of Enlightenment knowledge. This is because information functions like analogy and disrupts Enlightenment universality in its pluralities, which Steiner and Benjamin (as well as high modernism more generally) confuse with mechanistic positivism. The pluralities of information include the pragmatics of its interpersonal nature, the necessity it creates for representation by means of "nonvisualizable" statistics, its essential temporality. These three pluralities disrupt the simplicity, accuracy, and generalizability that are the Enlightenment criteria for scientific certainty I have repeatedly cited. The technical term for all these things information theory developed is "redundancy," which is not simply an inefficiency or error in communication but an essential component of communication. (Freud calls this the "overdeterminations" of psychological life; Derrida calls it the "iterability" of language; Benjamin sees in the ambiguous repetitions of redundancy the possibility of historical "redemption." As I have suggested throughout this book, an essential feature of analogies are their redundancies.) It is precisely the elimination of redundancy that is the purpose of the mathematical formalism of both Cartesian and Newtonian mechanics. This elimination is what abstract formalism *is,* and it explains why Enlightenment mechanics defines with great operational precision both matter and energy but cannot include information.

Similarly, redundancy in communication is not completely reducible to Shannon's mathematical formalism, which is why, as Hayles notes, his objectivist, "scientific" conception of information was not uncontested. Hayles describes with great tact and economy the alternatives offered to Shannon's mathematical formulations of information throughout the 1950s at the Macy conferences. This contest took the form of *semanticizing* information by historicizing it, and it is here—and especially in the concept of redundancy that arose out of both sides of this contest—that information's link with the postmodern can be discerned. (Its links with the high Modernist laments of Benjamin and Steiner over the loss of knowledge, experience, and presence can also be discerned in the contests over the formality of information.) One form this contest took is the opposition between Shannon and Lawrence Kubie, who criticized the scientific work of the Macy conferences from the vantage of psychoanalysis. "At the center of [Kubie's] explanation," Hayles writes, "was the multiple encoded nature of language, operating at once as an instrument that the speaker could use to communicate and as a reflexive mirror that revealed more than the speaker knew" (1994:459). Much could be written about the analogical relationship between information theory and psychoanalysis; suffice it here to repeat the analogy I drew between redundancy in information theory and overdetermination in psychoanalysis. Like redundancy, overdetermination breaches the Enlightenment project of defining reason in terms of Leibniz's "necessary and sufficient" truth and Descartes's "clear and distinct" ideas, the double project of generalization and individualism in Smith's analysis. Both of these binary articulations exclude the third category of information: *apprehensible truth* and *conveyable ideas*.

Hayles describes the more scientific of the contests over the concept of information at the Macy conferences in the persons of Shannon and Donald MacKay. Unlike Shannon, MacKay argued that information and meaning are closely connected and that connection could be discerned by emphasizing the reception of messages as much as the generation of messages. (In this focus on reception MacKay is repeating the great conceptual leap of Saussurean linguistics—that Modernist "proto-information theory"—which I have already mentioned in discussing Smith, its self-conception, in Greimas's words, as "a linguistics of perception and not of expression" [see Schleifer 1987:xix]. He is also repeating, at least analogically, Barthes's poststructuralist assumption, which I have also mentioned, that "a text's unity lies not in its origin but in its destination" [1977:148].) The problem with reception for classical science is the problem of subjectivity: while the "sender" of a message can always be taken as a transcendental subject assumed to be everywhere and nowhere in a text (as both Shannon and Stephen Dedalus suggest), the receiver of a message cannot quite so easily be universalized. Focus on the receiver raises the problem of optics as opposed to mechanics in the early-eighteenth-century controversy between Leibniz and Newton, which Wiener refers to in describing the reflexivity of information. It does so because information itself *redundantly* addresses sender and receiver. "Information," Wiener writes, "is a name for the content of what is exchanged with the outer world as we adjust to it, and make our adjustment felt upon it" (1967:26–27). Optics, he argues, cannot easily do away with the subject of experience because optics is precisely concerned with information, messages, and communication (1967:28). In a wonderful analysis that is both factual and rhetorical

Hayles describes how MacKay rescued "information affecting the receiver's mindset from the 'subjective' label" by proposing that Shannon was "concerned with what he called 'selective information'—that is, information calculated by considering the selection of message elements from a set," while he, MacKay, was arguing "for another kind of information that he called 'structural' . . . [which] has the capacity to 'increase the number of dimensions in the information space' by acting as a meta-communication" (1994:449).

Such "structural" information pluralizes messages and receivers; it is a form of redundancy, "a model," as Hayles says, "that triangulated between reflexivity, information, and meaning" in a way that "recognized the mutual constitution of language and content, message and receiver" (1994:450). In these terms it describes analogical thinking. Moreover, such "pluralization," if I can use this word, links information theory with what I am calling the postmodern. Postmodernism, as I have argued in *Modernism and Time* (chap. 1), can best be understood in relation to the second Industrial Revolution of the late nineteenth century. The second Industrial Revolution, as Fredric Jameson has noted, was "one of the most active periods in human history" (1981:251), which created vast wealth in terms of material goods, of intellectual accomplishments, and of human populations and led to what one historian describes as a "crisis of abundance" in the twenty years leading up to World War I (Kern 1983:9).[2] Such a crisis, as I mentioned in the

2. This period has come to be described as the "second Industrial Revolution," the transformation of the relatively small-scale industrialism of entrepreneurial or industrial capitalism to large-scale finance capitalism. For an extended discussion of the relationship between the abundance of the second Industrial Revolution and emerging forms of representation in the early twentieth century, see my study *Modernism and Time*. Part of my argument in that book is that a significant "product" of the second Industrial Revolution is the rise of the lower-middle class, a social formation similar but not identical to the petty bourgeoisie. This new "class"—Arno Mayer persuasively argues as a social formation it is a "classless class or half-class" (1975:422) similar to but not identifiable as a social class in Marx's or Weber's understanding—was a class of clerks and information workers such as teachers, advertising canvassers, and even entrepreneurs represented in the literature of the early twentieth century. (For a discussion of this class formation of nonmanual information workers, see *Modernism and Time,* chap. 3.)

For a historical survey of the vast wealth created by the second Industrial Revolution, see Frank Tipton and Robert Aldrich, *An Economic and Social History of Europe, 1890–1939* (1987: esp. chaps. 1–3). See also Carleton Hayes, who calls this period "the climax of the Enlightenment" (1941:328). "By 1900," Oron Hale notes, "Europe was the center of a booming world economy" (1971:55). "At the turn of the century," he continues, "Europe was experiencing one of those discontinuous leaps forward in technology and

introduction, demanded new ways of making sense out of experience, whose confusions weren't the result of need and dearth, as they were for great Enlightenment figures such as René Descartes and Adam Smith, but whose confusions stemmed from difficulties that arise from abundance and plenty.

The responses to such confusions—some say, a manifestation of these confusions themselves—can be understood under the heading of the "postmodern"; they can also help us to understand what Satya Mohanty means by "postpositivist view of objectivity" (1995:110). When the problem is abundance rather than dearth—that is to say, when redundancy or overdetermination or even the multiplication of instances of "analogy," as opposed to the reduction of phenomena (or "examples") to atemporal principles—is the problem, attitudes and questions arise that are different from those that conditioned the necessary and sufficient questions and answers of the Enlightenment. Edward Said describes such attitudes and questions as "worldly." In "The Politics of Knowledge" he writes that "there must be . . . a theoretical presumption that in matters having to do with human history and society any rigid theoretical ideal, any simple additive or mechanical notion of what is or is not factual, must yield to the central factor of human work, the actual participation of people in the making of human life" (1994:147). He goes on to say that "this kind of human work, which is intellectual work, is worldly, that it is situated in the world, and about that world" (147) and that it is

---

invention which had marked the industrial progress since the mid-eighteenth century. Electricity, petroleum for lighting and fuel, the internal combustion engine, the automobile and the airplane, refrigeration, the wireless telegraph, and motion pictures appeared as marvels of applied science affecting directly the lives of millions of the earth's inhabitants" (1971:56). In *The Culture of Time and Space* Stephen Kern offers a wide-ranging phenomenology of intellectual and quotidian life in this period. For a discussion of the relationship between the second Industrial Revolution and the sociology of postmodernism, see David Harvey (1989: esp. pt. 2). Harvey argues the continuity of early- and late-twentieth-century capitalism in terms of economic growth in the context of a larger argument that the distinction between modernism and postmodernism should be abandoned (or at least modified) in relation to a Marxist reading of the economic "base" of these phenomena. In a very different register Wiener traces the social transformations occasioned by the replacement of steam energy with electricity at the end of the nineteenth century (1967:185–222), technologies he associates with the first and second Industrial Revolutions, respectively. The critique of "the logic of general equivalents" in the work of Jean-Joseph Goux (1990:6; see also 1994) can easily be assimilated to the argument I pursue in *Modernism and Time,* which is inflecting my discussion here: namely, that the remarkable abundance of material, intellectual, and human resources associated with the second Industrial Revolution required transformations in the modes of explanation inherited from the Enlightenment and gave rise to the addition of "information" to the matter/energy binary.

engaged with culture in an "unprovincial, interested manner" (151). What Said describes in terms of worldliness, both "unprovincial" and "interested," sounds like—is *analogous* to—Wiener's definition of information in its complex and repeated interactions with the world.

This definition of information raises questions about Enlightenment simplicities I have exampled here in Adam Smith in powerful and troubling ways. The "experience" of modernity, meaning by that term the secular-scientific experience in the West since its beginning in the Enlightenment is (or was) governed by what Latour describes as the contradiction of modernity, "the double task of domination and emancipation" (1993:10). (This is clearly related to Mohanty's discussion of colonialism and postcolonialism.) In this contradiction can also be discerned the two great (if sometimes incompatible) achievements of the Enlightenment I examine in Smith, general semiotics and subjective idealism. Mohanty describes this contradiction in terms of idealism and positivism; Wiener describes it in terms of energy and matter (and also as "storage" and "process" [1967:166]); Latour describes it in terms of "natural law" and "political representations" (1993: 49); Said does it in terms of "unprovinciality" and "interests." Focusing more closely on information theory, Hayles describes this opposition in terms of "homeostasis" and "change." "Shannon's distinction between signal and noise," Hayles writes,

> had a conservative bias that privileges stasis over change. Noise interferes with the exact replication of the message, which is presumed to be the desired result. The structure of the theory implied that change was deviation, and that deviation should be corrected. By contrast, MacKay's theory had as its generative distinction the difference in the state of the receiver's mind before and after the message arrived. In this model, information was not *opposed* to change, it *was* change. (1994:452)

The identification of information and change underlines the transformation of the simplicity of the relationship between principle and example to the complexity of the relationships among analogies I am pursuing in this paragraph and in this book as a whole. Analogies do not reduce redundancies to the same: rather, they encompass the matter and energy of differences to convey ideas and apprehend truth.[3]

3. In a remarkable essay "Gödel's Theorem and Postmodern Theory" David Thomas describes the pluralization of oppositions I have gathered here by focusing on transcendental and decentered subjects of knowledge. Throughout his

Mohanty's attempt to discover "postpositivist" objectivity is important in relation to the very plurality of this listing. Many have been trying to find a language to describe this monstrous "reality" that our received languages of knowledge and power do not quite fit: Derrida's neologisms, Foucault's "genealogies," Davidson's and Kuhn's "schemes," the convoluted metalanguages of structuralism and the nonvisualizable mathematics of quantum mechanics, and even the term *negative materialism* I used in my book *Rhetoric and Death* and the "analogical thinking" I am using here[4]— all are attempting to "rescue" the achievements of modernity where the very abundance of their successes, the very *worldliness* of their success, has led to crisis. Information theory encompasses and, from time to time, articulates this situation—our postmodern situation, which is also modern and premodern. Thus, Wiener nominalizes the issue. "Whether we should call the new point of view materialistic," he writes, "is largely a question of

essay he treats matters of great importance to information theory: coding, the relationship between language and metalanguage; and, although he doesn't use this formulation, the nature of what Greimas calls the "still very vague, yet necessary concept of the *meaningful whole* [*totalité de signification*] set forth by a message" (1983:59; see Thomas 1995:258).

4. In *Modernism and Time* I even use the somewhat infelicitous term *non-transcendental disembodiment* to describe the centerless power of electricity, telephone, finance capital, and other aspects of the second Industrial Revolution. The articulation of "non-transcendental disembodiment" is an aim, I suggest there, of the analogies, which are presented throughout *Modernism and Time* as both a theme and a procedure governing its organization as a whole. It is the *semantic formalism* of such analogies—what Igor Stravinsky describes as the "reflective system between the language structure of the music and the structure of the phenomenal world" (1982:147) and what Benjamin describes as its "nonsensuous similarity" (1978:334) or, in Buck-Morss's translation, its "non-representational similarity" (1977:90)—that allows them to encompass the contradiction of disembodiment without transcendence. This is why Benjamin uses the literary and discursive figure of the tragic hero, whose "life, indeed, unfolds from death, which is not its end but its form" (1977:144), as an image of his understanding; it is why Bakhtin's conception of the "answerability" of art—and of other intellectual formations examined throughout both this book and *Modernism and Time*—does not simply reflect a "logic of abundance" but in fact *informs* it semantically and analogically. Such "material disembodiment," as I might also call it—the "materialism of the idea" Derrida mentions in relation to Mallarmé (cited in chap. 5); or, the "materialism of the incorporeal," as, I suggest in the postscript, Foucault might call it—is characteristic of the semiotics of finance capital (as opposed to Smith's industrial capital), of the decentralized power of electricity, and of information and information theory more generally. This informing process—this *information*—extends the "semantic formalism" I describe in part 1 to the "postformalist knowledge" of analogies and analogical thinking in this and the following chapter.

words: the ascendancy of matter characterizes a phase of nineteenth-century physics far more than the present age, and 'materialism' has come to be but little more than a loose synonym for 'mechanism.' In fact, the whole mechanist-vitalist controversy has been relegated to the limbo of badly posed questions" (1961:44). Perhaps the same can be said of the opposition between citizen and polity that Smith struggles with or that between information and experience or wisdom that Benjamin articulates.

In any case, in the face of abundance the precarious separation and balance of these pairs of opposites that governed with such ambiguous success Enlightenment knowledge, Enlightenment wealth, and Enlightenment subjectivity—gathered together in Smith's understanding of economics—break down. This, I think, is the burden of Latour's argument, even if he systematically reduces the postmodern to an expression of despair. Thus, he writes that,

> when the only thing at stake was the emergence of a few vacuum pumps, they could still be subsumed under two classes, that of natural laws and that of political representations; but when we find ourselves invaded by frozen embryos, expert systems, digital machines, sensory-equipped robots, hybrid corn, data banks, psychotropic drugs, whales outfitted with radar sounding devices, gene synthesizers, audience analyzers, and so on, when our daily newspapers display all these monsters on page after page, and when none of these chimera can be properly situated on the object side or on the subject side, or even in between, something has to be done. (1993:49–50)

Latour begins *We Have Never Been Modern,* as Benjamin begins "The Storyteller," by reading the newspaper and asking about how the monsters of categorical disparity he finds in the news can be tamed and, more strikingly, how it is that their disparate, positivist "wealth" does not simply give rise to the exhilaration of Smith (who imagines the invisible hand of the compositor) or the despair of Steiner (who imagines chaos and dissipation). The answer Wiener suggests is that Enlightenment knowledge has been transformed into postmodern information, which is indeed universal but whose universalities cannot dispense with temporal instances, semantics, and interests. Another World War I writer on information, Werner Heisenberg, notes in *Physics and Philosophy,* as we have seen, that Bohr's conception of "complementarity" encourages physicists "to apply alternatively different classical concepts which would lead to contradictions if used simultaneously" (1958:179). Such alternations describe the analogies and temporalities of information, which are universal but not transcendental. Such information, like many of the things Latour mentions—like the very postmodernity he descries—is "hybrid," worldly, and redundantly a response to and manifestations of the very abundances of contradiction and monstrosity that inhabit our world.

Practiced Apprenticeship and Successive Renewals
Disciplinarity and Collaboration in the Sciences and Humanities

I ended the preceding chapter with Bruno Latour's discussion of the hybrid monstrosity of cross-disciplinary knowledge in the modern world and Werner Heisenberg's quieter assertion of Bohr's conception of complementarity to comprehend that knowledge. In this chapter I return to terms from part 1—the analogy between syntax and semantics—to examine the roles of collaboration in the sciences and humanities. In the course of this discussion I also argue the analogical thinking of language studies allows for a postformalist knowledge that can effect certain kinds of cross-disciplinary understanding.

The categories of syntax and semantics create a possibility of contrasting different modes of explanation even if, in the asserted analogy between syntax and semantics—figured, as I have done, in the description of analogy in part 1 as a species of "semantic formalism"—both differences and similarities are bound up together in this assertion. Charles Taylor describes these contrasting modes of explanation closer to the terms of the "movement" of meaning across time and space effected by analogy in a thoughtful discussion of the work of Paul Ricoeur in narrative theory. One mode of explanation, which I am associating throughout *Analogical Thinking* with Enlightenment thought, is what Taylor calls "nomological," or "law-governed," science. Nomological science, Taylor argues, "concerns a form of explanation whereby the phenomenon to be explained is completely absorbed by the law or structure which constitutes its explanation" (1991:175). In this mode of explanation any "event" is explained by its "subsumption" by atemporal structures and laws that exist once and for all. Against this nomological schema, which is parallel, in my argument, to the abstract formalism of syntactics, Taylor posits "a very different type of relation between structure and event" whose "paradigmatic example is that of *langue-parole*" (1991:176), which describes the "postformalism" of the "kind of information that [MacKay] called 'structural' " (Hayles 1994:449) that I described in the preceding chapter. "A language," he writes,

> may be viewed as a structure of rules, or of possible formations and transformations. But this structure has purchase on the real only by virtue of *parole*. It is only through repeated acts of communication by members of a linguistic community that a structure has real existence. But "events" or "particular cases," which are speech-acts, are not in a simple relation of subsumption with the rule to which they are submitted. They may be in conformity with it, or they may deviate. This renewal is not however dictated by the nature of things; it is not a mere example, nor is it a particular case of a regularity. . . .
>
> For it is a matter of human acts aiming (in principle) at the realization of a structure, which may, however, not succeed or which may even be directed against the structures which must (in principle) rule them. Languages live only through successive renewals, each of which is a risk, for it runs the risk of not coming through this renewal unharmed. (1991:176)

If nomological explanation seeks the "certainty" of atemporal and universal law, then the model of language Taylor is describing—the model of what I am calling postformalist analogy—focuses on the community out of which knowledge arises *at a particular time.* Most of all, it suggests the communal and temporal aspects of knowledge. Recently, much work in the social study of science by people like Katherine Hayles, Bruno Latour, Robert Markley, Steve Woolgar, David Bloor, and the Edinburgh School have focused on this aspect of science studies. (In *We Have Never Been Modern* Latour begins by using the social study of science to raise important questions about the disciplinary nature of knowledge in our time. At the end of the first chapter of his book he asks: "Can we aspire to Enlightenment without modernity?" [1993:12], a question I also address in the instance of Foucault in the postscript. See also Markley 1993; and Woolgar 1988.) In this chapter I will use the work of these writers in order to discuss strategies for collaboration in the humanities and to discuss the ways in which those of us studying language and literature—that is, those of us studying the conjunction of syntax and semantics—can learn from intellectual practices of the nomological sciences.

Seeing and Witnessing: Literary Studies and the
Advent of Theory

Before I turn to the analogy between contrasting modes of analysis in the arts and sciences, I want to examine more closely the conjunction of syntax and semantics in the humanities under the category of "theory," since the advent of what has been called literary theory grows out of the attention to linguistics, semiotics, and information I have described in earlier chapters. "In the 1960s and early 1970s," Jonathan Arac has argued, "literary studies dissipated its disciplinary identity by pursuing 'theory' in such diverse areas as linguistics, psychoanalysis, anthropology, and phenomenology," even while "this hybrid mixture has made it a resource, a transfer point for renewal across a wide range of disciplines" (1989:1). It is such possibilities of "renewal," in Taylor's figure, that situates literary studies in its particular relationship to other disciplines. That is, the power and importance of theory in literary studies in the last two decades—and even the very "violence and irrationality of the attacks on theory" that Hillis Miller numbered among the phenomena that indicate the "triumph" of theory in his 1986 MLA Presidential Address (1987:285)—is, in fact, linked somehow to widespread reconsiderations of the nature of knowledge and explanation.

The use of the term *theory* in literary studies is curious in itself. An early use of the term in American criticism congruent with its contemporary use can be seen when W. K. Wimsatt asserted, in 1949, that the semantic basis of literary art was too broad to be encompassed within the study of aesthetics and required its own study in what he called "literary theory." "Literary theorists of our day," Wimsatt argued, "have been content to say little about 'beauty' or about any over-all aesthetic concept. In his most general formulation the literary theorist is likely to be content with something like 'human interest,' " even though "disinterestedness, we remember, is something that Kant made a character of art. . . . How the poet arrives at anything like the disinterest, the detachment, the self-contained objectification of which we hear the aesthetician speak (how the poet's 'rage' achieves its 'order'), must be a peculiar question, the answer to which will have an odd relation to the main doctrines of general aesthetics" (1950:228–29). In 1949 Northrop Frye called for the "scientific" study of literature in his essay "The Function of Criticism at the Present Time," which later became the "Polemical Introduction" to the *Anatomy of Criticism*. In both of these cases theory was an attempt to replace the aesthetic focus on the disinterested affectiveness of art by focusing, to some degree or other, on the relationship between literary meaning and interested writers and readers.

In this, Wimsatt's term *theory* is tied up with the problem of knowledge conceived as the object of disinterested scientific investigation. Jürgen Habermas describes this problem in narrating the origin of the term. "The *theoros*," he notes, "was the representative sent by Greek cities to public celebrations. Through *theoria*, that is, through looking on, he abandoned himself to the sacred events. In philosophical language, *theoria* was transferred to contemplation of the cosmos" (1971:301). In this narrative Habermas goes on to opposed this "scientific" conception of theory to its use in the nonscientific discourses of the "historical-hermeneutic" sciences in which theory contemplates meaning and not facts provided by observation (1971:306–8). By opposing facts and meaning, Habermas is erasing a crucial aspect of the work of the *theoros,* who were a collective, *collaborative* entity. That is, as Wlad Godzich has argued,

> the act of looking at, of surveying, designated by *theorein* does not designate a private act carried out by a cogitating philosopher but a very public one with important social consequences. The Greeks designated certain individuals . . . to act as legates on certain formal occasions in other city states or in matters of considerable political importance. These individuals bore the title of *theoros,* and collectively constituted a *theoria.* (It may be useful to bear in mind that the word is always a plural collective.) (1986:vii)

Their work, Godzich goes on to argue, was to bear witness for the community, to transform the private perception—the *"aesthesis"* of "the individual citizen, indeed even women, slaves, and children [all of whom] were capable of aesthesis, that is perception [which had] no social standing"—into a social and institutional fact. "Between the event and its entry into public discourse," Godzich concludes, "there is a mediating instance invested with undeniable authority by the polity. This authority effects the passage from the seen to the told" (1986:xv). Godzich is describing the very kind of "mobilization" that, as we saw in the preceding chapter, Latour isolates as a central unacknowledged factor in Enlightenment knowledge, even as he is isolating Latour's "visualization" under the double categories of seeing and witnessing. That is, the social mobilization of theory defined in this way *institutes* the private self-evidences of sight—as *aesthetics*—as public discourses of knowledge, so that witnessing expands its significance, analogically, from the act of seeing to the act of telling. (See also Jay 1993:30–32, 55.)

The complex conception of theory as the contemplation and discursive articulation of meaning—what I describe later in this chapter as the "notation" of witnessed knowledge—is congruent with Wimsatt's literary theory and Frye's argument that criticism should take its place among the social sciences. That is, if theory makes understanding and not the world its object, it does so by examining understanding—and the phenomenon of knowledge—outside of categories of aesthetic subjectivity. For this reason Miller, in his presidential address, defines *theory* as

> the displacement in literary studies from a focus on the meaning of texts to a focus on the ways meaning is conveyed. Put another way, theory is the use of language to talk about language. Put yet another way, theory is a focus on referentiality as a problem rather than as something that reliably and unambiguously relates a reader to the "real world" of history, of society, and of people acting within society on the stage of history. (1987:283)

As Godzich argues—in ways that resonate with the discussion of Cartesian "intuition" pursued in the postscript—this understanding of theory "forces a recognition of the incompatibility of language and intuition. [And] since the latter constitutes the foundational basis of cognition upon which perception, consciousness, experience, and the logic and the understanding, not to mention the aesthetics that are attendant to them, are constructed, there results a wholesale shakeout in the organization and conceptualzation of knowledge" (1986:x). This "shakeout," I am suggesting, recovers the similitude within equivalence; as Frank Lentriccia describes it, "theory is primarily a *process* of discovery of the lesson that I am calling historical; any single, formulable theory is a reduced version of the process, a frozen proposition which will tend to cover up the process it grew out of by projecting itself as an uncontingent system of ideas" (1985:108).

The advent of theory in literary studies has not gone uncontented. Thus, E. D. Hirsch describes what he calls "the Great Literary Theory Debate" as an "interest conflict" between those who seek to recover "primary interpretations"—namely, the intentional meanings of literary authors—and those who seek "secondary interpretation, or what Foucault calls '*resemanticizing* the text'" (1985:190). The struggle he sees in this debate is between "the needs and interests of undergraduates" who presumably simply want to get to "know" literature and its authors—who simply want to achieve the "humane [and aesthetic] pleasure of particular books"—and "the institutional advantages of secondary interpretation in the sphere of professorial publication" (1985:190–91). Within Hirsch's argument, however, the reference to Foucault's notion of "resemanticizing" texts suggests a description or definition of analogical thinking: such resemanticization describes the semantic formalism I discussed in chapter 2 and the postformalist knowledge that, as I argue in this chapter, can effect certain kinds of cross-disciplinary understanding. More generally, it describes the repeated "paraphrase which formulates in another fashion the equivalent content of a signifying element within a given semiotic system" (1982:159) by which Greimas and Courtés define nontraditional "interpretation," which governs the readings of part 3.

What is striking here is the manner in which both Godzich and Foucault associate the process of resemanticization with the *institutionalization* of knowledge within social formations. This is clearly the case, I believe, in the humanities, in which, as Hirsch notes, knowledge takes the form of "secondary texts" responding to already-semanticized "primary" texts. But even in the sciences, in which so-called primary texts seem to be phenomena themselves, and thus not clearly similar to "texts," the "given" of phenomena—"data"—is itself organized in a manner that is at least analogous to the textualization I am calling semantic, insofar as it results from superimposed collaborations of researchers as well as individual observations (see Eco 1983:204–5, for the relationship between scientific "universes" and semiotic texts). As Latour argues, the seeming observable "discrepancies" around which scientific knowledge organizes itself "proliferate" not in the immediate phenomenal experience of reality, "not by looking at the sky, but by carefully superimposing columns of angles and azimuths. No contradiction," he continues, "no counterpredictions, could even have been made visible. Contradiction . . . is neither a property of the mind, nor of the scientific method, but is a property of reading letters and signs inside new settings" (1986:20).

Latour's practical definition of *theory*—confusing as it does the seeing and the witnessing of knowledge—underscores the ways in which analogy reads signs in new settings. And it is precisely the work of theory within literary studies to encompass a larger range of reference than the more formal sciences do and to function, as Arac says, as a "transfer point for renewal across a wide range of disciplines" (1989:1). The definition of theory as polemical, witnessed knowledge creates, as Paul Ricoeur says, "a resemblance between relations rather than between terms per se" (1988:151). This "understanding"—the understanding of analogical thinking—has been particularly clear in literary studies because the question of apprehending meaning "inside new settings" defines literary studies altogether. "The object that defines this field of study—'literature'—," Samuel Weber argues, "has traditionally been distinguished from other 'objects' of study precisely by a certain *lack* of objectivity. . . . And such a lack of objectivity has, from Plato onward, confronted the study of literature (or of art in general) with the problem of its *legitimation,* and hence, with its status as, and in regard to, *institution(s)"* (1987:33).

For this reason the combination of seeing and witnessing, gathered together in the concept of theory, has been a focus for rethinking the aestheticization of knowledge embedded in the traditional Enlightenment criteria defining understanding in terms of its coherence (generalization), simplicity, and correspondence to empirical fact. Each of these criteria emphasizes a single aspect of Enlightenment understanding: coherence emphasizes its logic, and empiricism emphasizes its object, just as simplicity emphasizes its self-standing wholeness. "Faith in reason," Alfred North Whitehead wrote in *Science and the Modern World,* "is the trust that the ultimate natures of things lie together in a harmony which excludes mere arbitrariness. . . . To experience this faith is to know that in being ourselves we are more than ourselves: to know that our experience, dim and fragmentary as it is, yet sounds the utmost depths of reality: to know that detached details merely in order to be themselves demand that they should find themselves in a system of things: to know that this system includes the harmony of logical rationality, and the harmony of aesthetic achievement" (1967:18). Here Whitehead describes knowledge itself as systematic, aesthetically whole, and corresponding to reality.

Whitehead is participating in and articulating canons of Enlightenment knowledge. Such knowledge, above all, traffics in "common sense." Thus, for the Enlightenment, as Gilles Deleuze argues in *Kant's Critical Philosophy,* knowledge is possible because of the self-evident harmony of the human faculties—the harmony of reason, judgment, and imagination, corresponding with the generalizing noncontradiction, empirical accuracy, and elegant simplicity of Enlightenment knowledge itself. In Kant, Deleuze writes,

> common sense appears not as a psychological given but as the subjective condition of all "communicability." Knowledge implies a common sense, without which it would not be communicable and could not claim universality. Kant will never give up the subjective principle of a common sense of this type, that is to say, the idea of a good nature of the faculties, of a healthy and upright nature which allows them to harmonize with one another and to form harmonious proportions. . . . *Even reason,* from this speculative point of view, possesses a good nature which allows it to be in agreement with the other faculties: the Ideas [Kant writes in the *Critique of Pure Reason*] "arise from the very

nature of reason; and it is impossible that this highest tribunal of all the rights and claims of speculation should itself be the source of deceptions and illusions." (1984:21–22)

For Kant the "very nature of reason" must be a transcendental source of truth and self-evidence.

It is precisely this received sense of knowledge—its harmony, its disinterestedness, its measure against preexisting empirical data—that theory critiques. It does so by reconceiving knowledge as dependent not on the intelligible noncontradiction of phenomena nor on the detached self-standing subject or nature of experience nor on the preexisting reality of the object of knowledge. Instead, it is dependent on modes of analogical thinking authorized by the collaborative activity of the *theoros*. That is, it suggests what Latour has called the "underwriting" of understanding accomplished by the superimposition of more than one set of data, more than one system of logic, more than one subject of experience. In describing the "inscriptional" nature of scientific understanding—an understanding very different from Whitehead's and very different, too, from Habermas's distinction between cosmological and hermeneutical science—Latour argues that the text of knowledge is underwritten by "its adequation, fit, superimposition" to other claims of knowledge which are also textual (1988:13). This is true, Latour asserts, whether that text be literary-aesthetic, scientific-empirical, or purely logical (1988:21). Elsewhere, Latour describes this as the simple mechanism underlying Kant's Copernican revolution. Geology, he argues, invented "a new visual language" to understand the stratification of the earth. Without such a language "the layers of the earth stay hidden and no matter how many travelers and diggers move around there is no way to sum up their travels, visions, and claims." With the new "language" of geology—its rendering as textuality, the transformation of the evidence of eye to the witnessing of discourse—understanding becomes possible. "The Copernican revolution," Latour concludes, "dear to Kant's heart, is an idealist rendering of a very simple mechanism: if we cannot go to earth, let the earth come to us, or, more accurately, let us all go to many places on the earth, and come back with the same, but different homogenous pictures, that can be gathered, compared, superimposed and redrawn in a few places" (1986:15). Latour is replacing—or really supplementing—Kant's reason with the immanent plural relationships that semiotics describes and analogy enacts. Moreover, he is suggesting the ways in which literary studies is only a special case of institutional knowledges, all of which—including the "natural sciences" I mentioned in chapter 1 and return to in this chapter—can be understood, as Benveniste says, "as double from the fact that they are connected to something else" (1971:39), insofar as they manifest themselves within the social formations of historical institutions.

The places at which "the same, but different homogenous pictures . . . can be gathered, compared, superimposed and redrawn" (1986:15) that Latour describes is for literary studies the explicitly discursive *institutions* of knowledge in which superimpositions of readings and the contestation of understandings take place. Gaston Bachelard has called this "the polemical character of cognition" (cited in Weber 1987:xiii), and it describes an understanding of interpretation—and of *theory* itself—not as the formal description of phenomena or signs "independent of possible 'interpretations' " (Greimas and Courtés 1982:159) but as a plural (i.e., collaborative) and thereby postformal, analogical paraphrase of something that *already* signifies within another system of signification. In this—as in Heisenberg's attempts to account for subatomic mechanics, Freud's attempt to account for the economy of unattended psychological forces, Saussure's attempt to account for the nature of signification, and contemporary literary theory's attempt to account for literary meaning, literary form, literary power— knowledge and explanation always exist in relation to other instituted forms of understanding and knowledge that are always susceptible to renewal. Knowledge and explanation so conceived call for a dialogics that traverse the opposition, in Habermas and elsewhere, between scientific and nonscientific discourse.

The Disciplinary Identity of the Humanities

The elaborate etymology of theory as the combination of seeing and witnessing can help us to "see" that the relationship between the humanities as an intellectual discipline and the humanities as a "transfer point"—a site of cross-disciplinary collaboration—is complex and vexed. On the one hand, as Latour has argued, disciplines by their nature are time bound, collaborative, and a function of the cultures in which they develop. As he notes in *Science in Action,* "an *isolated* specialist is a contradiction in terms. Either you are isolated and very quickly stop being a specialist, or you remain a specialist but this means you are not isolated" (1987:152). On the other hand, despite the fact that disciplines *are* a product of—or at least are imbricated in—the cultures in which they develop, they still resist the possibilities of collaboration across disciplines. That is, insofar as knowledge is discipline specific, interdisciplinarity is highly problematic; knowledge in one discipline does not necessarily—and, in fact, cannot—constitute knowledge in a different discipline. Thus, Donald Davidson writes in "The Material Mind": "I take it for granted that detailed knowledge of the neurophysiology of the brain will make a difference . . . to the study of such subjects as perception, memory, dreaming and perhaps of inference. But it is one thing for developments in one field to affect changes in a related field, and another thing for knowledge gained in one area to constitute knowledge of another" (1986:247).

That disciplinary forms of knowledge—like *theory* itself—are both isolated and the product of a community creates problems for our work in language, semiotics, and literature. In fact, the model of our work in the humanities complicates this situate even further because we have inherited from the Enlightenment a sense of the subject of knowledge as overwhelmingly individual and overwhelmingly isolated. Michel Foucault touches upon this in his essay "What Is an Author?" when he contrasts the changing subjects of humanistic discourse and scientific discourse in the Enlightenment. "A reversal occurred," he writes,

> in the seventeenth or eighteenth century. Scientific discourses began to be received for themselves, in the anonymity of an established or always redemonstrable truth; their membership in a systematic ensemble, and not the reference to the individual who produced them, stood as their guarantee. . . . By the same token, literary discourses came to be accepted only when endowed with the author-function. We now ask of each poetic or fictional text: from where does it come, who wrote it, when, under what circumstances, or beginning with what design? (1994:347)

The great model of this description of the humanities is Descartes, who asserts that reason is closely associated with the individual. Thus, he writes, "My plan has never gone beyond trying to reform my own thoughts and construct them upon a foundation which is all my own" (1985:118; see Gellner 1992:2). The assumption governing this description is that the mind and soul of the Cartesian individual stand "outside" time, what has been called the "ghost in the machine," and it leads Descartes to imagine that his philosophy began when he realized he didn't have to get out of bed in the morning to do his intellectual work. A second model for our discipline is another Enlightenment model, "the reader of a novel," whom Walter Benjamin describes as "isolated, more so than any other reader. . . . In this solitude of his," Benjamin continues, "the reader of a novel seizes upon his material more jealously than anyone else. He is ready to make it completely his own, to devour it, as it were" (1969:100).

Both of these descriptions of our disciplinary work, that of thinking and that of reading, create the impression that these isolated activities are natural, individual, unwitnessed so to speak, and context free. It is time, I think, for those of us who are questioning—not abandoning, I hasten to add—the Enlightenment ideals upon which these descriptions are based to find ways to make our disciplinary practices conform to our analyses. I try to present my students with a similar caveat when I tell them that not only writing but, above all, our thinking and reading take the discipline of apprenticed practice. In the same way, I say, that they shouldn't imagine they can play the piano simply because they can hum a tune, so they should realize the disciplines of language in which we participate require much practice and testings in order to develop skillfulness. When I am talking to colleagues in the history of science, math, and biology, I am faced with a similar task of asserting that literary and cultural studies *are,* in fact, disciplines, and, like those other disciplines, they require what I am calling apprenticed practice in order to approach mastery. At the same time I am faced with the task of explaining to colleagues in history, physics, and even in English down the hall that the discovery or construction of knowledge— I prefer to describe it as the *notation* of knowledge, which, combining as it does the recognition and inscription of Latour's "visualization," the seeing and witnessing of theory, avoids the question of origins—is conditioned by social institutions that are external to the disciplines that articulate knowledge. In other words, in the humanities more than in the sciences we are faced with describing the seeming contradiction which I have mentioned and which inhabits *theory*: the isolated nature of disciplinary work and the collective nature of the disciplines themselves.

The key terms of the description I am presenting—*skillfulness, apprenticeship, collaboration*—are submerged in the atemporal individualism and universalism that Ernest Gellner demonstrates are embedded in Enlightenment knowledge. Louis Hjelmslev, whom I cited in chapter 1, in discussing scientific semiotics, participates in these Enlightenment assumptions when he presents what he takes to be the traditional opposition between the sciences and the humanities. "Humanistic, as opposed to natural phenomena," Hjelmslev writes, "are non-recurrent and for that very reason cannot, like natural phenomena, be subjected to exact and generalizing treatment" (1961:8). Thus, he argues, traditionally the humanities conceived of itself as pursuing a different method from the sciences, "namely, mere description . . . without being interpreted through a system" (1961:8–9). Hjelmslev goes on to argue that the systematic study of language by linguistics requires the methods of science, and, as he notes, his *Prolegomena* is, in fact, a vast systematization of Saussure's analysis of language.

My point here, however, is that the opposition between the particularities of the humanities and the generalizations of the sciences that Hjelmslev articulates—an opposition that, in important ways, conditions the canons of Enlightenment universalism, individualism, and ahistoricism, which, as I suggested in the preceding chapter, came to "crisis" at the turn of the twentieth century—leaves out the temporalities and nonuniversal pluralities of apprenticeship, of the acquisition of skills through practice, and of the collaboration that governs these activities (see Weber 1987 and Bambach 1995 for institutional and historical discussions). The idea of disciplinary collaboration I am presenting here, along with the idea and practice of theory as a collective, collaborative enterprise, *precede* the systematics of "exact and generalizing" science without recourse to such individualistic attributes as "genius," "intuition," or "instinct." Collaboration, then, like the "semantics" that opposes itself to "syntactics"—and, I am arguing, like analogical thinking more generally—is always temporal, always plural, and, most important, occurs *before* the impersonality of system that Foucault, like Hjelmslev, presents in what he calls the "always redemonstrable truth" of science. Such recurrences, as I have suggested, presuppose the abstract formalisms of syntactics and systems rather than the meanings and values of semantics.

Collaboration, I am arguing, is different from method—the impersonal systematicity of Descartes's *Discourse on Method*—precisely because it does not lend itself to the generalizing abstractions of formalism. Yet it is also different from the "intuitions" of private and individual genius. Like Hjelmslev, as we have also seen, Emile Benveniste, distinguishes between the "orders" of naturalistic and humanistic phenomena in terms of the "simplicity" of physiological and biological data and the complexity of "phenomena belonging to the interhuman milieu" that constitutes the "facts" of culture (1971:38–39; see chap. 1 of the present book for the full citation). The facts of culture Benveniste is describing are, above all, *semantic* facts: they possess, paradoxically, the particularities of shared meaning and value that Charles Taylor describes. Elsewhere in *Problems in General Linguistics* Benveniste notes that "we can never get back to man separate from language and we shall never see him inventing it. We shall never get back to man reduced to himself and exercising his wits to conceive of the existence of another" (1971:224). I suppose that Descartes, that remarkable mathematician, is exercising his wits in this way. But my point (and that of Benveniste) is that the meanings and values inhabiting semantics are, in Greimas's formulation, "neither pure contiguity nor a logical implication" (1983:244): they are neither the pure intuitions of genius nor the abstract formalisms of nomological system. Instead, paradoxically, they seem to reside in the excluded middle—the excluded temporalities and pluralities—of apprenticeship, practice, collaboration, and, above all, in the semantic formalisms and postformalist understanding of analogical thinking. The best example of such semantics is the always-possible metaphorization of any meaning, the fact that language *always* can lend itself to analogy. Greimas describes this more generally as the "edifice" of language appearing "like a construction without plan or clear aim" (1983:133) because "discourse, conceived as a hierarchy of units of communication fitting into one another, contains in itself the negation of that hierarchy by the fact that the units of communication with different dimensions can be at the same time recognized as equivalent" (1983:82). In this, Greimas is giving a technical and "systematic" account of the relation between structure and event that Taylor describes in language. And the best example of postformalist understanding is the pragmatics of discovering, in the conjunction of semantics and syntax in language study, the "transfer point for renewal across a wide range of disciplines" that Arac describes (1989:1).

Robert Markley's figure for this paradoxical pragmatic "systematicity" of meaning, namely the complex of knowledge and power caught up in the social institution of money, aptly captures the problem of the disciplinary identity of the humanities that I am trying to examine in relation to the disciplinary practices of the natural sciences. (In this he joins Adam Smith and Latour—as well as the "economics" of Descartes and Foucault in the postscript—in a focus on money as a token of meaning.) "Money," Markley says, "is the symptom that structures both scientific and humanistic inquiry" (1994). But like other "objects" of study Davidson and Kuhn describe that do not remain exactly "identical" in different disciplinary contexts—or like the "same" words that become analogically similar to themselves, which J. F. Ross describes—money as a *symptom* does not function in the same way in the sciences and humanities. What Markley conveys by focusing on money, which is both a fact of social life and a semiotic phenomenon, is that we who work in English studies and discourse theory are able to understand phenomena as meaning, that we have, through the apprenticed practice of our discipline, achieved an attentive sensitivity to the rhythms of signification, the patterns of meaning that are the substances and conditions of "culture"—including the disciplined culture of our intellectual life. This, after all, is what our discipline can teach, if only its students (including ourselves) assume the patience and humility that come with the role of the subject, in a phrase developed by Jacques Lacan, who is presumed not to know. It examines the semiotics of value in relation to systems of fact. Even what Markley describes as the knowledge we can gain from institutional science, the *technē* of generating funds, becomes, in this narrative, disciplinary knowledge supplementing blindness: another version of symptomological semantics.

Certainly, Markley's assertion that money in America bears the enormous authority of a neurotic symptom captures this problem insofar as Freud's analyses of neurotic symptoms is a more or less systematic attempt to semanticize (physiological) formalism. In their definition of *interpretation* in *Semiotics and Language,* as we have seen, the two different concepts Greimas and Courtés present nicely parallel Taylor's distinction, with which I began this chapter, and shed light on the ways that psychoanalysis can help us to understand the nature of the disciplinary identity of the humanities. According to their "classical" concept of interpretation, "every system of signs may be described in a formal way that does not take into account the content and is independent of possible 'interpretations' of these signs" (1982:159). In this conception—which governs the logic of Cartesian mathematics—"semantic interpretation" comes after and follows from abstract formalism, which is general and universal. This understanding of interpretation preserves our commonsense idea of the referential function of interpretation and sign systems more generally: the world to which language refers *preexists* the language that describes it, just as the necessities of formal logic preexist the phenomena that exemplify those logical necessities. Interpretation, then, consists of finding a language that *conforms* to preexisting *forms;* interpretation is always exemplary.

The second concept of interpretation, Greimas and Courtés argue, "is completely different." Within this perspective—which they identify with Saussurian linguistics, Husserlian phenomenology, and Freudian psychoanalysis and I am identifying with the postformal disciplinary study of language and literature—"interpretation is . . . a paraphrase which formulates in another fashion the equivalent content of a signifying element within a given semiotic system" (1982:159). In this second understanding form and content are not distinct, but, rather, every "form" is, alternatively, a semantic content as well, a "signifying form," so that interpretation offers an analogical paraphrase of something that *already* "signifies within a system of signification." In this conception of *interpretation* the semantic content isn't dependent on preexisting forms. Rather, both content and form— semantics and syntax—arise together, collaboratively and analogically, in what I have called the *notation*—that is, the *recognition* and the disciplinary *inscription*—of meaning and value. Such notation, I believe, is central to Freud's development of psychoanalysis. (See Weber for a description of "*another* kind of [disciplinary] institution" modeled on Freud's sense of "ambivalence," which "entails not merely the static opposition of conflicting emotions, but rather a constantly shifting dynamic of drive and prohibition" [1987:149, 148].)

The conjunction of syntax and semantics—both their (formal) opposition and their (temporal) combinations—distinguishes the disciplines of humanitic study from the nomological sciences. Such a conjunction creates the possibility of analogical thinking, which is neither haphazardly arbitrary nor logically formal. Moreover, it creates a semiotics of value, whether the signifier of value is the notation of knowledge or the social power of money. In important ways that, I take it, critics of humanistic accounts of the sciences such as Norman Levitt and Paul Gross cannot understand, our disciplinary knowledges have a larger range of reference than technical sciences precisely in their ability to encompass the kinds of analogical thinking I am describing throughout this book. We can see, for instance, the semiotics of money in what looks simply like the formal technical description of phenomena because, as Benveniste says, facts of culture are necessarily semantic insofar as they "refer" to other, analogous, systems of meaning. But the price of this range is the very polysemy that allows us to see the language of semiotics in economic activity while not being able to manipulate the mathematical symbols of formal economics. This price is the burden of postformalist knowledge—the very forms and formulations that demand a choice between semantic "goods," a choice, that is between descriptions of knowledge as either discovered or constructed. Markley calls this "post-Kantian structures of knowledge" (1994). Above all, these are *semantic* structures, and the positive and unique nature of this semantics—the *temporality* of semantics—precludes the precisions of formal manipulation. Thus, as we have seen, Thomas Kuhn argues that

> proponents of different theories are . . . like native speakers of different languages. Communication between them goes on by translation, and it raises all translation's familiar difficulties. The analogy is, of course, incomplete, for the vocabulary of the two theories may be identical. . . . [S]ome words in the basic as well as the theoretical vocabularies of the two theories—words like "star" and "planet," "mixture" and "compound," or "force" and "matter"—do function differently. Those differences are unexpected and will be discovered and localized, if at all, only by repeated experience of communication breakdown. (1977:338)

Kuhn is describing the problem of interdisciplinarity Davidson mentions: the ways that the "function" of disciplinary knowledge-tokens spoil in translation. If Davidson is describing the "identical" object of study for different disciplines, Kuhn is describing the problematic nature of such identity within the temporal development of the same discipline.

Disciplinary Collaboration

The conjunction of semantics and syntax in our discipline of language and literature—their opposition and combination—helps us to see this problem in ways that are more difficult to obtain in other disciplines. It allows us to see polysemy and analogies of meaning—what linguists studying both semantics and syntax precisely call levels of signification. Thus, if the semiotics of meaning and the "discipline" of value are what we can teach, they also allow us to see what we can learn from the nomological sciences. In this regard Markley's argument that science in higher education is more closely linked than the humanities to the money system of our culture suggests that the disciplinary practices of the sciences offers the humanities ways to reimagine the subject of disciplinary knowledge, a subject that can be conceived as *collective* rather than individual and as *multi-modal* in its articulations. The social institutions of money and exchange point in this direction, and so do the collectivity and trangenerational activity of apprenticeship and remembrance that Benjamin describes in the essay I have cited, "The Storyteller." (Benjamin also describes this idea of collectivity in "The Task of the Translator," an essay that complements Kuhn's observations in provocative ways.) Werner Heisenberg, I think, is trying to describe such "post-Kantian" knowledge when he asserts that true but contradictory descriptions of the world can *alternate* rather than be taken as simply true, once and for all (1958:179). In the concept of "alternation" Heisenberg offers the conjunction of Davidson's and Kuhn's disciplinary and temporal descriptions of objects of knowledge. The term Latour uses for this conjunction, as we have seen, is the "superimposition" of forms of knowledge. The "proliferation" of scientific knowledge in the Renaissance, he argues, occurred "not by looking at the sky, but by carefully superimposing columns of angles and asimuths. No contradiction, or counter prediction could ever have been visible. Contradiction . . . is neither a property of the mind, nor of the scientific method, but is a property of reading letters and signs inside new settings that focus attention on inscriptions alone" (1986:20).

Such superimposition is a nice alternative to the impermeable divides between science and literature that are often posited, the insurmountable differences between *modes* of knowledge that Davidson and Benveniste describe. It is, I think, a modified concept of Kuhn's "translation." Moreover, it points to what I imagine that we, working in the humanities, can learn most from contemporary scientific disciplines. The structures of knowledge in the sciences, as I see it, are at once Kantian and post-Kantian; they might even be, in an important way, pre-Kantian as well. That is, the structures of their knowledge, far more than ours I think, are governed by what I am calling apprenticed practice. Practice is methodical: it is the active formalism of playing scales, conforming to syntax, ordering the world through periodic tables. (Saussure's phonology, like Trubetzkoy's and Jakobson's "distinctive features," approaches the systematicity of Mendeleyev's periodic table.) Apprenticeship, on the other hand, entails the temporally specific mentorings of what Benjamin calls "counsel." Such structures of knowledge in the sciences alternate and superimpose the roles of subjects supposed to know and those who suppose they do not know—subjects, that is, who know different things. Like playing the piano or listening to a story in order to repeat it, structures of apprenticeship presuppose trust and authority and responsibility within a community of workers; and, if money changes hands, it does so in the mode of psychoanalysis, in which such exchange is also a tool in apprenticeship. The institutions of science have more formal places for apprenticeship in their curricula and especially in their research than we do in the humanities, even if the very nature of our discipline, its conjunctions of syntax and semantics, allows us to examine these formal places for apprenticeship more self-consciously, in first-person narratives and analyses.

The disciplinary structures of nomological sciences prevent such examination of the relation between practice and apprenticeship because the sciences (as disciplines) are more fully committed than the humanities to Enlightenment modes of thinking. Latour argues that these Enlightenment modes of thinking conflate the categories of Kantian, post-Kantian, and pre-Kantian thought through a kind of unconsciousness: the willful (and "fruitful") ignoring of the conjunctions (both oppositions and combinations) that I am arguing characterize the disciplinary identity of the humanities, its analogical thinking. Latour argues that the "modernity" of Enlightenment modes of thinking is based upon the simultaneous assertion and subversion of "pure" categories of inquiry, disciplines, and thought—such as (though these are not his examples) the absolute distinction between form and content, structure and event (in Taylor's example), syntax and semantics. What *is* Latour's example is the absolute distinction between nature and culture, the sciences and humanities that I am distinguishing in this chapter. Latour describes, with great insight, the double Enlightenment project of "domination and emancipation." "We have to rethink the definition of modernity,"

Latour writes, "interpret the symptom of postmodernity, and understand why we are no longer committed heart and soul to the double task of domination and emancipation" (1993:10).

The nomological sciences are *disciplined* both to participate in versions of collaboration and apprenticeship and to be blind to the temporalities of these activities in presenting universalist results. In *Science in Action* Latour describes the ways science "forgets" the "uncertainty, people at work, decisions, competition, controversies" that go into science (Latour 1987:4) so that the result of scientific inquiry is like the "black box" of cyberneticians. Whenever faced with great complexity, he writes, "in its place [cyberneticians] draw a little box about which they need to know nothing but its input and output. . . . That is, no matter how controversial [the histories of these black boxes], how complex their inner workings, how large the commercial or academic networks that hold them in place, only their input and output count" (1987:2–3; throughout his work *network* is one of Latour's term for what I am calling "collaboration").

A subject of disciplinary knowledge that can be conceived as collective and multi-modal inhabits Bruno Latour's and Steve Woolgar's description of the collaborative work of science in *Laboratory Life*. In their study they describe the interactions of scientists working together and against one another, what they call "the idiosyncratic, local, heterogenous, contextual, and multifaceted character of scientific practices" (1986:152). They note four modes of collaboration discernible within different kinds of "conversational exchange" (1986:160) among scientists. What these conversations entail, they argue, are "complex negotiations" between and among people who bring different knowledges, skills, accomplishments, and social authority to the laboratory. For instance, in a conversation in the lab between two scientists, Wilson and Flower, which Latour and Woolgar analyze at length, we are told that "Wilson has control over the availability of the substances [peptides he has manufactured in his own lab]; Flower has the necessary expertise to determine the amounts of these substances" (1986:157). In other words, these collaborators bring different "things" to their work together and alternate the roles of master and apprentice.

The first of the four modes of conversational exchange Latour and Woolgar describe is the sharing of "known facts." "These kinds of exchanges," they write, "serve an information-spreading function which enables group members continuously to draw upon each other's knowledge and expertise to improve their own" (1986:161). The second mode takes place during "practical activity": "these are the verbal components of a largely nonverbal body of exchanges during which reference is constantly made to the correct way of doing things" (1986:161). A third kind of exchange "appeared to focus primarily of theoretical matters" (1986:162). Finally, "a fourth kind of conversational exchange featured discussion by participants about other researchers" in which, "instead of assessing a statement itself, participants tended to talk about its author and to account for the statement either in terms of the authors' social strategy or their psychological make-up" (1986:163). These categories seem to exhaust the possibilities of workplace exchange and collaboration in terms of empirical facts, practical procedures, the logic of possibilities of knowledge, and, finally, simple gossip. Moreover, they easily situate themselves upon Greimas's semiotic square.

empirical facts ⟷ practical procedures

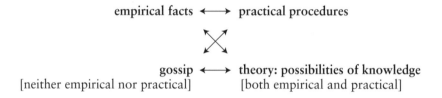

          gossip ⟷ theory: possibilities of knowledge
[neither empirical nor practical]   [both empirical and practical]

Greimassian semiotics allows us to see the ways that these knowledges are imbricated in one another; to see how they create their own networks of analogical meanings. Moreover, the two levels of Greimas's square both separate and bring together—they superimpose—the oppositions between fact and method, semantics and syntax, that Latour argues in *We Have Never Been Modern* Enlightenment thinking more generally does *unconsciously*. Again, the terms I am multiplying here—*superimposition, networking, imbrication*—are all descriptions of collaborative activities, analogical modes of meaning.[1]

What is striking about the categories Latour and Woolgar present is the

    1. For a discussion of Greimassian semiotics in relation to scientific knowledge, see Schleifer, Con Davis, and Mergler 1992: chap. 1. Greimas himself brings together (or "superimposes") these categories in his first description of the semiotic square in which he alternatively opposes white versus nonwhite and white versus black (Greimas and Rastier 1968:104). The first is a formal (logical) opposition, while the second is a semantic opposition. The "nominalization" of *nonwhite* into *black* is what I mean by focusing on semantics, and it creates according to Greimas the transformation of "the *modal predicate* into a *modal value*" (1987:129). The semiotic square, then, by presenting a *formal* description of *semantic* value—by analogizing formalism and semantics—self-consciously enacts the collaboration of what I am calling semantic formalism that is neither pure contiguity nor a logical implication.

ways in which the "subjects" of these knowledges constantly shift. In describing conversations about practical activity, for instance, they note that "these exchanges take place between technicians, or between researchers and technicians (or between researchers acting as technicians)" (1986:161). The roles of master and apprentice are repeatedly transformed. This is precisely what the Cartesian model of the subject of thinking—the project focused solely on "the reformation of my own opinions" but not on the *position* of the thinker—cannot accommodate; it is what the model of the isolated reader of a novel Benjamin describes does not allow. Moreover, the shifts themselves are neither logical nor completely random: they are not "purely" empirical. Rather, they follow the trajectory of Greimas's square, "neither pure contiguity nor a logical implication" (1983:244). The most striking contrast Latour and Woolgar describe, for instance, is that between the "logic" of possibilities embodied in "theoretical" talk and the seeming accidents of gossip embodied in narrative talk. In his contrast of "information" with "wisdom," Benjamin describes similar interactions in the work of storytelling. Going beyond the mere transmission of information embodied in manuals and newspapers, whose subject is the transcendental subject of Enlightenment reason, the talk of collaborating scientists takes the form of apprenticeship, which not only combines fact and method (the elements of the first level of Greimas's square and, more concretely, of practice) but more radically combines *personal* idiosyncrasies and *impersonal* knowledge (the elements of Greimas's second level of apprenticeship). Benjamin describes such apprenticeship, without naming it, in his description of storytelling. Storytelling entails, he argues, experience, craftsmanship, wisdom, and interpersonal counsel. These four qualities—they correspond, willy-nilly, to the facts, procedures, theory, and personal gossip that Latour and Woolgar describe—can help define disciplinary collaboration. That is, they point to how facts are changed and renewed in the face of shared experience, what techniques we might develop to foster such collaboration, what is at stake in collaboration, and the temporal locus of shared work.

In "The Storyteller" Benjamin is elaborating a wonderful description of collaboration across generations under the figure of storytelling. In this essay he defines storytelling precisely in the ways that stories—as opposed to novels—involve the collaboration between the present generation and those who preceded us. "There is no story," he writes, "for which the question as to how it continued would not be legitimate" (1969:100). This is because while the novel traffics in "information" which, in its nature, is only subject to "verification" (1969:89), stories transmit "experience," "counsel," and "wisdom." "If today," Benjamin writes, "having counsel" is beginning to have an old-fashioned ring, this is because the communicability of experience is decreasing. In consequence we have no counsel either for ourselves or for others. After all, counsel is less an answer to a question than a proposal concerning the continuation of a story which is just unfolding. To seek this counsel one would first have to be able to tell the story. . . . Counsel woven into the fabric of real life is wisdom. The art of storytelling is reaching its end because the epic side of truth, wisdom, is dying out. (1969:86–87)

Such wisdom, as Benjamin suggests, is above all collective and communal. It is based upon experience that can be shared and craft that can be passed on. Moreover, it is itself transmitted in the form of personal counsel. The wisdom and experience of storytelling can be shared because they can be apprehended as analogues for the experience of those who listen. The very craft of storytelling—its collaborative retelling, its repeated witnessing, its temporality—is analogical.

In these definitions—as in the retelling of a story by Isak Dinesen I set forth in chapter 6—Benjamin is decrying the transformation in philosophy during the Enlightenment that Rorty describes, "the Cartesian . . . triumph of the quest for certainty over the quest for wisdom. From that time forward," Rorty goes on, "the way was open for philosophers . . . to attain the rigor of the mathematician . . . rather than to help people attain peace of mind. Science, rather than living, became philosophy's subject, and epistemology its center" (1979:61). Certainty, rather than wisdom, became the object of philosophy, just as information became the object of solitary subjects of experience and knowledge. That is, the epistemology that Rorty describes in philosophy's quest for certainty is the function of an individual subject, one who stands outside the experience he comprehends—the Enlightenment subject is always the unmarked masculine—seeking a kind of complete and individual mastery that exists once and for all. It seeks the "certainties" of formal syntax and nomological system rather than the wisdom, born of time-bound experience within communal life and transmitted by means of repeated analogues, that is semantic and for that reason neither "established," once and for all, nor always "redemonstrable."

It is precisely the "mastery" of certainty—Benjamin calls it the "explanations" the novel and newspapers pursue—that the collaborative activity of storytelling eschews in its attempts to articulate, in "chaste compactness" (1969:91), events that can possess, analogically, more than one subject, that in fact *require* more than one subject. As an example, Benjamin cites the story of Psammenitus from Herodotus, the defeated Egyptian king who sees his daughter and son captured by his enemies yet still remains "mute and motionless, his eyes fixed on the ground." Afterward, Benjamin says, when "he recognized one of his servants . . . in the ranks of the prisoners, he beat his fists against his head and gave all the signs of deepest mourning" (1969:90). When he recounts this story, Benjamin offers several interpretations by Montaigne and others. Herodotus, he suggests, "offers no explanations" but gives up his story to those who will come to read it in other times and places. "This is why," Benjamin concludes, "this story from ancient Egypt is still capable after thousands of years of arousing astonishment and thoughtfulness" (1969:90).

Just as the collaborations of scientists exhaust the activities of the workplace in terms of empirical facts, practical procedures, the logic of possibilities of knowledge, and, finally, gossip, so the collaborations of shared narratives—of storytelling—exhaust the possibilities of experience in terms of the layering of stories that complete, momentarily, one another in their narrative facts, discursive procedures, possibilities of interpretation, and the ways they offer local and personal counsel that must be taken up by a new storyteller. This is why Benjamin ends his essay by describing storytelling in terms, quoted from Paul Valéry, of "the accord of the soul, the eye, and the hand of someone who was born to perceive" and evoke the signs of a story. "With these words," Benjamin says, "soul, eye, and hand are brought into connection. Interacting with one another, they determine a practice" (1969:108). This interaction—parallel to that of theory, fact, and procedure that Latour and Woolgar describe in science—brings together what Benjamin calls "gestures trained by work" (1969:108) in collaborative activity that eschews the mastery of isolated thinkers, isolated readers, and—as in laboratories—isolated workers. Above all, the collaborations in the humanities that Benjamin describes—like those in the laboratory Latour and Woolgar describe—are governed by temporality, memory, and a sense that no one exists alone. This is the knowledge that we can learn from the sciences: that even semiotics—even with what Lévi-Strauss calls its attempt to create a "Kantism without the transcendental subject" (1975:11)—can traffic in wisdom, which is to say can conceive its subject as collective and communal and its objects as susceptible to analogical multiplication. The way to achieve such wisdom, I think, is above all to *remember* the temporal aspect of knowledge, its "worldliness," the fact that knowledge emerges in the activities of time.

Let me conclude this chapter with a story of my own collaborative work. In working on *Contemporary Literary Criticism* and *Criticism and Culture* with my friend and colleague, Robert Con Davis, we developed a particular method of collaborative writing. One of us would draft a section of these books and then pass on a disk with the draft electronically encoded. The next person would rework the text and pass it back, and we'd go back and forth, master and apprentice. We discovered that, since there were no markings for any of the changes one or the other of us made, the only way we could "own" a particular text is if we could remember it. I couldn't *see* what passages R.C. deleted from my work, so that when I read over the reworked text I couldn't judge it against the first draft but only in terms of whether or not it made sense and only against my memory of the first draft. With each draft, then, each of us was faced with the facts of the text that, after the passage of time, ceased to originate solely in any particular person. Only those deleted passages that we remembered and remembering, added back to where they had been, could survive. In several instances we found ourselves taking out and putting back in the same passage over and over until, finally, we had to discuss together our various motives—both personal and impersonal—for inclusion and exclusion. But most of the time such discussions were unnecessary: we simply shifted roles from writer to reader and back again. Thus, like the story that Benjamin describes as the product of "that slow piling one on top of the other of thin, transparent layers which constitutes the most appropriate picture of the way in which the perfect narrative is revealed through the layers of a variety of retellings" (1969:93), we developed a method of collaborative writing of hand and eye that follows the temporality of storytelling and remembrance. Or perhaps, in a more accurate description, we found ourselves moving from position to position on Greimas's square, encountering discursive facts, enacting practical procedures of writing and revision, theoretically reading the combination of fact and procedure, and, occasionally, getting down to personal concerns and the social and psychological strategies of gossip. In the end we produced texts whose subjects weren't simply the aggregate of two isolated writers and whose knowledges, we knew, could never be "finished" but could go on and on in repeated revisions and analogical rethinkings not only between us but between those books we were writing and other people who, coming later, might read and master them in practices of apprenticeship.

Such practices create the successive renewals that Taylor talks about; they create the very facts—the *analogical conjunctions*—of disciplinary activity and disciplinary knowledge. That knowledge is subject to repeated renewal even though at a particular moment it is also—"alternatively," as Heisenberg says—nomologically *true*. This paradox of "truth" is the paradox of "value" that has run, like a barely perceived bass, throughout this chapter and, indeed, throughout this whole book. *Value*—I once thought *valence* might have been a better description (Schleifer 1987:xxi)—is a term in Saussure that is both linked to meaning and distinguished from it: a site of the conjunction of the abstract formalism and semantic formalism of syntax and semantics, the economies of value point toward postformalist understanding. In an important way value is the "successive," "repeated," above all "temporal," aspects of meaning that depend, momentarily but objectively, on the repeated acts of members of a community. Such acts and values are the repeated renewals resulting from the alternating facts of isolation and community, which Taylor describes, that articulate themselves repeatedly and analogically. They arise from practices of counsel, apprenticeship, and collaboration over time.

Part III

Interpretation

Chapter 5

Yeats's Postmodern Rhetoric

As I have suggested throughout this book, the work of analogical thinking serves historical moments but also, existing within a society of individuals, it serves more than a single moment—it involves the very "future" that language and collaboration make possible. That is, while the meanings and pragmatics of the way that analogies "come into play precisely at those points where one wishes to speak of language itself or of the relation between language and the world" (Burrell 1973:224), the meanings and actions of analogy also serve other generations and other historical moments, not simply as forms for knowledge and association but also as a form of mastery to bequeath, as a kind of "cultural" inheritance, to those who come afterward. This, as I have argued in the preceding chapter and will examine again in chapter 6, is a form of collaboration among people existing in different places and at different times. It is because of this possibility of analogizing experience—of grasping the similar in the disparate—Walter Benjamin suggests, that a "story from ancient Egypt is still capable after thousands of years of arousing astonishment and thoughtfulness" (1969:90).

In describing the relationship between capitalism and nature in *One-Way Street,* Benjamin offers the analogy of generational relationships. "Who would trust a cane wielder who proclaimed the mastery of children by adults to be the purpose of education?" he asks. "Is not education above all the indispensable ordering of the relationship between generations and therefore mastery, if we are to use this term, of that relationship and not of children?" (1978:93). In this passage Benjamin brings to mind Paul Ricoeur's description of "the Analogous, which is a resemblance between relations rather than between terms per se" (1988:151). Here, as in much of his work, Benjamin brings together different generations in one glance or phrase to underline the temporal disparity encompassed by culture. In "N [Re The Theory of Knowledge, Theory of Progress]" he spells out further the collaborative and institutional implications of knowledge I have been examining. Responding in his notes to a letter from Max

Horkheimer in 1937 in which Horkheimer accused Benjamin of being idealistic in his assertion of "incompleteness . . . , if completeness isn't included in it," since "past injustice has occurred and is done with. The murdered are really murdered" (1989:61), Benjamin replies:

> The corrective to this way of thinking lies in the conviction that history is not only a science but also a form of remembrance. What science has "established" can be modified by remembrance. Remembrance can make the open-ended (happiness) into something concluded and the concluded (suffering) into something open-ended. This is theology; however, in remembrance we have an experience which forbids us from conceiving of history fundamentally a-theologically, despite the fact that we are hardly able to describe it in theological concepts which are immediately theological. (Cited in Wolin 1989:225; also translated in Benjamin 1989:61)

For Benjamin's term *theological* I would substitute *witnessed:* remembrance—even the small remembrances R.C. and I participated in when we collaborated in our writing—forbids us from conceiving history and knowledge as fundamentally unwitnessed. That is to say, I would add that Benjamin's "form of remembrance," the ordering of the relationship between generations, constitutes witnessed knowledge in its creation and imputation of value across particular experiences. This imputation apprehends particular experiences as analogical even in their particularity, so that the value it articulates is not universal but can be apprehended as "general," occasions for analogy, a dialogue of the alternative explanations of *interpretation* as Greimas and Courtés define it. The interpretations of analogy create a place for the activities of imputations that are always repeated but never the same. They do so provisionally, by allowing those who come after to finally judge the worth and value of the interested struggle to institute disciplinary knowledges and generalizable truths. In the study of language and literature—syntax and semantics—we confront experience that forbids us from conceiving of knowledge itself as only and always disinterested.

The burden of part 3 of this book—its examination of the relationship between modern and postmodern modes of apprehending literary texts—pursues, in what Clifford Geertz calls the "thick descriptions" of its interpretations, the ways that literature and criticism have attempted to resist the secularization of nomological science and the seeming absoluteness of Enlightenment knowledge by pursuing—by *retelling*—possibilities of the sacred within modern life. In this pursuit, I am suggesting, "postmodern"—or, as I prefer, the post-Enlightenment—modes of understanding resist the conception of history as fundamentally atheological even as it attempts to gather together modes of apprehension that are not immediately, or traditionally, understood as "theological." This problem and pursuit is most explicitly clear in chapter 6, which examines *The Postmodern Bible,* and it is appropriate that this is so, since that chapter of part 3 corresponds most fully to the collaborations I have examined in part 2. Such social collaborations, as the short genealogy of theory I presented in the preceding chapter suggests, institute and authorize a transpersonal sense of the sacred that, at least to my mind, makes sense within the secular truths the Enlightenment has bequeathed to us. But Yeats's bardic semiotics, examined in this chapter, and the intertextuality of American letters, examined in chapter 7, also attempt to recover versions of the sacred within our Enlightenment culture, ways of apprehending knowledge as forms of renewal in collaborative analogies of truth and value.

In this chapter I examine a complex, double conception of rhetoric implicit in Yeats's poetry as a kind of analogical thinking, discourse calling for the kind of rereading and retelling that I have discussed in the preceding chapters. This conception of rhetoric is neither universal nor accidental but arises at a particular historical moment within the limits of particular discursive possibilities. It arises, I am suggesting, within the rhetoric of modernism yet suggests or points to the related phenomenon of postmodernism. The relationship between modernism and postmodernism—like the relationship between abstract and semantic formalism I examined in chapter 2 or the relationship between syntax and semantics I examined in chapter 4—forms a complex analogy, temporalized in the *post-*. The chapters of part 3 examine the work of analogy by exploring the complexity of the connection between modernism and postmodernism in Yeats's poetics, in the collaborative work of appropriating and retelling the "pre-Enlightenment" text of the Bible for our time, and an intertextual examining of a relatively contemporary work, Norman Mailer's *Executioner's Song.* Taken together, these chapters repeat the focuses on language, collaboration, and interpretation of *Analogical Thinking* as a whole in their attempts at the rereadings—the analogical "post-readings"—of disciplined interpretation.

Modern and Postmodern

In the famous definition of the "mythical method," T. S. Eliot describes and exemplifies the complexity of the Modernist rhetoric I am examining. "In using the myth," Eliot writes, in manipulating a continuous parallel between contemporaniety and antiquity, Mr. Joyce is pursuing a method which others must pursue after him. . . . It is simply a way of controlling, of ordering, of giving a shape and a significance to the immense panorama of futility and anarchy which is contemporary history. It is a method already adumbrated by Mr. Yeats, and of the need for which I believe Mr. Yeats to have been the first contemporary to be conscious. . . . . It is, I seriously believe, a step toward making the modern world possible for art. (1975:177–78)

What will concern me here is less Eliot's understanding of Joyce's achievement than his description of the "panorama" of contemporary life and its articulation in language. For it is my contention that the mythical parallel that Eliot describes is, in fact, what he explicitly denies that it is in his review of *Ulysses,* simply a kind of scaffolding Joyce uses to be discarded after the futility and anarchy of contemporary history rises up and is represented in language.

In this Eliot is repeating a recurrent gesture of Modernist rhetoric: he is delimiting phenomena that is not capable of being reduced to "order"— which is not even susceptible to linguistic order—and he is asserting that, nevertheless, it is analogous to the classical order of myth that somehow underlies its "surface" disorder. Robert Langbaum offers the standard narrative account of this when he suggests that the

"mythical method," as Eliot calls it, allows the writer to be naturalistic, to portray modern chaos, while suggesting through psychological naturalism a continuing buried life. . . . The mythical method gives a doubleness of language to parallel our own doubleness (doubleness between the apparent and buried) of consciousness and selfhood. (1977:89–90)

The problem with such an account, as Langbaum himself suggests, is that it *naturalizes* the terror and disgust inherent in Eliot's response to contemporary history. But, more than this, it naturalizes the important antinaturalistic impulse in Modernist language. Modernism may, in fact, as Langbaum argues, replace the naturalism and realism of late-nineteenth-century literature with its own "psychological naturalism," but a more interesting way of examining literary modernism—especially in light of the postmodern phenomena that follows (or accompanies) it—is to see its continuity with the antinaturalism of the Symbolist movement of the 1890s. Daniel O'Hara has called this antinaturalist, antiromantic impulse in Yeats the "demonic sublime," and, tracing Yeats's treatment in literary criticism since the end of World War II, he sees the culmination of Yeats's profound influence on the ways criticism reads in Paul de Man's distinction between natural "image" and esoteric "emblem" in Yeats (1984). Most important, the antinaturalism of the Symbolist movement is *analogical:* it treats language, as Clive Scott has argued, no longer "as a natural outcrop of the person but as a material with its own laws and its own peculiar forms of life" (1976:212), as a kind of *magic.* Such treatment, as I have argued elsewhere (1985b), focuses on the syntactics of literature, the signifier rather than the signified, syntax rather than semantics.

In other words, the apocalyptic antirepresentation of modernism "marks"—in the semantic formalism of linguistic markedness—what Jacques Derrida describes in Mallarmé's work as the articulation or circumscription of the "ideality" of nothingness. Here idea and intellection are *without* content or the representation of determined content: spirit transcends any content, any material determination, any taint of representation in an operation that is

> not a unified entity but the manifold play of a scene that, illustrating nothing—neither word nor deed—beyond itself, illustrates nothing. Nothing but the many-faceted multiplicity of a lustre which itself is nothing beyond its own fragmented light. Nothing but the idea which is nothing. The ideality of the idea is here for Mallarmé the still metaphysical name that is still necessary in order to mark nonbeing, the nonreal, the nonpresent. . . . This "materialism of the idea" is nothing other than the staging, the theater, the visibility of nothing or of the self. It is a dramatization which *illustrates nothing,* which illustrates *the nothing,* lights up a space, re-marks a spacing as a nothing, a blank: white as a yet unwritten page, blank as a difference between two lines. (Derrida 1981b:208)

The antirepresentational impulse in modernism, its Symbolist focus on the play of signifiers and the concomitant positing of "the nothing" behind that play, most clearly demonstrates its analogical mode of apprehension: in this case absence itself is hypothesized as a free-standing entity that is metonymically analogous to the world. This impulse and mode of apprehension,

I think, most closely articulates the analogy between modernism and post-modernism.[1]

The great difference between the two—between modernism in its Symbolist moment and postmodernism—is the difference between the metaphysical name Derrida describes and the "staging" of that name. In fact, in this passage Derrida describes the antirepresentational metaphysics of modernism, its turning away from the immense panorama of futility and anarchy of the contemporary world by turning to *another* world of what Yeats called, in 1893, the "subtlety, obscurity, and intricate utterance . . . . of our moods and feelings [which] are too fine, too subjective, too impalpable to find any clear expression in action or in speech tending towards action" (1970:271). This turn, as Derrida says elsewhere, "is a departure from the world toward a place which is neither a *non-place* nor an *other* world. . . . This universe articulates only that which is in excess of everything, the essential nothing on whose basis everything can appear and be produced within language. . . . Only *pure absence*—not the absence of this or that, but the absence of everything in which all presence is announced—can *inspire,* in other words, can *work*" (1978:8). This is the "work" of the negative I mentioned in the introduction, the "metaphysical" work of Symbolism: it includes Eliot's (and Conrad's and Yeats's and even Lawrence's) visceral abhorrence of the material plenitude of the world (the futility and anarchy of the Congo or Ireland's filthy modern tide or ape-neck Sweeney's animal movements) and a concomitant antirepresentational aesthetic that implies the possibility of inscribing and discerning ideality beneath and behind the ruined fragments of experience. Such negativity is antipositivist, anti-Enlightenment: it creates room for possibilities against self-evidence, an analogical system of signification different from but related to the meanings at hand.

---

1. Compare this description to Daniel Albright's interdisciplinary study of Yeats in *Quantum Poetics: Yeats, Pound, Eliot, and the Science of Modernism.* "Most of us," he writes, "when we read Yeats's poetry, pay close attention to the ravishing *images*—the Japanese sword, the bird made of gold, the old Norman tower. But in some ways the true subject of the poems consists not of these formal particulars, but of a hovering formlessness behind them: Yeats was less concerned with *images* than with the imagination itself, a shapeless matrix of shapes, a retina that could be knuckled into emanating waves of sparks and fields of intenser darkness. . . . Though critics once described Yeats's poems as perfected artifacts, urns of words, no poems are less iconic than Yeats's: they are histories of heaving imaginative processes, standing waves" (1997:31). Albright's whole study, pursuing the complementarity of Bohr's wave/particle distinction within the poetics of early-twentieth-century poetry, is itself a form of analogical thinking, both across and within disciplines.

But, if Derrida describes the metaphysical "name" of Symbolism and its turn toward some other "place," he also describes the fully imminent operation—the history of its imaginative processes—that creates that metaphysics as a theatrical effect, the imminent relationship between naming and turning (see Melville 1986: chap. 1). In these terms the difference between postmodernism and modernism is the difference between the articulation, or staging, of *nothing* in discourse and the hypostatization—the metaphysical naming—of *the nothing* as a kind of transcendental "object" of linguistic appropriation. For the postmodern the articulation of "nothing," in one way or another, is hardly a crisis; it hardly imagines, as Yeats had said, that "where there is nothing, there is God." For the postmodern the crisis of representation that Symbolism addresses and the further crisis of materialism—the "body of that death" Mallarmé describes (in Symons's translation [1958:70])—in relation to the spirit and language is old hat, hardly news, simply something else. It has none of the social and political programmatics—what Fredric Jameson calls "the protopolitical vocation and terrorist stance" (1984:xviii)—of the older modernism.

That crisis was most starkly expressed (not self-consciously staged) in the Symbolist movement in literature—of which, Arthur Symons said, Yeats was the chief representative in English (1958:xix). It was so because the crisis of modernism is best understood as predicated on a conception of the *inadequacy* of language to experience, the inadequacy, that is, of any "natural" signifier to the transcendental signified of an hypostatized *nothing*, what Yeats variously called the "immortal moods," "the Divine Essence," or simply "perfection" (1968:148) that Symbolism attempts to delineate. Its method, however, is the *elaboration* of the signifier, the development of intricate syntactic strategies to circumscribe and thus *negatively* represent the unrepresentable, the unspeakable. But remove the transcendental signified from this project—the "perfected emotions" that Yeats speaks of early in his career—and we are left only with the "theatrical" play of signifiers, a radical version of the "pastiche" that Jameson sees as characterizing the postmodern. "Pastiche," he writes, "is, like parody, the imitation of a peculiar mask, speech in a dead language: but it is a neutral practice of such mimicry . . . devoid of laughter and of any conviction that alongside the abnormal tongue you have momentarily borrowed, some healthy linguistic normality still exists" (1991:17). Postmodern pastiche speaks a "dead language," while the Modernist Symbolist gesture responded to the futility and anarchy of the contemporary world with what Yeats calls its *antithetical* languages—and I would call its analogical languages—of parody, disdain, and vision. Its rhetoric was predicated on the mythical "depths" of antinatural vision and intuition: in de Man's description of Yeats's articulation of emblems discovered *within* natural "images," this poetic discourse "substitutes 'names and meanings' for the thing itself and, in gnostic fashion, searches for Being not in the divinely created thing, but in language as the vessel of divine intellect" (1984:170). Such "names and meanings" underline the *linguistic* nature of analogy I discussed in the introduction, what David Burrell describes as analogy's ability to "function within our language but whose serviceability is not restricted to their role within the language" (1973:224). Remove the depths de Man describes, the transcendental signifieds as divine intellect—make *the nothing* simply nothing—and the linguistic strategies of Modernist representations seem remarkably postmodern, remarkably close not to the "celebration" of futility and anarchy that postmodernism sometimes seems to be but to their quiet acceptance, which the postmodern always also—always already—is. In other words, modern and postmodern are analogues of each other—I speak of this in more detail in the following chapter—in which, as Ricoeur says, the resemblance is "between relations rather than between terms per se" (1988:151), the relations between possibility and self-evidence.

Analogical Rhetorics

Of course, the transcendental signified, the "metaphysical name," cannot be removed. It can only be shown not to have been "there" in the first place. Such a showing is what Derrida means by the staging and dramatization of the antirepresentational "play of a scene that . . . illustrates nothing." The mode of the staging of Modernist discourse leads to the larger question of rhetoric—and more specifically to "postmodern" rhetoric. Hugh Kenner has examined the rhetorical power of modern poetry—and especially the Symboliste rhetoric Derrida is describing—in terms of the strategies Modernists developed to set words "free" from the historical occasions of their enunciation, to make them seem to be unwitnessed. Kenner argues that Symbolism creates its meanings and effects by imitating or "counterfeiting" the way the passage of time erases the occasion of enunciation, the "vehicles" bearing its metaphoric "tenor." (Albright makes a similar argument in terms of the presentation in Modernist poetics of the usurpation of the text of poetry by "pre-text" and "post-text" [1997:5].) The example Kenner narrates is from *Cymbeline*: "Golden lads and girls all must / As chimney-sweepers, come to dust." After describing the "magic" that "irradiates the stanza" so that "we, the heirs of Mallarmé and Valéry and Eliot, do not simply pass over 'golden' but find it richly Shakespearean," he notes that in Shakespeare's Warwickshire "golden boys" are the name for dandelions, and they are called "chimney-sweepers" when they go to seed. The Modernist or Symbolist strategy, then—its postmodern rhetorical staging—is to turn *linguistically* to the other world, the "non-place" Derrida describes. "We may want to say," Kenner argues,

> that Shakespeare wrote about happenings in the world, the world that contains mortal men and sunlight and dandelions, and that a post-Symbolist reading converts his work into something that happens in the language, where "golden" will interact with "dust" and "wages" and "lads" and "girls" and "chimney-sweepers," and where "dust" rhymes with "must," mortality with necessity. Thus the song seems to us especially fine when we can no longer say what the phrase "golden lads" was meant to name. (1971:122, 123)

The post-Symbolist reading Kenner describes offers the analogical "resemblance" of linguistic possibility and self-evident happenings in the world. By means of this narrative Kenner can *situate* the linguistic representation or suggestion of a depth of transcendental significance too fine and impalpable to seem to have material embodiment within a historical context of enunciation.

In this way the question of representation in language—the question of rhetoric—hangs over modern studies of literature and modernism in general in terms of the occasion of enunciation. Moreover, it does so in Eliot's terms of mythical depth as opposed to linguistic and experiential "surfaces." Such a conception of depth, or of a metaphysical naming, allows the world and its materialism—Conrad's imperialism, the religious politics of Ireland, the sheer multiplicity of the America Eliot fled—to fade away and reveal beneath the "body of that death" transcendental value, what Yeats describes in "Michael Robartes Remembers Forgotten Beauty" as "the loveliness / That has long faded from the world." But it does so only by repressing its own rhetoricity in momentary analogies. In other words, I am suggesting that the difference between depth and surface characterizes the difference between modernism and postmodernism in terms of rhetoric of analogical figures and relationship in which the figure does not subsume what it stands for. In postmodernism the atemporal, universal depths of Enlightenment modernity float to the surface and on the surface play and stage themselves linguistically and analogically.

The difference I am describing between modern and postmodern is based upon two seemingly incompatible senses of language and rhetoric.

Language presents what O'Hara calls the symbolic and "unselfconscious linguistic formations" of "the great narrative myths of the culture" (1981: 170), and rhetoric studies linguistic strategies to articulate the preexisting significance it unselfconsciously describes—the immaterial transcendental signifieds that inhabit Yeats's vision or the atemporal principles and laws that inhabit the phenomena of Enlightenment science. But language also creates, or stages, the *effects* of meaning themselves—linguistic *meaning-effects*— the felt, "given," sense of meanings beyond the complete control of its users, what O'Hara calls the "semantic innovation" of metaphor in "self-reflective" discourse (1981:170). In this context rhetoric studies the staging of meaning as a linguistic effect created by language's scaffolding con-figurations—created, that is, by the analogical play of signifiers. In the first case rhetoric is creating relations between things; in the second it is creat-ing "a resemblance between relations rather than between terms per se" (Ricoeur 1988:151), specifically the way in which analogy allows us to speak of "what we can do with the language as a whole" (Burrell 1973:224) by superimposing fields of semiotic system and collaborative social action upon one another.

The opposition of these two senses of language and rhetoric is of great urgency because it suggest two ways of reading, two modes of interpreta-tion. We can choose to understand both literature and our world in terms of myth and symbol, in terms of the causation, as Eliot says, of a controlling order analyzed, quite literally, in depth, in which *depth* itself does not call for rhetorical analysis, the analysis of what Derrida has called "the rheto-ricity of rhetoric" (1986:109). Or, as I will suggest, we can stay on the surface of things in a kind of postmodernism to discover scaffolded topogra-phies and analogical configurations of textual play in situating our under-standing—including understanding of the "effect of depth" itself that lan-guage gives rise to—in terms of a postmodern rhetoric of modernism. For what is scaffolded in Modernist literature, after all, is the particular dis-course of modern rhetoric, the panorama Eliot describes in his original title for *The Waste Land,* "he do the police in different voices." That is, the discourse of literary modernism at least partially articulates the so-called anarchy of history not in terms of human intentions, "buried" or "parallel" orders of shape and significance, harmonies of voice and base—in a word, not in terms of the emotions of monumental secret and originary causes behind things—but in terms of palpable effects, analogies of rhetorical effects, residing on the accidental surfaces of discourse.

In any case this is where postmodernism, in criticism as well as litera-ture, draws our attention: to the *surface* of things, to analogies of surfaces.

Richard Rorty calls the form of attention "textualism" rather than "idealism," the pragmatics of asking how things work, what local *effects* they have, and how those effects are related to other effects, rather than what they mean. "Pragmatism," Rorty writes, "is the philosophical counterpart of literary modernism, a kind of literature which prides itself on its autonomy and novelty rather than its truthfulness to experience or its discovery of pre-existing significance. Strong textualism," he concludes, "draws the moral of modernist literature and thus creates genuinely modernist criticism" (1982:153). In another essay Rorty contrasts pragmatism to an earlier tradition that "thinks of truth as a vertical relationship between representations and what is represented." Pragmatism, on the other hand, "thinks of truth horizontally . . . This tradition does not ask how representations are related to nonrepresentations, but how representations can be seen as hanging together" (1982:92), that is, as effectively and pragmatically functioning.

It is in this sense of the pragmatics of the momentary, repetitious configurations of meaning that I have defined analogical thinking and Jameson defines postmodern rhetoric. Postmodernism, he notes, contains two important features. "First," he says,

> the falling away of the protopolitical vocation and the terrorist stance of the older modernism and, second, the eclipse of all of the affect (depth, anxiety, terror, the emotions of the monumental) that marked high modernism and its replacement by what Coleridge would have called fancy or Schiller aesthetic play, a commitment to surface and to the *superficial* in all the senses of the word. (1984:xviii)

Such a conception of superficial pragmatism, although Rorty doesn't say it, characterizes postmodernism beyond Jameson's description. In postmodernism, Jean-Francois Lyotard notes, the narrative function is "dispersed in clouds of narrative language elements—narrative, but also denotative, prescriptive, descriptive, and so on," a dispersal that Lyotard goes on to describe as "a pragmatics of language particles" or "valencies" intersecting (1984:xxiv)—that is, "hanging together." Arthur Kroker and David Cook define the pragmatics of the "postmodern scene" more hyperbolically, figuring it as a "disembodied eye" that "is nothing less than a pure sign system: it cannot be embedded in a chain of finalities because the floating eye as a sign-system signifies the cancellation of vertical being" (1986:79). In a different idiom Charles Newman characterizes the pragmatism of postmodernism as an "*inflation of discourse,* manifesting itself in literature through the illusion that technique can remove itself from history by attacking a concept of objective reality which has already faded from the world, and in criticism by the development of secondary languages which presumably 'demystify' reality, but actually tend to further obscure it" (1986:10). These descriptions share a definition of understanding in which cause gives way to effect as the mode of explanation; how phenomena work, how they are *configured* (i.e., how they hang together) rather than their secret cause, is the nature of explanation. (It is for this reason that I identify such postmodern rhetoric with post-Enlightenment thought in *Modernism and Time* [2000: chap. 1].) Like modernist Symbolism, this rhetoric focuses on the signifier rather than the signified, but it does so not in the service of the recovery of the signified somewhere else—what Yeats had called "the abundance and depth of Nature" (1968:87)—but, rather, in the service of simply that "play" on the surface.

This is apparent in another "Modernist" writer contemporaneous with Eliot, Joyce, and Yeats who describes and exemplifies the pragmatic, postmodern play of the surface in modernist discourse, Ferdinand de Saussure. In the last chapter of *The Course in General Linguistics,* Saussure argues against the causal explanation of descriptive linguistics in favor of a kind of Darwinian chaos and accident, the purely accidental nature of any particular language form. "No characteristic" of language, he writes, "has a right to permanent existence; it persists only through sheer luck" (1959:229). "Mere phonetic modifications," he adds, "which are due to blind evolution, result in alternations. The mind seizes upon the alternations, attaches grammatical values to them, and spreads them, using the analogical models which chance phonetic developments provide" (1959:231). The mind seizes phonetic accidents retrospectively, not as causes but as superficial phenomena to be put to some use, analogous to existing linguistic phenomena.

While such a pragmatics characterizes postmodernism, the moment of literary modernism is characterized by the *analogical* confrontation—the nonreductive confrontation—of these two different conceptions of explanation and significance, the confrontation of naming and staging or, in de Man's famous description of "Among School Children," the intersection of grammatical and rhetorical meaning (1979a:11–12). Eliot's anxious need to find a grounding method in the chaos of Joyce's and his own vision, like Yeats's need to articulate a visionary, transcendental resolution of experience not only in the apocalyptic Symbolist poetry of the 1890s but even in such a high Modernist poem such as "Among School Children," seems to me to encompass the similarities and differences—the analogy—between the old conception of metaphysical meaning and the new conception of pragmatic function. Perhaps it is the enabling analogy of the practice of literary modernism. But the transformation from cause to effect, from causal to functional explanation, or, in Saussure's terms, the transformation from a mode of understanding based upon the diachronic discovery of a simple origin to a mode of understanding based upon a synchronic apprehension of relationships between and among phenomenal data, is at the heart of what I am calling the postmodern rhetoric—the analogical rhetoric—of modernism.

Apostrophe and Analogies in "Among School Children"

This is most clear in Yeats's "high" modernism, and, again, Eliot is instructive. In 1940, with characteristic generosity, Eliot came to praise Yeats after his death and described in his work another version of the mythical method, a kind of "impersonality" of the lyric poet "who," Eliot writes, "out of intense and personal experience, is able to express a general truth; retaining all the particularity of his experience, to make of it a general symbol" (1961:299). "In becoming more Irish," he says of Yeats, "he became at the same time universal" (1961:301). This is high praise indeed, and by the end of Eliot's essay he himself is mythologizing Yeats, marking him as "one of those few whose history is the history of their own time, who are part of the consciousness of an age which cannot be understood without them" (1961:308).

Now, certainly, Yeats participates in this kind of "mythological method," what Auden calls more modestly the transformation of the occasional poem into "a serious reflective poem of at once personal and public interest" (1950:313). But the "method" of this mythology is horizontal rather than vertical, even despite all of Yeats's talk of "the deeps of the mind," of the Shakespearean ideal of "depth only," of vision and trance. In "Among School Children," for example, Yeats certainly "universalizes" his experience in much the same way Eliot universalizes his wife's neurotic discourse in "A Game of Chess." But, like Vivien's language—"Speak to me. Why do you never speak. Speak"—Yeats's situation in the classroom questioning is seemingly accidental, provided by the chance developments of the Irish Free State. Moreover, below the scaffolding of his myths and vision, is the sheer phenomenal power of the poetry hanging together, discovering coherence in what he calls "the Path of the Chameleon," the bewildering incoherence of his particular experience. Thus, more important than the aesthetic questions at the end of the poem is the order of love the mind finally seizes upon (its shape and significance), which Yeats stages throughout his poem, configuring the accidents of his experience—the nuns, mothers, and lovers imagined in the classroom—into the transcendental discourse of

Plato, Aristotle, Pythagoras. In this Yeats, like Leopold Bloom before him, articulates a kind of female discourse of nun, mother, lover in what he imagines to be a universal male philosophic voice; he devises an "antithetical" language in which the accidents of a schoolroom filled with girls and women can transcend that situation to give rise to "representative" human values figured in male philosophers and artists. But, most generally, he makes the surface of his experience, like the surface discolorations of the lapis lazuli he writes about, function to create his rhetorical effects, the effects of (transcendental) meaning.

Take, for instance, what most critics understand as the center of the poem, the apostrophe at its end:

O Presences
That passion, piety or affection knows
And that all heavenly glory symbolize—
O self-born mockers of man's enterprise.

The passion, piety, or affection that knows the object of the apostrophe, "Presences," each corresponds to the occasions of desire described in the poem, the lover's passion, the nun's piety, the mother's affection. But more interesting is the fact that the apostrophe itself is a representative example of—a rhetorical strategy in—the antirepresentational mythologizing force of Modernist discourse. Apostrophe, Jonathan Culler has argued, offers "a poetic presence through an image of voice, . . . the pure O of undifferentiated voicing" (1981:142). As such, apostrophe is radically antinatural; it is against narrative, time, and history. As Derrida has said, it cannot be assimilated to the accusative case of speech or to language in general: it is "not a category, a *case* of speech, but, rather the bursting forth, the very raising up of speech" (1978:103). In these terms it is, in Greimas's structuralist analysis, a "surface" linguistic phenomenon approaching—signifying— the "deep meaning" of the "primal cry" of undifferentiated language (cited in Schleifer 1987:153) that I examine more fully in the postscript. That is, apostrophe substitutes what Culler describes as "a temporality of discourse for a referential temporality." "In lyrics of this kind," he says,

> a temporal problem is posed: something once present has been lost or attenuated; this loss can be narrated but the temporal sequence is irreversible, like time itself. Apostrophes displace this irreversible structure by removing the opposition between presence and absence from empirical time and locating it in a discursive time. (1981:150)

The temporal problem of "Among School Children," of course, is the problem of temporality itself, the poet's aging, and what Yeats calls in his diary note for the poem, "the old thought that life prepares for what never happens" (cited in Parkinson 1964:93). Instead of absences, its apostrophe posits and addresses—it *names*—"Presences" that give a shape and significance to history. That is, in "Among School Children" apostrophe transforms images begetting fresh images, on and on and on, in the furious complexity of post-Enlightenment *events*—what I am calling here "postmodernism"—into transcendental presence. It does so, as Culler says, by creating not "a predicable relation between a signifier and a signified, a form and its meaning, but the uncalculable force of an event" (1981:152). Such an event is the linguistic occurrence of a symbol or a myth, situated analogically, as O'Hara describes symbolism, "on the border between the realms of language, dreams, and the sacred" (1981:170). (In *Executioner's Song* one of the people in Gary Gilmore's life, Pete Falovan, describes prayer as a similar kind of event that is not susceptible to nomological understanding.) Just as Yeats figures the disappointment and anger at approaching death in terms of birth in the almost archetypal gesture of modernism of stanza 5—a gesture of asserting "vital" depths below the meaningless surface of experience figured in the representation of a child as a "shape" upon its mother's lap—so apostrophe delimits transcendental, unpresentable Presences as the object of situated address.

It does so in an *analogical* discourse: death is articulated by describing birth in a language that makes life itself, "that must sleep, shriek, struggle to escape," a vast chaos whose only virtue is as a naturalistic storehouse of images that can be transformed to Symbolist emblems of the unarticulable. Such an apostrophic discourse is remarkably violent: it includes the object of address only by violating it in ways that Yeats's rhetorical question violates the affection of mothers and mothering:

> What youthful mother, a shape upon her lap
> Honey of generation had betrayed, . . .
> Would think her son, did she but see that shape
> With sixty or more winters on its head,
> A compensation for the pang of his birth,
> Or the uncertainty of his setting forth?

The violence here is borne by conceiving "compensations" for affection only in terms of a logic of cause and effect—the same logic that governs the paradoxes of the final stanza and Yeats's Symbolist project more generally.

The bitter furies of complexity that children—and lovers and other images—occasion might well be answered by an image of skipping on waves rather than fighting them or a conception of the sea as buoyant rather than "dolphin-torn" and "gong-tormented." They might as well be answered by reading the analogue of Yeats's modernism, the postmodern stagings in his Modernist discourse.

Still, like Langbaum's reading of Eliot and Yeats, most of the canonical critics of "Among School Children" have described the ending of the poem in terms of symbol and depth rather than in terms of surface and buoyancy: Cleanth Brooks speaks of "the vision of totality of being and unity of being" in the last stanza of the poem (1947:185); Richard Ellmann suggests that the poem at least hints at "an escape from mortality" (1954:229); and Frank Kermode describes the final image of the poem as "the work of a mind which is itself a system of symbolic correspondences, self-exciting, difficult because the particularities are not shared by the reader" (1957:83). All of these understandings of the poem share Culler's sense of the nature and function of apostrophe, its ability to control and order and shape experience verbally, creating discursive mastery over the bitter furies of complex temporality by positing a depth beneath the surface of time and history. Even de Man, in his controversial use of "Among School Children" to assert the aporia that the opposition between grammatical questioning and rhetorical questioning occasions—an analysis which, were it brought to the questioning of youthful mother, would betray an analytic energy that disregards the human cost of Yeats's vision—even de Man suggests in his argument that the apostrophe at the poem's end is a transcendental, universalizing touchstone of understanding.

All of these interpretations point to what Lyotard calls the "sublimity" of modernism, its attempt "to present the fact that the unpresentable exists. To make visible that there is something which can be conceived and which can neither be seen nor made visible" (1984:78). This, I think, describes Yeats's own sense of depth, his sense that "Shakespeare's people make all things serve their passion . . . : birds, beasts, men, women, landscape, society are but symbols, and metaphors, nothing is studied in itself, the mind is a dark well, no surface, depth only" (1965:194).

But here, Yeats is also describing the pragmatics of his own symbolism, the fact that poetry, as he understands it, *finds* its symbols at hand in the same way language, in Saussure's description, seizes upon the accidents of phonetic development and attaches meaning to them. The poem, as I have already noted, began, as Yeats himself wrote to Olivia Shakespear, is a "curse upon old age" (1955:719), an articulation of the *impossibility* of the transcendental, universalizing apostrophe with which it ends (or even de Man's thematizing of that impossibility): its curse simply articulated a broken heart. Of course, such a recourse to origin—to a "cause"—is precisely what I am arguing analogical rhetoric of postmodernism eschews, but it is instructive in Yeats's case. It is so because, as Lyotard says, the postmodern is "that which, in the modern, puts forward the unpresentable in presentation itself; . . . that which searches for new presentations, not in order to enjoy them but in order to impart a stronger sense of the unpresentable" (1984:81). Yeats's apostrophe attempts to transform the images of experience into a symbol of unpresentable Presences. But in this attempt he presents the unpresentable in presentation itself—namely, the arbitrary nature of his signs within analogical discourses that do not seem quite so arbitrary and do not quite completely separate language from the world.[2] The poem presents the accidents of experience—mothers and birth, nuns and children, aging lovers—as occasions for an apostrophic speech about unpresentable, blossoming labor.

That is, the postmodern in Yeats's modernism is the radical contingency of the images he hangs together in his poetry, their existence as local analogies aspiring to the condition of transcendental truth. All the examples of apostrophe that Culler offers besides that of the ending of "Among School Children"—Blake, Shelley, Rilke—are contrasted with narrative and historical description. "If one brings together in a poem a boy, some birds, a few blessed creatures, and some mountains, meadows, hills and groves," Culler writes,

> one tends to place them in a narrative where one thing leads to another; the events which form ask to be temporally located. . . . But if one puts into a poem *thou shepherd boy, ye blessed creatures, ye birds,* they are

2. Throughout *Modernism and Time* I examine this relationship in terms of what Igor Stravinsky describes as the possibility of discovering "a reflective system between the language structure of the music [of Beethoven] and the structure of the phenomenal world" (1982:147). Thus, I argue that "art, as Stravinsky suggests, follows the logic of its particular 'language,' the logic implicit in the media with which it 'structures' experience" (2000:20). Besides presenting its own "logic," however, the arts "also present—*alternatively*—a 'reflective system' between the language structure of the art and the structure of the phenomenal world. Above all, such 'reflection' is *analogical:* as Stravinsky's term 'structure' suggests in both the case of art and of experience, art does more than simply reveal the 'structures' implicit in experience; it also organizes that experience as well—momentarily configures and answers it" (2000:20). Stravinsky's use of *structure* is nicely congruent—*analogically* congruent—with MacKay's description of "structural" information described in chapter 3.

immediately associated with what might be called a timeless present but is better seen as a temporality of writing. (1981:149)

"Among School Children" does both: it offers the historically located description—what Albright calls the "pre-text"—of the "images" that nuns, mothers, and remembered lover worship, all of which, as Kermode says, are very difficult precisely because they are accidental, famous, so to speak, for fifteen minutes, unpresentable "particularities not shared by the reader" (1957:83). And the poem also offers the apostrophe to the transcendental and timeless Presences somehow buried "beneath" these accidents of history, implied by these accidents as a primal cry implies some inarticulate "deep" meaning, because otherwise—postmodernly—all that would be left would be material accidents subject to the meaningless changes of time.

In this way, in an analogical presentation of modern and postmodern, the poem narrates its own mythological method of transforming historical occasion to symbolic event. The specific method of this apostrophic mythologizing, however, is the local violence of transforming the subjects of desire from female to male, so that in stanza 6 the figure of Plato—itself assumed from the "accidental" simile in the second stanza of Plato's parable—becomes the figure of piety, Aristotle the figure for the mother, and Pythagoras the figure for the passionate lover. Plato, Aristotle, and Pythagoras are linked signifiers in a metonymic chain. In other words, Yeats seizes upon the accidents of his experience and imposes the hierarchical order of sexual difference, marked in the "universalization" of the unmarked male terms, and transforms the chaotic metonymies of female life—mother, child, nun, lover—which mixes spiritual and material existence indiscriminately, into the transcendental synecdochical order of male philosophic discourse. Image becomes Presence as female becomes male, and with this transformation the metonymy of "nuns and mothers" become the activity of symbolization, Presences symbolizing the unpresentable, "all heavenly glory." Such glory, like the transformation of schoolgirls of the poem sewing and reminding Yeats of Maud Gonne to the "son" of stanza 5, creates a male preserve as its universalizing mythical method: it makes the world possible for art by making experience male experience, even as Maud Gonne's "present image floats into the mind" as formed not by the accidents of the experience she chose for herself and had thrust upon her but by Quattrocento finger. It makes it possible by articulating the accidental materialism of metonymy into the ideal order of synecdoche and, even more, the order of material female signifiers functioning as "forgotten" vehicles for unmarked, transcendental (i.e., male) signifieds.

Here, then, is an apostrophe of modernism not unlike Eliot's mandarin definition of the mythical method. The apostrophe itself, as Culler argues, "makes its point by troping not on the meaning of a word but on the circuit or situation of communication itself" (1981:135) in the same way that analogy allows language to situate itself in relation to the world: apostrophe transforms the resemblance between things into the analogical resemblance between relationships. Apostrophe, Culler goes on, proceeds by "deflection"; that is, it moves horizontally, even though, as he says, critics turn aside from apostrophes with embarrassment and attempt "to repress them or rather to transform apostrophe into description" (1981:13). Like Yeats, Modernist critics repress rhetoric and transform the stagings of apostrophe into metaphysical namings. Greimas, as I have mentioned, describes poetic phenomenon in technical semiotic terms—namely, "the shortening of the distance between the signifier and the signified . . . to reachieve the 'primal cry,' " which is, he argues, an "illusory signification of a 'deep meaning,' hidden and inherent in the plane of expression" (cited in Schleifer 1987:153). Modernism traffics in deep meanings, while postmodernism locates meaning itself—including so-called deep meanings—analogically on the contingent, worldly surface of experience and discourse. This is why, I believe, that recent literary criticism—heirs to the structuralism of Saussure and his followers, including Greimas, as well as the collaborations of theory—achieves Rorty's "genuine modernist criticism" in its focus on the analogy between postmodernism and modernism, its alternation of Enlightenment and post-Enlightenment modes of interpretation, its focus on the effective play of discursive surfaces rather than the search for adequate causes.

An Edifice of Surfaces

"History is necessity," Yeats wrote in a late diary entry, "until it takes fire in someone's head and becomes virtue or freedom" (1962:336). Such fire, however, is "simply" an analogy, a discursive effect residing on the surface of things. In just the way "Among School Children" seizes upon the language of experience to create a discursive *effect* suggesting a "truce with time," "an escape from mortality," a vision of unity, so modernism makes a virtue of necessity and creates at least the illusion of coherence within futility and anarchy. The futility and anarchy of modernism, however, are measured against the depths of mind and meaning and what is lost— Enlightenment certainties articulated by Descartes and others—just as the pain and uncertainty of child rearing is measured against images and promises of "what never happens."

With a twist of the wrist, however, modernism eschews depths for surfaces and thinks of truth rhetorically, playfully, phenomenally; it thinks of it *analogically*. With a postmodern gesture the panorama of contemporary history becomes "fun." As Nietzsche says in *The Gay Science*, "all people who have depth find happiness in being for once like flying fish, playing on the peaks of waves; what they consider best in things is that they have surface: their skin-coveredness" (1974:217). Yeats never quite conceived of the sea as a surface, preferring always to imagine what its depths threw forth. Yet his shells and gods and dolphins, like the children and nuns and philosophers of "Among School Children," take their place, analogically, within the topology of figures and edifice of surfaces constituting modernism. What I have done in situating these figures within the poem—and within the Modernist enterprise—is to read the surface rhetorically and analogically, as not only Saussure but also his poststructuralist readers have taught us, as a configuration, a way of making, not finding, sense in the world and making it, perhaps, possible for art.

Chapter 6

The Postmodern Bible, Collaboration, and Storytelling

Again, the kingdom of heaven is like unto a merchant man, seeking goodly pearls; Who, when he had found one pearl of great price, went and sold all that he had, and bought it.
   Again, the kingdom of heaven is like unto a net, that was cast into the sea, and gathered of every kind: Which when it was full, they drew to shore, and sat down, and gathered the good into vessels, but cast the bad away.
   —Matthew 13:45–48

In this chapter I will examine the relationship between collaboration and post-Enlightenment modernity—what I described in the preceding chapter as postmodernism—by focusing on two analogical meanings of the parables from Matthew that serve as my epigraph: Jesus' likening the discovery of the Kingdom of Heaven to the discovery of "one pearl of great price" and his likening of the Kingdom of Heaven to an indiscriminate harvesting of fish, which only later is measured and judged. Analogical thinking encompasses the kind of hypotactic discourse that Jesus engages in here, bringing together disparate things not to order them, once and for all, but to place them in temporal and allegorical sequencing that, at its best, might well produce a constellation of "goodly pearls" but at its worst produces only meaningless repetition. The relationship between eternity and time—in more secular terms, the possibility of love and community and friendship in a world that seems just to go on and on in meaningless repetitions—is what is at stake these days in the term *postmodern.* I believe that the publication of *The Postmodern Bible,* in 1995, written by the Bible and Culture Collective, composed of ten scholars from different disciplines and different institutions, is—or will be—a crucial locus for describing the constellation and meaning, if any, of that relationship.

The Postmodern Bible

To this end I will comment about postmodernity and collaboration in relation to *The Postmodern Bible,* a study that is remarkable in its ambition to create a scholarly text in the humanities written by what its collective author(s) call its "variegated and, on occasion, contentious 'we,' . . . [who occasionally faced] the instability and composite nature of our individual identities" (1995:11). The Bible, the collective notes, is "an especially apt forum for [a collective] since its composition too was collective, its chapters never signed, its cultural milieu predating the advent of the modern authorial self and copyright law" (1995:16). Thus, both personally and professionally—in terms of subjective experience and objective knowledge—the collective continues, "we have struggled with problems of identity and purpose, and we have learned how to read and write corporately, differently, in a way that is appropriate for our time and place" (1995:16). Such a collective enterprise is rare in the humanities, and its very procedures—its concern with local understanding, its blurring of subjectivity and objectivity, above all its questioning of basic assumptions of Enlightenment knowledge, its reason, its criteria for judging truth, and its understandings of who, precisely, is the "subject" of reason, knowledge, and experience itself—are closely related to the idea of the postmodern altogether. That is, I believe that the great task of the humanities in the new century is to reconceive the subject of knowledge as plural as well as singular. It is our task, now, to develop the possibility and the methods of collective knowledge. Science has already done this, as I have argued in chapter 4, though without any self-reflection on—without any "theory" of—the collectivity of its enterprise. Likewise, the great art forms of our time—television and film, as opposed to the novel of the Enlightenment, written and read in private—embody what might be called unconscious collectivities. (I believe pre-Enlightenment sacred texts, such as the Bible, might well embody "conscious" collectivities—or at least modes of apprehension in which the opposition between conscious and unconscious is of little import.)

A central concern of postmodernity, as the Bible and Culture Collective suggests, has to do with both "identity" and individualism, on the one hand, and "objectivity" and the simplicity of truth on the other—two major tenets of modernity when it is understood as coinciding with the secularization of understanding and experience in the Enlightenment, that of a free-standing individual subject of knowledge and atemporal, universal objects of knowledge (see Gellner 1992: chap. 1). Postmodernism, as I have suggested—at least as an intellectual concept—calls these assumptions of the Enlightenment into question: this is why I prefer *post-Enlightenment* to the vaguer term *postmodern*. "Modernism," as Bill Readings suggests, following Jean-François Lyotard, "is not an epoch, but a mode of thought about time, which rests upon two elements: time as succession and an ultimately atemporal subject" (1991:161).[1] The experience of postmodernism, both exhilarating and despairing, calls into question both the nature of "objective" truth outside the accidents of temporal occurrences and the "atemporal" subject of understanding that also stands, singly, outside the accidents of time. The "postmodern" Bible, the Collective suggests, has to be read and reread, because the *time* of its reading affects the nature of its message. And, because it is read and reread, the subjects of its understanding can only be plural—even if its reader is the "same" person over time.

Thus, *The Postmodern Bible* offers readings of the Bible from the vantages of different schools of literary criticism—"reader response," "structuralist," "feminist," etc.—and in the many voices of a collective, it aims, as it says, "to contest an epistemology and a set of disciplinary practices that privilege the autonomous self, an ideology that values private ownership, and a professional discursive practice that legitimates the dissemination of knowledge in one form at the expense of another" (1995:16). To this end it offers a

> postmodern critique of the Enlightenment legacy [that] seeks to make us more sensitive to differences, better able to think about incommensurability and change, and aware of the socially constructed character of knowledge and the various means of its production. [Such a critique] also attempts to engage indeterminacy, chaos, and ambiguity—not as the failures of modernity but as its inevitable other side. (1995:10)

This critique, though the collective doesn't articulate this, attempts a version of the analogical thinking I have been pursuing throughout this book in terms of the very critique of the Enlightenment legacy that it and, I have suggested, analogical thinking perform.

The Enlightenment, Modernity, and Postmodernism

My aim in this chapter is to examine the nature of postmodernity in relation to time and collaboration. I will pursue this aim by focusing on a number of

1. For a useful overview of the concept of postmodernity, in addition to the references in the preceding chapter, see the essays collected in Steven Seidman, *The Postmodern Turn.* The literature on postmodernity is huge: David Harvey, *The Condition of Postmodernity;* Linda Hutcheon, *A Poetics of Postmodernism* and *The Politics of Postmodernism;* Andreas Huyssen, *After the Great Divide;* among many other studies, offer historical, literary, and cultural discussions. An early but still useful collection of essays is Hal Foster, *The Anti-Aesthetic: Essays on Postmodern Culture.*

things: I will look at some of the prefatory material to *The Postmodern Bible,* including its dedication and the epigraph to its introductory chapter; I will look at Stephen Moore's allegorization of the story of the miracle of the fishes in examining Lacan in the chapter on "Psychoanalytic Criticism"; I will return to Walter Benjamin's essay "The Storyteller," in which he examines the collaborative nature of storytelling in terms of its transgenerational element, what he calls elsewhere, in relation to Kafka, its "transmissibility, its haggadic element" (1969:144); and, finally, I will glance at a remarkable story—a love story, really—by Isak Dinesen called "The Pearls," which confronts the transpersonal tradition of aristocratic culture with nineteenth-century bourgeois individualism to examine the ways we love and hold those who are closest to us.

The confrontation between bourgeois values and what might be, in fact, a fanciful aristocratic ethos that Dinesen portrays in her story might help me begin by occasioning another description of the relationship between modernism and postmodernism different from that of the preceding chapter, since it is situated on the level of social life rather than the level of language and rhetoric. The confrontations of bourgeois and aristocratic ethos in Dinesen are repeated throughout her work, as they are, as we have seen, in the thematics of Yeats as well, and they delineate an important element of high modernism. Modernism, I believe, can be understood as a plaintive cry of the end of a particular tradition in our culture characterized by the uneasy combination of Enlightenment ideology and aristocratic political power. One thing that makes this combination "uneasy" is the problem of individualism within Enlightenment ideology, the subject of knowledge as free-standing, singular, and universalizable. It is within this ideological tradition, I think, that George Steiner situates himself when he writes in *Real Presences* a passage that The Bible and Culture Collective uses as its epigraph to the first chapter of *The Postmodern Bible:* "In the humanities," he writes, "collective formulations are almost invariably trivial (what worthwhile book after the Pentateuch has been written by a committee?)" (1989:36). I take *Real Presences* to be Steiner's most religious study—surely, its title suggests this—and I take it to be itself a plaintive Modernist cry of loss over a tradition that maintained the felt "presence" of cherished beliefs that combined, again uneasily, the egalitarian humanism of the Enlightenment and patriarchal ethnocentrism, Latour's definition of Enlightenment modernity as the "double task of domination and emancipation" (1993:10). In politics this tradition was articulated in the high liberalism of late-nineteenth-century Europe.

Within Western culture, larger than this political strain, these beliefs included aesthetic intuitionism (1989:37), best exemplified, in Steiner's words, by the "brimful of meanings which will not translate into logical structures or verbal expression" (1989:217), "a covenant between word and world" (1989:93), and a sense of transcendental universalism, hope, and faith (1989:230–32). All of these things, Steiner suggests, are resolutely anti-postmodern, and they imply, for him at least, three things: the trivial nature of collaborative work, empirically recoverable intellectual differences between men and women (cf. 1989:206–8), and essential differences in modes of thought between Western and non-Western cultures. I think there is a direct relationship between the vision of Enlightenment, always felt in Steiner, and such assertions concerning autonomy, empiricism, and reason.

In any case, a decade earlier, in his book on translation, Steiner had a different sense of our modern world that was less lamenting than the cry against the lost presences of postmodernism he presents in *Real Presences*. In *After Babel* Steiner asserts that "counter-factual conditionals" and "future tenses" are "fundamental to the dynamics of human feeling" (1975:216). Such a sense of futurity—like that which I mentioned at the beginning of the preceding chapter as well as Hjelmslev's definition of meaning as "purport" described in the introduction—governs the language of the collective dedication of *The Postmodern Bible,* with its jumble of tenses: conditional wishing, past-tense description, and present-tense inspiration. "Nine of us," it says, "wish to dedicate our collaborative effort in this volume to the tenth member of our collective, Wilhelm Wuellner, on the occasion of his retirement from a long and productive career of teaching and scholarship. We have benefited enormously from his careful critique and personal integrity. Wilhelm's ready humor, willingness to risk, and commitment to collaborative process inspires us and gives us hope" (1995:v).

The juxtaposition of Steiner and the dedication marks the aims and limitations of *The Postmodern Bible* and its senses of modernism and post-modernity. The "substance" of the postmodern that its first chapter asserts is unrelentingly positive. The postmodern, we are told, transforms modes of understanding. It recovers the local—and with the local, as in the dedication, the "fundamental dynamics" of the future as well, in its firm hope that "the next generation [will make] *its* collective statements, [construct] the intelligibility of its own time, and [make] our own attempts at such collective critique old hat" (1995:19). And it offers the exhilaration of what has come to be called "constructivism," Roland Barthes's assertion that meaning resides in the destination rather than the origin of texts (1977:206). In this way the introductory chapter of *The Postmodern Bible* describes a positive sense of how the critique of Enlightenment universalisms and the rereading of the Bible from the present rather than the past is a significant and exciting part of what it calls the "intelligibility" of postmodernity.

But what its working definition of the postmodern leaves out is the nihilism and non-sense of the postmodern, precisely what Steiner laments. This negative sense of postmodern intelligibility and postmodern freedom can be seen in a passage from Kafka, whom Benjamin was describing in terms of textual "transmissibility" in a world, as Benjamin says, in which "the consistency of truth has been lost" (1969:143).

> It seemed to K. as if at last those people had broken off all relations with him, and as if now in reality he were freer than he had ever been, and at liberty to wait here in this place, usually forbidden him, as long as he desired, and had won a freedom such as hardly anybody else had ever succeeded in winning, and as if nobody could dare to touch him or drive him away, or even speak to him; but—this conviction was at least equally strong—as if at the same time there was nothing more senseless, nothing more hopeless, than this freedom, this waiting, this inviolability. (1974:139)

Here in *The Castle* Kafka is describing what is missing as a *theme* of *The Postmodern Bible,* the despair that resides alongside of the exhilaration of making the Bible intelligible for our world. It may be—I for one surely hope not—that even the collective enterprise at the heart of this project despairs of a goodly pearl of truth within postmodern unintelligibility and settles for the "triviality" that Steiner names.

In fact, it seems to me that our task, in recovering or constructing the intelligibility of our time, is to discover ways of valuing collaborative enterprise. One example of such enterprise—of what I would like to imagine is a collective, transpersonal spirit not exactly beyond despair but analogically alternating with it—is present in the citation of Stephen Moore's discussion of Lacan in relation to story of the miraculous catch of fish in Luke 5. The procedure of the collective quoting one of its member's voices individually through citation occurs throughout *The Postmodern Bible,* and it offers a fine sense of postmodern voicing altogether, in which voices are alternatively possessed and dispossessed, with hope and despair playing against each other, forming analogies with each other. Such possession, as I hope to show, helps define Benjamin's sense of storytelling precisely insofar as he describes the "same" stories being told at different times, to different purposes, in different voices—as he describes, that is, the analogically "similar" within the same. Moore, and the collective quoting Moore, enacts such storytelling in his allegorical reading of the miracle of the fishes in Luke. After describing both Lacan's figure of "hoop net" for the unconscious and the huge catch that Simon gets by following Jesus' advice to let out the nets, Moore notes that,

> faced with the subaqueous representatives of his own unconscious writ(h)ing grotesquely in the analytic net . . . , Simon yields his own soft underbelly to the analyst's knife, lets himself be cleaned like a fish, spills his guts at the analyst's feet ("he fell down at Jesus' knee saying 'Go away from me, Lord, for I am a sinful man!' "). Filleted, Simon is forced to acknowledge that he too is a split subject. But only that he might better serve as bait. "From now on you will be taking human beings alive . . . ," Jesus reassures him. (*Postmodern Bible*, 200–211; citing Moore 1992:123)

Whose story is this? The collective's? Moore's? Lacan's? The Bible's? My own? Who is the analyst here? What does it mean to say, as both Lacan and *The Postmodern Bible* say, that the subject is "split"? Earlier, in the chapter on "Poststructuralist Criticism"—the Moore/Luke/Lacan story appears in the chapter on "Psychoanalytic Criticism"—the collective offers a description of "deconstructive" allegorizing:

> Other contemporary literary and philosophical theories, while they abandon univocity and tolerate polysemy, retain a nostalgia for meaning. Deconstruction deflects this desire with a renewed "allegorizing" of the text—not the classical allegory of a truth hidden beneath the folds of the text's literal surface, but a "ludic allegory" . . . of surfaces that play upon one another, on intertextual juxtapositioning. For this sort of allegory, there are only surfaces. The text is a weave or trace that endlessly unravels itself. (1995:135)

As I will argue in the next chapter, such "intertextual juxtapositions" take the form of analogical juxtaposition just as, as I argued in the previous chapter, they articulate themselves within the play of rhetorical surfaces. In a sense Moore's narrative is such an analogical weaving, and in the chapter on "Psychoanalytic Criticism" we are offered the further interplay of secular and sacred texts as Jesus is figured as wielding a knife.

But these understandings of both poststructuralism and postmodernism—Moore's allegorical reading of Luke and the collective's definition of deconstructive, postmodern allegory—seem to me too easy because they do not mark what is at stake in these enterprises of psychoanalysis and salvation in the way that analogy (as opposed to allegory) necessarily marks its stake by not relinquishing its example in favor the principle exampled once and for all. Thus, even in the "splitting" Lacan and Moore speak of it is not clear what is being broken apart: Simon's sinfulness, some might argue, is precisely of a piece. What is broken, I imagine, is experience into time: the "strange temporality" Lacan talks of in *The Four Fundamental Concepts of Psycho-Analysis,* in which "something other demands to be realized—which appears as intentional, of course, but of a strange temporality" (1977:25). The "other" to be realized—the collective calls it "the 'otherness' of the father, of language, and of culture" (1995:204)—is that other time of other people's lives, the analogical otherness of *post-.* This is why Benjamin's Marxist/Messianic reading of stories is so important. Benjamin suggests that the splitting Moore allegorizes is, above all, temporal and that the splitting of meaning and value—the value of love, as I will suggest in reading Dinesen in a moment, but which could also be read, less secularly than I do, in more sacred texts.

This splitting of meaning and value results from the strange temporality that Lacan mentions. That temporality in Benjamin gathers together different generations, which have different experiences: it gathers them together literally in our familial households and neighborhoods—though one negative mark of the postmodern are our "Sun Cities," which segregate generations—and more globally in our cultural inheritances. But at the same time it presents each generation with what Benjamin calls its own "experience," which he describes precisely as what can be passed on from generation to generation so that it is "characteristic," Benjamin says, "that not only a man's knowledge or wisdom, but above all his real life—and this is the stuff that stories are made of—first finds transmissible form at the moment of his death" (1969:94). Such experience, for Benjamin, is specific to each generation and frees each generation from envy for any time but its own (1969:253–54). To paraphrase Lacan, then, in my own (and Benjamin's) words, the strange temporality in modernism and postmodernism—the strange temporality of the analogy that plays *between* them—creates or underlines the "split" between the time we are born into and the time of our lives.

Such a split is negative as well as positive. In fact, another negative mark of the postmodern—Benjamin is explicit about this—is the transformation of experience into temporally unmarked information, which I examined in chapter 3. The aim of the novel, he argues, is above all to convey "information" and "explanation," while that of the oral story is to convey "wisdom" and "experience." The "birthplace of the novel," Benjamin says, "is the solitary individual, who is no longer able to express himself by giving examples of his most important concerns [and] is himself uncounseled, and cannot counsel others" (1969:87). Storytelling, on the other hand, is above all a social and communal activity: it is "passed on from mouth to mouth" (1969:84); it is the source of "tradition" (1969:98); and it is dialogical, an encounter with an other that creates the possibility of recovering value in the world. "After all," Benjamin writes, "counsel is less an answer to a question than a proposal concerning the continuation of a story which is just unfolding. To seek this counsel one would first have to be able to tell the story" (1969:86).

For Benjamin storytelling creates the possibility of recovering and transmitting experience; he suggests that the genius of storytelling is its ability to preserve and enact value across time by creating powerful collaborations across time. But the price of this recovery is a sense of allegory that is inhabited fully by the destructions, as well as "deconstructions," of time: allegory, Benjamin argues, marks time in "the jagged line of demarcation between physical nature and significance" (1977:166); it presents "reality in the form of the ruin" (1977:177), meaning allegorized in the destructions of time. "The characters of the *Trauerspiel* die," Benjamin writes, "because it is only thus, as corpses, that they can enter into the homeland of allegory" (1977:217). In these instances, he says, "allegory loses everything that was most particular to it" and "goes away empty-handed" (1977:232, 233). Thus, in "The Storyteller" he situates the *power* of stories precisely in deathbeds when things are gathered up and passed on at the price of death.

Later, however, he describes the essence of a story's meaning—is it "recovered," as Steiner might say? or "constructed," as Barthes would say?—as the handprints of its tellers, the responses of its listeners. Storytelling, he suggests, is a collaboration between teller and listener whose times of experience are different. Thus, he quotes Morris Heimann's assertion that "a man who dies at the age of thirty-five . . . is at every point of his life a man who dies at the age of thirty-five." "Nothing," Benjamin says, in glossing this text,

is more dubious than this sentence—but for the sole reason that the tense is wrong. A man—so says the truth that was meant here—who died at thirty-five will appear to *remembrance* at every point in his life as a man who dies at the age of thirty-five. In other words, the statement that makes no sense for real life becomes indisputable for remembered life. (1969:100)

Remembered life for Benjamin, like analogy itself, which comes "into play precisely at those points where one wishes to speak . . . of the relation between language and the world" (Burrell 1973:224), is a form of collaboration between ourselves and those who came before us. Such collaboration, as Benjamin presents it, requires a kind of "allegorization" that is close to analogy: collaboration is based upon similarities, not identities; it proceeds, as Diane Elam argues, by virtue of solidarity rather than identity politics (1994). This is why, I suspect, that Benjamin's allegories, unlike many in *The Postmodern Bible,* include the mark (or "trace") of despair about finding the connection between "word and world" that Steiner describes, the harmony between word and world that Kant assumed. That is, in Benjamin's allegory, like that of deconstruction, which *The Postmodern Bible* describes, the "center" of meaning (as in the novel [1969:99]) or the "kernel" of thought or the "heart" of an idea does not exist. Rather, Benjamin explicitly compares storytelling to the formation of a pearl, describing the "slow piling one on top of the other of thin, transparent layers . . . of a variety of retellings" in the story (1969:93) in order to figure how the goodly pearls of storytelling and analogical allegory layer different things—and, above all, different times—without homogenizing difference.

In this temporal conception of signification the recovery or construction of meaning *has to be* collaborative, what Benjamin calls "a secret agreement between past generations and the present one. Our coming was expected on earth" (1969:254). That expectation was the faith those who came before us had that they would be understood, that their best intentions—even those only "recoverable" later, by us—would be acknowledged and fulfilled, that by luck or by skill they would be able to so prepare us with their experience and wisdom that we would collaborate with them to create what Benjamin calls "the chain of tradition which passes a happening on from generation to generation" (1969:98). The vision of collaboration in Benjamin is of great importance. The figure he often uses to describe its product is *constellation,* and it seems to me that it creates the possibility of post-Enlightenment values—*postmodern* values—which do not repress our despair as much as *The Postmodern Bible* sometimes does in its impulse toward "good news," even while, at the same time, it doesn't universalize, to the point of trivialization, the Enlightenment subjectivity that Steiner clings to so desperately. "Ideas are to object," Benjamin writes, "as constellations are to stars. This means, in the first place, they are neither their concepts nor their laws. They do not contribute to the knowledge of phenomena, and in no way can the latter be criteria with which to judge the existence of ideas" (1977:34). Neither concept nor law nor knowledge, constellation for Benjamin, is the apprehended connections among things without universalizing such connections.[2] Such connections are the glue of analogical thinking: just as Ricoeur describes analogy attending to resemblance between relations rather than between terms (1988:151), so in Benjamin's description of storytelling the apprehensions might change, but the connections are repeated at different times and in different situations as stories are repeated and fulfilled.

The multi-tensed dedication to *The Postmodern Bible* gathers together Benjamin's sense of constellation, even while Moore's Lacanian allegory, borne on the power of its figurative "hoop net," creates a gathering that is too authoritative in its metaphors and too assertive in its allegory. Thus, for instance, we are never told in what sense Simon is "filleted" or Jesus is an analyst wielding a knife, even while we are not left to complete these figures *for* Lacan or the Bible or Moore. This allegorical narrative, unlike those Benjamin describes in "The Storyteller," leaves us no particular things—the comprehended remembrance of the thirty-five-year-old man, the face of the dying, or what he calls "chaste compactness which precludes psychological analysis" (1969:91)—around which to constellate or coalesce, repeatedly and collaboratively, its analogical meanings. Throughout its texts the Bible, both Old and New Testaments, provides such things, as readers as disparate as Erich Auerbach, Jacques Derrida, Søren Kierkegaard, Elaine Scarry, and Georges Bataille have suggested. I have offered two such analogical things from Matthew in my epigraph—the Kingdom of Heaven figured as a fishing net, and the Kingdom of Heaven figured as a merchant seeking goodly pearls. What is striking about the figures for the Kingdom of Heaven that Jesus articulates in his parables is that, like Benjamin's constellations, they are not reducible in their number, focus, or temporality.

2. In *Ideology of the Aesthetic* Terry Eagleton offers this description of Benjamin's sense of the "constellation" of ideas. "The idea," Eagleton writes, "is not what lies behind the phenomenon as some informing essence, but the way the object is conceptually configured in its diverse, extreme and contradictory elements. Benjamin's dream is of a form of criticism so tenaciously immanent that it would remain entirely immersed in its object. The truth of that object would be disclosed not by referring it in rationalist style to a governing general idea, but by dismantling its component elements through the power of minutely particular concepts, then reconfiguring them in a pattern which redeemed the thing's meaning and value without ceasing to adhere to it" (1990:328). In *Modernism and Time* I try to present a more fully rhetorical understanding of Benjamin's sense, one that emphasizes the "analogical" understanding I am describing throughout this book (see 2000: chap. 2). Such analogies in Benjamin, I argue there, are fully inhabited by time.

Storytelling

Since I have spent some time on the analogical figure of a fishing net, hoping to suggest something of the unrelenting metonymy of postmodernism—the nihilism traceable in its incessant repetitions—I will turn to the goodly pearl of Isak Dinesen's high Modernist story "The Pearls"—whose title in Danish, Robert Langbaum mentions, is "The History of the Pearl" (1975:161). The alternation of plural and singular in these titles, like the dialectic of battle and marriage in the story or the dialectic of the "anti-aesthetic" and aesthetic of postmodernism and modernism, underlines the complexity of constellation in Benjamin and the complexity of collaborations in our cultural work.

In this story Jensine, young daughter of a rich bourgeois family, marries a poor aristocrat, Alexander. On their wedding trip to Norway she learns that he fears nothing—neither the danger of the mountains nor, later, the danger of war with Germany—and that he has a cavalier attitude toward debts, which was unheard of in her family. "He was not braving, or conquering, the dangers of this world," Dinesen writes, "but he was unaware of their existence. To him the mountains were a playground, and all the phenomena of life, love itself included, were his playmates within it. 'In a hundred years, my darling,' he said to her, 'it will all be one' " (1961:109). Once, when "he recounted how he had gambled in Baden-Baden, risked his last cent, and then won," Jensine thought silently to herself: "he is really a thief, or if not that, a receiver of stolen goods, and no better than a thief" (1961:110). Then she decides to conquer him by making him fear for her, but, no matter how recklessly she behaves on their mountain climbs, he fears for her safety no more than he fears for his own. One day, however, she discovers the one thing he does fear: that she might break the string of pearls he had received from his grandmother and had given to her on their wedding day. When she does break it, she has it repaired by a local cobbler, who, like so many characters in Dinesen, was once a poet. Because Jensine sees that the cobbler imagines she does not trust him with the string of fifty-two pearls, she doesn't bother to count them after they are repaired.

When they return to Copenhagen, she does count them and finds there is an extra pearl on the necklace, one worth more than all the rest. She writes to the cobbler, and he tells her that he had it from another necklace he had repaired. Then she realizes that he is, like her husband, a receiver of stolen goods, and "at last she thought: 'It is all over. Now I know that I shall never conquer these people, who know neither care nor fear. It is as in the Bible; I shall bruise their heel, but they shall bruise my head' " (1961:122–23). After this moment of despair she stares at her own face in the mirror and is presented with just the kind of split Moore and Lacan describe. As Dinesen says:

> the two young women stared at one another intensely. Something, she decided, was of great importance, which had come into the world now, and in a hundred years would still remain. The pearls. In a hundred years, she saw, a young man would hand them over to his wife and tell the young woman her own story about them, just as Alexander had given them to her, and had told her of his grandmother.
>
> The thought of these two young people, in a hundred years' time, moved her to such tenderness that her eyes filled with tears, and made her happy, as if they had been old friends of hers, whom she had found again. (1961:123)

In this ending "The Pearls" transforms Enlightenment competition—the war of all against all—into the constellation of marriage and into generosity without accounting. It transforms personal love into familial love, or even something larger—what Wallace Stevens calls in his secular language "a planet's encouragement" (1972:382) but which could easily be assimilated to more conventionally sacred accountings. It does so by transforming "The Pearls" into "The History of the Pearl," a single pearl of great price around which transgenerational love constellates itself and creates an analogical collaboration between the world and language.

That is, Dinesen's story, highly aesthetic in its effect, is a Modernist narrative of constellations and collaborative temporality. The time of the contest, wife against husband, is that of the individualism and universalist self-expression that Steiner imagines governs the work of the humanities. Readers of the Bible—especially postmodern readers—know better: just as Jensine completes her husband's grandmother's story by imagining herself split, not by a fillet knife but by a sense of transgenerational value in which what comes after fulfills the promises of the present, so this collaborative project of a "postmodern" Bible fulfills the promise of the Bible by finding its intelligibility in the time that has come. This, I think, is the import of the dedication the Bible and Culture Collective chose for itself and, in choosing, marked both the singularity and plurality of collaboration.

That split in collaboration inhabits the subject of knowledge in this enterprise of *The Postmodern Bible*. This split subject of collaboration mirrors both the split within the hoop net of psychoanalysis and the split that Dinesen's delicate story describes within our love for one another. By marking a split Dinesen's story traces time's destructiveness as well as the good news of love, just as the dedication to *The Postmodern Bible* signals retirement as well as engagement. Modernism notes the necessity of such a split with nostalgia and lament, when it doesn't, like Steiner, eschew the temporality of collaboration for the so-called real self-present voice of authority. Derrida, in an early essay, contrasts what I would call this Modernist nostalgic collaboration with a postmodern affirmation of free play without truth or origin (1972). (Derrida calls it "Nietzschean," which, perhaps, is another name for the postmodern.) Such Derridean affirmation, however, all too easily can be seen as writhing or writing in an analytic net. Affirmation, I think, can be traced more closely in the analogical thinking that allows the temporal collaboration of storytelling: in the Bible, in the postmodern Bible, in our stories of love, in the many voices inhabiting a reading like this one, and even in analogical allegorizing itself, as in my allegorizing of Dinesen's story, making it a narrative of Benjamin's meaning—a story that "tells" Benjamin's meaning. Such affirmation almost entirely (but not quite) erases from its telling the mortality, the seeming "accident" of death, which in a hundred years will make everything equal to everything else in meaningless repetition: as Benjamin said, such an allegory presents "reality in the form of the ruin." In her high modernism Dinesen "aestheticizes" experience, makes it individualist and transforms ongoing time into arrested meaning, yet her story also marks what Lyotard calls the postmodern within modernism— "not modernism at its end but in the nascent state," that which "puts forward the unpresentable in presentation itself; that which denies itself the solace of good forms" within aesthetic presentation (1984:78). The alternations between these things—nostalgia and affirmation, nihilism and good news, the singularities and pluralities of post-Enlightenment postmodernism, the alternation between modern and postmodern in Kafka, Dinesen, and even our reading of the Bible—might well help us define what is at stake in developing interpersonal and temporal modes of collaboration in our understanding, experience, and judgment. It might well allow us to comprehend the best moments of our individual and collective lives as pearls to be saved and to be passed on, even while we know—in that scandal to Enlightenment canons of reason, truth, and simplicity—that such "salvation" is local, timely, and plural in its repetitions.

Chapter 7

Analogy beyond Intelligence
Dreiser, Mailer, and the Nature of Intertextuality

No writer succeeded in doing the single great work which would
clarify a nation's vision of itself as Tolstoy had done perhaps
with *War and Peace* or *Anna Karenina,* and Stendhal with *The
Red and the Black,* no one novel came along which was grand
and daring and comprehensive and detailed, able to give
sustenance to the adventurer and merriment to the rich, leave
compassion in the icechambers of the upper class and energy as
alms for the poor. . . . Dreiser came as close as any, and never
got close at all, for he could not capture the moment, and no
country in history has lived perhaps so much for the moment as
America. After his failure, American literature was isolated—it
was necessary to give courses in American literature to
Americans, either because they would not otherwise read it, or
because reading it, they could not understand it.
—Norman Mailer, *Cannibals and Christians*

Literary Criticism

About a third of the way through *Cannibals and Christians* Norman Mailer
reproduces a talk he gave at the Modern Language Association meeting some
time in the early 1960s. This talk can function as the starting place for what
will be the focus of this chapter, an examination of the nature of intertextuality as a mode of analogical thinking. Just as chapter 5, which focuses
on the arbitrary nature of the sign in Yeats's poetry, examines the semiotics
of the Modernist lyric and chapter 6 examines collaboration in postmodern
readings of the bible and Isak Dinesen, so this chapter, focusing on Norman
Mailer and Theodore Dreiser, examines the analogies of "interpretation" in
terms of literary history and intertextual reading. Such an intertextual reading grows out of what Paul de Man has called the "advent of theory," which
occurred "with the introduction of linguist terminology in the metalanguage
of literature" (1986:8)—it occurred, as I argued in chapter 4, with the
introduction of interdisciplinarity into literary studies—and it conceives of
"literature" as a system best apprehended as a more or less impersonal

collaboration among authors within a tradition. Thus, an intertextual focus on literary interpretation gathers together or constellates the analogical themes of this book, language, collaboration, and interpretation.

In this analysis I am following Mailer's own lead. In his MLA lecture he presents an intertextual understanding of American literature by opposing two different ways of understanding American letters, one based upon literary categories (figured as "Dreiser" and "Wharton") and another based upon class conflict (figured as "cannibals" and "Christians"). This double presentation will help me offer an intertextual reading of Mailer's great book, *The Executioner's Song,* in relation to another remarkably ambitious American novel, Dreiser's *An American Tragedy,* and, at the same time, it will help me to define both Mailer and Dreiser in a more radically intertextual position, that of a claimed *absolute* difference from the novel of manners in America. This absolute difference, in turn, will define a particular American intertextuality—a particularly American reading of literary culture—as a kind of violent understanding of literature and experience altogether. Here again, as in the preceding chapters of part 3, I examine the relationship between modern and postmodern in the figures of Dreiser and Mailer.

In his MLA talk Mailer imagines himself presenting a twenty-minute lecture dealing with "The Dynamic of American Letters." Immediately, then, he presents analogical contexts and levels of interpretation in his talk, a discourse that is simultaneously direct and indirect, a lecture in which a lecture is staged. In this presented and imagined lecture he utters "my first sentence as lecturer: 'There has been a war at the center of American letters for a long time'" (1966:96), which exists, like the analogical uses of the "same" word that I discussed in the introduction, on different levels, within different contexts. The war in American letters, he notes, is a class war between an upper-middle-class looking for "a refinement of itself to prepare a shift to the aristocratic" and "a counter-literature whose roots were found in poverty, industrial society, and the emergence of a new class" (1966:96).[1] Mailer goes on to define this war in literary terms—"Naturalism versus the Genteel Tradition it has been called" (1966:98)—and to figure the warfare as

---

1. The "new class" Mailer mentions, although he doesn't make this argument, is the emerging lower middle class of the second Industrial Revolution. In *Modernism and Time* I argue that the emergence of this class of "information workers"—clerks (like Joyce's Farrington, Forster's Leonard Bast, or "the young man carbuncular" in *The Waste Land*), advertising canvassers (Leopold Bloom), school teachers (Ursula Brangwen, Cecil Fielding)—along with European imperialism are two global themes of twentieth-century Modernist literature (2000: chap. 3).

that between Edith Wharton (and her avatar Truman Capote [1966:100]; see McCord 1986:68–77) and Theodore Dreiser. But after the failure of Dreiser, Mailer suggests, the warfare itself degenerates into the opposition between cannibals and Christians, the "Camp" discourse of Terry Southern and the morality of Saul Bellow: "literature was down to the earnest novel and the perfect novel, to moral seriousness and Camp. Herzog and Candy had become the protagonists" (1966:100).

The Christians themselves, Mailer concludes, degenerate further than Herzog. "American consciousness," he writes, "in the absence of a great tradition in the novel ended by being developed by the bootlicking pieties of small-town newspaper editors and small-town educators, by the worst of organized religion" (1966:102), while the sons of immigrants, motivated by resentment and disappointment, "took over the cities," plundered them as

> cannibals selling Christianity to Christians, and because they despised the message and mocked at it in their own heart, they succeeded in selling something else, a virus perhaps. . . .
> Yes, the cannibal sons of the immigrants had become Christians, and the formless form they had evolved for their mass-media, the hypocritical empty and tasteless taste of the television arts they beamed across the land encountered the formless form and all but tasteless taste of the small-town tit-eating cannibal mind at its worst, and the collision produced schizophrenia in the land. (1966:102–3)

The warfare between cannibals and Christians could stand for the conflicts that inhabit, analogically, Dreiser's *American Tragedy* and Mailer's *Executioner's Song*. Dreiser, after all, situates Clyde Griffith's early life within the "worst of organized religion" in the Griffith ministry, and Mailer situates Gary Gilmore's early life within the schizophrenic Mormon world of Utah, which seemingly offers no alternative between the wholesome life of Max Jensen, the young Mormon whom Gilmore kills, and the life of bikers and incest that Gilmore's nineteen-year-old lover, Nicole, inhabits. Moreover, both books articulate the distinction between cannibals and Christians in terms of the American geography of East versus West, and Mailer even divides his book into two global sections, "Western Voices" and "Eastern Voices" (with the latter, apparently, including the voices of California). Still, unlike *American Tragedy*, Mailer's book is ultimately collaborative in its voices—perhaps "postmodernly" collaborative—in its refusal of a central presiding narrator.

Intertextual Dynamics

But more to my point is the fact that the "dynamic" of American letters that Mailer describes is an intertextual dynamic, a kind of analogical thinking that brings things together, as we do when we apprehend constellations without resolving them into either harmony or strife. Mailer's dynamic of American literature describes, intertextually, both the relationship between particular texts—*Herzog* and *Candy,* for instance—and the relationship of literary texts to the discursive network of American culture, the culture of immigrants and aristocrats, of class struggle and class warfare. Thus, it articulates what Jonathan Culler has called both the weak and strong forms of intertextuality. These two understandings of intertextuality are, at one extreme, the precise intertextuality of reference to "a single anterior action which serves as origin and moment of plenitude" (1981:110)—reference, that is, to some *preceding* text that is taken to be the source and resource of the text at hand. At an extreme of literary criticism this kind of reference becomes the "influence" study of traditional literary history. At another extreme of critical reading Culler describes a "strong" intertextuality, which is the intertextuality of discourse as such, the networking of semiotics and information theory and the larger networking of cultural forms of collaboration and understanding I have described in the earlier sections of this book.

Both of these intertextual strategies define institutions of literary studies and practices of literary interpretation, and they mark the link I have suggested throughout *Analogical Thinking* between what I describe in the postscript as things and events, the analogy between what the Enlightenment took such pains to keep separate, nature and culture. At one extreme literary studies, as John Frow describes it, focuses on the *particular* in historical as well as textual terms. This strategy is exemplified in Hans Robert Jauss's focus on "the situation of the text in relation to a unified horizon of expectations which is not purely literary but which forms a homogeneous structure determining the production and reception of new texts" (1986:125; see Jauss 1982). These structures, like the mindless clichés of the immigrant media moguls Mailer descries, *include* literary genres and, more specifically, particular previous literary texts. At another extreme literary studies focuses on the "general discursive field." This strategy is exemplified in Julia Kristeva's examination of the intertextual relations "between literary discourse and its raw material" (1986:127). In this instance, Frow notes, "instead of the social *determination* of the literary norm, we have the social text as *content* of the literary text" (1986:127; see

Kristeva 1980), the book about "a nation's vision of itself," as Mailer describes it (1966:98).

In this analysis intertextuality is apprehended in terms of two alternative frames of reference. On the one hand, intertextuality is conceived as *external*, an interrelationship of preexisting social "texts," including both particular literary works (*The Red and the Black, In Cold Blood*) and social forms (genres, the economics of publishing, the literacy of readers, etc.). On the other hand, it is conceived as *internal*, the diacritical discursive interrelationships that Saussurean linguistics has taught us generate meaning altogether (the binary oppositions between "cannibals" and "Christians," "East" and "West," "text" and "text"). Frow goes on to argue that "intertextuality is always in the first place a relation to the literary canon (to the 'specifically literary' function and authority of an element) and only *through* this a relation to the general discursive field" (1986:128). But, if this is true of Dreiser (or, at least, of Mailer's reading of Dreiser's opposition to the novels of manners of Wharton and James), Mailer himself, as I shall argue, achieves a more thorough intertextuality *between* these conceptions and approaches by analogizing them in a form of collaboration between fiction and history, novelist and "characters," text and culture.

That is, these two strategies of reading are changed (even while the relationships between them remain analogically the same) in Mailer's double argument about American culture and American literature—in the dynamics that run across these two accounts of the "Dynamic of American Letters." America, Mailer says, lacks the "external" tradition of particular national works that creates a literature outside the assignments of the classroom, a "useful" literature that can teach its citizens how to live. From within that lack America creates its own virtually impossible internal discourse—a dynamic discourse born out of the dynamic of American letters. This internal American discourse is the energy of the continent figured in its living "for the moment," a relation to time and event that destroys all tradition and, specifically, the European tradition of letters that America has assumed as its own literary model. Such a discourse is different from either mode of intertextuality Culler and Frow describe, the *external* intertextuality of Jauss's reading of the social collaborations that create literature, or the *internal* cacophonous play of voices without a stable content or center in which to ground itself within Kristeva's semiotic reading of literature. Rather, these two intertextual forces play analogically in Mailer's work to create his own version of the "nation's vision of itself" in *The Executioner's Song*. I will locate these two forces in the particular novel of Dreiser, *An American Tragedy*, and in the general comments about novels that Gustave Flaubert makes to help define the modernist-aesthetic literary tradition. But their presence in Mailer delimits another kind of interplay, what I might call a *postmodern* intertextuality played against the violence of the energetic version of American intertextuality or a "post-Enlightenment" analogical comprehension played against the received hierarchies of aesthetics and even semiotics itself. In either case Mailer offers a (postmodern, post-Enlightenment) discourse of the moment, of the event.

In *The Executioner's Song*, written fifteen years after he presented his MLA talk, Mailer himself joined—or really rejoined—the war at the center of American letters by answering the gentility of Capote's *In Cold Blood*, which he specifically mentions in his lecture, with his own attempt at clarifying the nation's vision of itself. Mailer's book is itself intertextual in both of the senses I have outlined. It is, I believe, a rewriting and resituating of Dreiser's *An American Tragedy*, but, like the ambition of that earlier book in Mailer's estimation, it also attempts to give sustenance to Americans by capturing the moment of another intertextuality, the warfare and interplay in America between voices of small-town Christians (like Jauss) and urban cannibals (like Kristeva), between the West and the East. Mailer analogically figures such warfare in the reduction of intertextuality to schizophrenia and the reduction of discourse to television: the "momentary" vision of America that *The Executioner's Song* offers is a television event, a public execution, which articulates what I will describe as a kind of intertextual, analogical overload. Still, as such it can help us to read and reread Dreiser's achievement in *An American Tragedy* and the intertextual dynamic of American letters altogether.

A Book about Something

> So let us say the war was between Dreiser and Edith Wharton,
> Dreiser all strategy, no tactics; and Wharton all tactics.
> Marvelous tactics they were—a jewel of a writer and stingy as a
> parson—she needed no strategy.
> —Norman Mailer, *Cannibals and Christians*

The two traditions in American literature Mailer describes, figured in the persons of Dreiser and Wharton, can help us to understand Mailer's attempt to do what he thought Dreiser could not do, namely to present America a vision of itself. What Mailer achieves in *The Executioner's Song* is a book that captures the modernity—or really the postmodernity—of American culture by presenting what Dreiser called an American *tragedy* as a media event. That is, *The Executioner's Song* rewrites the "tragedy" of Clyde Griffith's American life in the form of what Flaubert calls "a book about nothing," a book whose events, finally, are *inconsequential* because its protagonists and its happenings are so thoroughly ordinary. "There are in me," Flaubert writes in his famous letter to Louise Colet in 1852,

> literally speaking, two distinct persons: one who is infatuated with bombast, lyricism, eagle flights, sonorities of phrase and the high points of ideas; and another who digs and burrows into the truth as deeply as he can. . . .
> What seems beautiful to me, what I should like to write, is a book about nothing, a book dependent on nothing external, which would be held together by the strength of its style . . . ; a book which would have almost no subject, or at least in which the subject would be almost invisible, if such a thing is possible. The finest works are those that contain the least matter; the closer expression comes to thought, the closer language comes to coinciding and merging with it, the finer the result. (1980:154)

Dreiser, throughout his work, but especially in *An American Tragedy,* is a person of the first kind Flaubert describes. More than anything else, he wants to achieve a book about something, what Mailer describes as "a nation's vision of itself," in the bombastic ambition of his fiction rather than the "finer" stylistic achievement Flaubert describes. For Dreiser, as for Mailer, the *energy* of vision is more important than its discriminations.

For a book about nothing, like the semiotic turn in literary studies from interpretation to examining the *conditions* of interpretation (including semiotic intertextuality as a condition of interpretation in which language and thought merge and coincide), is a turn from subject matter to the exquisite intelligence that *reads* the minute signs that govern and condition social life. It is a turn from explication to semiotics, from aesthetics to theory. Thus, Wharton ends *The Age of Innocence,* for instance, without action and in the silent "reading" of events. At the end of the novel Newland Archer sits before his aged lover's house and refuses to act. Instead, he reads the servant's closing of the shutters "as if it had been a signal he waited for" (1968:361), and then he leaves. What Wharton offers instead of bombast—just as Flaubert does in *Sentimental Education*—is the "making sense" of an accidental gesture, creating a semiotic reading out of the "nothing" of habitual action. This is what Saussure calls the "zero sign" in the intertextual interplay of linguistic and semiotic elements in which "a material sign is not necessary for the expression of an idea; language is satisfied with the opposition between something and nothing" (1959:86). In a book about nothing, *nothing*, meaningless gestures, the *absence* of action—the very arbitrary nature of the sign I examined in semiotics in part 1 and in Yeats in chapter 5—are so situated within a semiotic system that *nothing* takes its place within a system of meaning to convey possible significance. The "style" of linguistic interplay between something and nothing creates the *condition* of possible meaning. It creates the semiotic possibility that *nothing*—by means of its analogy with *something*—can come to signify.

A book about something, on the other hand, takes experience to be more than the interplay of signs, more than the intertextuality of all meaning in the second, "cultural" definition of intertextuality I have offered. It takes experience to be the *positive* effects of such interplay, the "sonorities of phrase and high point of ideas" that Flaubert speaks of, the "bombast" that infatuates him. Such bombast is that of asserted interpretation—of *witnessed* interpretation—rather than the silent recognition of the semiosis that conditions and is internal to all discursive tactics and formations. *An American Tragedy,* like much of Mailer before *The Executioner's Song*—like "The Dynamic of American Literature"—is such a bombastic discourse. For this reason Clarence Darrow describes in the experience of reading it not the feeling of reading a story but, rather, "that of a series of terrible physical impacts that have relentlessly shocked every sensitive nerve in the body" (1971:5), an experience that, as Irving Howe says, "pulls one, muttering and bruised, into the arena of [Dreiser's] imagination" (1964:820). Thus, H. L. Mencken describes Dreiser's style as "wholly devoid of what may be called literary tact," containing writing he calls "dreadful bilge" (1971:13, 15).

In these terms there are two novels in Dreiser, just as there are in Flaubert, which play against each other unconsciously, analogically, intertextually. When Dreiser plots inarticulate experience, he achieves, as Mailer says, a kind of power of vision. But when he seeks to explain his vision, to articulate its "truth"—when he aspires to the intelligent sensitivity of Wharton in a novelistic discourse that, in Mailer's terms, could "reason out" how things work—he cannot pass on the knowledge he has gained. Dreiser, Mailer writes, is "like some heroic tragic entrepreneur who has reasoned out through his own fatigue and travail very much how everything works in the iron mills of life, but is damned because he cannot pass on the knowledge to his children" (1966:97). Dreiser, he says, cannot pass on his vision to the "cannibals" for whom he wrote because, since he had "no eye for the deadly important manners of the rich, he was obliged to call a rich girl 'charming'; he could not make her charming when she spoke, as Fitzgerald could" (1966:97). Dreiser cannot articulate the semiosis of "charm," the interplay of language that creates the meaning-effect /charm/. Instead, he "commodifies" it, as Fredric Jameson says, or he "substantifies" it, as Greimas says, in the "necromancy" of bombastic attribution. In this way he could not bring that intelligence and understanding to the events, the plot, of his novel.

But the *quality* of that bombast—what makes Dreiser, for Mailer, superior to Wharton—is precisely the fact that he doesn't "dig" or "burrow" into the conditions of silent understanding by presenting, without action, the scene of recognition. Rather, he presents the force of events *to be recognized* and attempts to articulate explanations of these events that are proportionate to their power and energy. In this is the central paradox of Dreiser, whom Jameson calls "our greatest novelist" (1981:161): his verbal understanding never coincides with the events it attempts to understand. Jameson describes this as "a strange and alien bodily speech . . . interwoven with the linguistic junk of commodified language" (1981:160–61). But it is the *interplay* of these two languages—the "bodily speech" absent from Wharton's centers of consciousness and recognition and the "commodification" of understanding making the subtle semiotic interplay of meaning into objective, "substantified" discourse—that creates Dreiser's particular intertextual power. This interplay represents, synecdochically, the power of America itself. That is, Dreiser expresses the energy of "eagle flights" rather than the discriminations of truth, intelligence, semiosis, precisely in the central unintelligibility, the essential indiscriminate commodified explanations of his discourse. Thus, Mencken goes on to assert that, while Dreiser regarded himself as "an adept at the Freudian necromancy"—"he frequently uses its terms," Mencken says, "and seems to take its fundamental doctrines very seriously"—"he is actually a behaviorist of the most advanced wing. What interests him primarily is not what people think, but what they do. He is full of a sense of their helplessness" (1971:16). That is, Dreiser creates a bombastic discourse within which exists not truth or semiotic play or exquisite readers of truth and semiotic play but, rather, the play of events beyond intelligence. The gesture of explanation without intelligibility—in a word, the gesture of "neocromancy" aping authors of the novel of manners such as Wharton—generates the power of his discourse, the meaning-effect of power beyond intelligence.

For all the bombastic examples of explanation in *An American Trag-edy*, for all the bombast of a rational discourse shading into ludicrousness, into what seems only a parody of Whartonian exploration of motives and the conditions of action—of a rational discourse shading into "junk"— such discovered "jewels" of explanation are not what interests Dreiser in the way they interest the "Eastern" (i.e., Californian) voice of Barry Farrell in *The Executioner's Song*, when he "discovers" the significance of Gary Gilmore's eyes (1979:827–29). Rather, as Julian Markels notes in a remark-ably insightful study of *An American Tragedy*,

> When Dreiser locates the drowning two-thirds through the 800-page novel, having told in minute detail the grim story of his hero's life beginning at age twelve, critics on the scent of naturalism assume that he has been spending his time building up a great weight of environ-mental forces that are to crush Clyde and explain the murder. But none of the mountainous information about Clyde's early life is even rele-vant to explain the murder. (1971:49)

The information is not relevant because Dreiser does not aim at what we have seen Benjamin call "explanation." Rather, he seeks to articulate char-acters who are, as Markels says, "so to speak, below the threshold of consciousness" (1971:51). That is, "by his characteristic arrangement of episodes, Dreiser creates a firm pattern for the inscrutable, patternless drift of experience" (1971:50).

The failure of explanation is the vehicle of signification in Dreiser, its own kind of zero sign conveying randomness rather than pattern, not a semiotic unconsciousness to be read, as Freud reads it, in slips and stutters but the utter unconsciousness of accidental event. It is precisely the inarticu-lateness of his explanations—precisely the lack of proportion between events and interpretation—that presents, bombastically, the energy of Drei-ser's vision. In other words, Dreiser himself offers, in the interplay of event and interpretation that never can encompass the event itself, a form of bombast that does not "clarify" but does present and enact the nation's vision of itself. The very fact that Dreiser fails at intelligence is part of his power and strength—a *condition* of his strength.

Virtually every chapter in *An American Tragedy* begins with some kind of explanation—some kind of necromantic interpretation—and more often than not they seem to be the kind of "bilge" Mencken speaks of. In fact, the problem with the novel—its dullness and pretentiousness—might well be a problem with chapters, with what linguistics call the "segmentation" of its discourse. Chapters begin by attempting to understand and explain what is going on—to summarize the preceding chapter or proleptically to summarize what will come—and it is precisely these attempts that make Dreiser seem such an inept Wharton. One can randomly open the novel to such explanations. For instance, chapter 45 of book 2 begins with notably inept figures.

> There are moments when in connection with the sensitively imaginative or morbidly anachronistic—the mentality assailed and the same not of any great strength and the problem confronting it of sufficient force and complexity—the reason not actually toppling from its throne, still totters or is warped or shaken—the mind befuddled to the extent that for the time being, at least, unreason or disorder and mistaken or erroneous counsel would appear to hold against all else. In such instances the will and the courage confronted by some great difficulty which it can neither master nor endure, appears in some to recede in precipitate flight, leaving only panic and temporary unreason in its wake. (1964:463)

Leaving aside the strong sense, when reading this passage in isolation, that Dreiser seems to be describing the difficulty of the novelist's task—or, at least, the difficulty of the novel of explanation and manners that he apes in such passages, the novel that attempts constantly to marshal the tactics of a metalanguage to explain and understand the behavior and relationships of its characters—leaving that aside, we still are presented with an almost unreadable passage, a parody of explanation.

Such a passage is comparable to the kinds of explanations Clyde Griffith—or Dennis Boaz in his "California" discourse of "synchronicity" in *The Executioner's Song*—might give himself, a kind of aping of what popular culture validates as appropriate explanation. Thus, Clyde describes Sondra, in a passage written in ambiguous indirect discourse, as "in her small, intense way, a seeking Aphrodite, eager to prove to any who were sufficiently attractive the destroying power of her charm" (1964:320). And in a passage from *The Executioner's Song* that is more clearly Boaz's indirect discourse he "began to ponder the tougher side of Gary. Macho to a certain extent. Of course, he had to use a gun to prove his power. Lived in ultimates. Must have been a very sensitive child" (1979:527). Dreiser's explanation of Clyde's behavior, like Clyde's perception of Sondra's "charm" and Boaz's perception of Gilmore's "macho" side, is the second kind of intertextuality I mentioned at the beginning of this chapter, that between a text and the diacritical system of invested cultural values in which it is embedded. Thus, at the beginning of chapter 45 Dreiser simultaneously assumes the conceptual framework of Freudian necromancy and the discourse of allegory (reminiscent of some of Poe's psychical figures in "The Fall of the House of Usher") to find a language to articulate Clyde's inarticulate experience. The fact is, Clyde is less *intelligent* than a character in James or Wharton, less aware of the discourses that control his consciousness, less conscious of the kind of global intertextuality that Kristeva describes. And Dreiser shares this limitation with his character. The novel of manners is the novel of semiotics, in which characters read, more or less, the intertextual *conditions* of sign-making that governs their behavior and their environment. Dreiser apes this novel in his explanations, his necromancy, his attempts to transform the accident of Clyde's life not into a sign but into a positive event, a commodity, a tragedy.

Yet, despite the constant gesture toward explanation—the constant *model* of the novel of manners that Dreiser apes with ludicrously bad results—this novelistic project is, as I have said, not the strength of his vision. That strength is the very bombast of his writing, which demonstrates, seemingly beyond Dreiser's own understanding, the *power* of events beyond understanding. The tragedy of Clyde's life—like the power of Dreiser's novel—is not its explanation but the palpable fact that explanations cannot sufficiently explain the insurmountable gap between the energy of Clyde's desire and the poverty of his understanding. In other words, the very attempt to encompass the inarticulate movement of events within some intelligible framework works, in Dreiser, seemingly beyond his own intention, to function as its own zero sign, which creates the effect of energy and desire that is unconscious to characters and, seemingly, to Dreiser himself.

Chapter 45, for instance, goes on to describe the "inner conflict" of Clyde in a heavy-handed way. Dreiser's description of Clyde's mind is itself representative of his attempt to comprehend inarticulateness, to situate "nothing" as a positive content. "The center or mentating section of his brain," he writes,

> at the time might well have been compared to a sealed and silent hall in which alone and undisturbed, and that in spite of himself, he now sat thinking on the mystic or evil and terrifying desires or advice of some darker or primordial and unregenerate nature of his own, and without the power to drive the same forth or himself to decamp, and yet also without the courage to act upon anything. (1964:464)

Yet for all the awkwardness of this conceit, and this chapter as a whole, it finally asserts in its very crudity not simply the reality of the "inner conflict" that Clyde undergoes—surely Wharton could have presented this more effectively—but the reality of Clyde's being overwhelmed by events that language cannot encompass or control. Manners cannot stem this desire in the way it stems the desire of Newland Archer; manners, reading, semiotics, social life, simply do not have the resources even to articulate the "Giant Efrit" that whispers to Clyde, tells him to "whisper, whisper—let your language be soft, your tone tender, loving, even. It must be if you are to win her to your will now. So the Efrit of his own darker self" (1964:472).

Mailer's Song

> I hear America singing, the varied carols I hear, . . .
> Each singing what belongs to him or her and to none else,
> The day what belongs to the day—at night the party of young
>   fellows, robust, friendly,
> Singing with open mouths their strong melodious songs.
>   —Walt Whitman, "I Hear America Singing"

Although Mailer perceived in 1966 the strength of Dreiser's achievement, he could only discover the kind of semiotic and intertextual understanding of Dreiser I have been describing after he embarked on *The Executioner's Song* in 1979 and gave up, in that work at least, his own bombast. Thus, he answers the bombastic poem in *Cannibals and Christians* entitled "The Executioner's Song"—a poem first published in the magazine *Fuck You* that describes killing, grave digging, and bowel movements—with his own quiet and seemingly anonymous *old prison song* as the epigraph to his book about Gilmore (1979:1052). Even in *Cannibals and Christians* he notes that his desire to write a long novel "may be here again, and if that is so, I will have yet to submit to the prescription laid down by the great physician Dr. James Joyce—'silence, exile, and cunning,' he said. Well, one hopes not; the patient is too gregarious for the prescription" (1966:5). The patient did prove too gregarious for cunning, America too exciting for exile, yet Mailer learned a kind of silence to let the noise and momentary bombast of America articulate itself.

That is, Mailer discovered, as Dreiser never did with European and Jamesian models standing before him, that he was dealing with a subject that did not lend itself to cunning explanation—that there were, in fact, aspects of human and social life that were not susceptible to intelligent responses. What the story—not the tragedy—of love and death in Gary Gilmore's life and, more generally, in American life demonstrated to Mailer was the poverty of intelligence and the necessity of a kind of silent listening even if the noise he heard did not make sense. As he told William Buckley on "Firing Line":

> This material made me begin to look at ten or 20 serious questions in an altogether new fashion, and it made me humble in that I just didn't know the answers. I mean, I've had the habit for years of feeling that I could dominate any question pretty quickly—it's been my vanity. And it was an exceptional experience to spend all these months and find that gently but inevitably, I was finding myself in more profound—not confusion—but doubt about my ability to answer to give definite answers to these questions. But what I had instead is that I was collecting materials that I would think about for the rest of my life. In other words, I was getting new experience. I thought it might be very nice for once just to write a book which doesn't have answers, but poses delicate questions with a great deal of evidence and a great deal of material and let people argue over it. (Qtd in Hellmann 1981:60)

What Mailer discovered was that a vision of America, unlike a vision of Russia or France, cannot produce answers and explanations but, instead, offers events and experience. This is the knowledge that Mailer sees that Dreiser, writing above all a book about "something," lacks.

In this way, then, *The Executioner's Song* situates itself against the interplay between energy of event and semiosis, between something and nothing. It situates itself against precisely what *An American Tragedy,* for all its ambition, could not accommodate: the *momentary* dynamic in American letters between Wharton's tactics and Dreiser's strategy. *The Executioner's Song,* in an important way, is a book about nothing—a book about Gary Gilmore's own attempt to create significance in the face of overwhelming pain through the "accidental" murders of strangers. These murders are accidental events in a sense very different from Clyde Griffith's murder. In Dreiser it seems clear that Clyde murders Roberta without intentionally—that is to say, without consciously—choosing to do so. In Mailer, Gilmore clearly kills Jensen and Bushnell "intentionally," but it is equally clear that *any* particular people would have served his purpose just as any material sign—including the zero sign—will serve semiosis. Gilmore's murders are embodiments of the arbitrary nature of the sign.

For Mailer the sign is *arbitrary* in the way it is arbitrary in Wharton but not in Dreiser. The remarkable thing about Mailer's book is that, more than Wharton, more than Flaubert even, more than Joyce (who claimed to have memorized the whole of *The Sentimental Education*), one can open *The Executioner's Song* to *any* page and discover there a "sign" that can constitute the interpretive center of the book as a whole. That is, *The Executioner's Song* maintains a network of *internal* intertextuality. For instance, in describing the love between Nicole and Gary, Mailer offers this paragraph early in his book:

> All she wanted was more hours with him. She had always appreci-
> ated any minute she had to herself, but now she would get impatient
> with wanting him to be back. When five o'clock rolled around and he
> was there, the day was made. She loved opening that first beer for him.
> (1979:86)

As in Joyce and Flaubert, here is a kind of apotheosis of free indirect discourse, a discourse, unlike that of Dreiser (and like that of Wharton), that presents but does not authorize interpretation. There is no bombast in the assertion of the *symbolic* force of opening the beer, yet one can read in this signifier—if one is sensitive enough—the sign of the relationship between Nicole and Gary, their class and sexual situation and the limita-tions of what they can imagine for themselves.

Yet, more than in Wharton, this arbitrariness is temporal as well as spatial; it embodies the accidental nature of what Mailer calls America's relation to the moment. *The Age of Innocence,* as a book about nothing, narrates the failure to seize the moment, Archer's repeated failure in youth and age. In this it follows the pattern of Flaubert, of Joyce's *Dubliners,* of even the patience and passivity of Austen's heroines. In other words, the novel of manners, like structuralism itself, conceives of the diacritical in-tertextual play constituting semiosis as *primarily* spatial: semiosis is *situ-ated* in a "center of consciousness" that reads (or learns to read) the world's signs. *An American Tragedy,* a book about something, narrates a similar moment's failure, but here it is a failure in action and the timing of action rather than a failure determined by intelligence and reading. Dreiser brings intelligence to bear on the so-called tragedy he narrates—he apes the situ-ated tactical reading of experience by drawing, as Mencken notes, on con-temporary received understandings of behavior—but his novel is not about such tactics but, rather, about a larger comprehension of America, not the tactics of a situated class but the strategic warfare between classes.

In *The Executioner's Song,* however, the moment is a determinant in every sign—every sign asserts meaning in the face of the accidents of time—even though, as in Dreiser, the signs are not local readings of experience but attempts at global understandings. Thus, Nicole's beer is significantly different from Archer's hesitation: it is *situated* at the end of the workday for working-class people not by the intelligence of its perceiver but by a *commercial* sign system, what Jean Baudrillard calls the "commodity as system" (1979:92). In *The Executioner's Song* every sign is arbitrary because it is commodified in the assertions, conscious or unconscious, of its users. As such an asserted sign, it both exists outside of any temporal pattern and exists as a sign—a signifier—of its own moment, witness to the analogical difference embedded within the same. By means of such signs—again consciously or unconsciously—all the characters of *The Executioner's Song* seek to flee temporal determination through semiotic acts, just as Clyde Griffith seeks to flee the accidental determination of his birth through the bombastic act of murder and Dreiser himself attempts to present a universal, tragic vision of America in his commodified language. The main characters of *The Executioner's Song*, the "Western" Gilmore and the "Eastern" Schiller, pursue semiotic repetition—re-presentation—with as much energy as Clyde pursues social promotion. Gilmore, like Gatsby, wants to live over the past life he lost in prison by dating women significantly younger than himself, and he imagines a metaphysics of reincarnation to allow the actions of life to be repeated. Schiller sees the Gilmore story as the opportunity to "remake" himself as a writer, to overcome the image of an ambulance chaser he has acquired, just as he sees his upcoming second marriage as a way to remake the pattern of his personal life. But all the characters of *The Executioner's Song*—both Eastern and Western Americans—seek to comprehend experience by understanding the moment as a "spot" of time susceptible to spatialization. Boaz constantly understands experience in terms of "synchronicity," while Farrell seeks to understand Gilmore as a type of "Harry Truman, mediocrity enlarged by history" (1979:828); the Mormons see marriage as itself simultaneously earthly and heavenly, while Dr. Woods, Gilmore's psychiatrist, seeks to understand him in terms of the drug Prolixin: "whole fields of the soul could be defoliated and never leave a trace" (1979:400).

These are examples of intertextuality as a kind of commodification of discourse. To read Nicole's beer, as I have, as a sign of the narrative is an internal intertextuality taking its place metaphorically interplaying with the many beers—usually stolen by Gilmore (and thus usually functioning as a kind of synecdoche)—that inhabit Gilmore's life. Yet it is also external, an embodiment of American culture *at a particular moment* whose beer commercials repeatedly commodify leisure and relaxation under the sign of *beer*. In this way *The Executioner's Song*, like other postmodern fiction, is an implicit manifestation of a television culture. As Arthur Kroker and David Cook note in *The Postmodern Scene*, "the *language of signification* and its surrealistic reversals is the basic codex of the real world of television culture. Cars *are* horses; computers *are* galaxies, tombstones or heartbeats; beer *is* friendship" (1986:275). Nicole's very "understanding"—the repetitious/spatial understanding as a sign in relation to something else, something *not there*—is governed by the moment of commodification, not the apprehended action of semiosis.

Here, I think, is the significance of the special status of indirect discourse in *The Executioner's Song* and the often noticed spacing of its paragraphs (the "blank as the difference between two lines" Derrida finds in Mallarmé [1981a:208]). "The trick," Phyllis McCord has noted,

> is that the narrator is himself fragmented into these points of view, for he does not make connections; only the characters or the reader does. Rather than the usual seamless web of omniscient historical narration, there are only gaps between the discourses. A "visible" reminder of this is in fact invisible: the white space between paragraphs or short groups of paragraphs on nearly every page of the novel. (1986:73: see also Hellman 1981:62)

Unlike *An American Tragedy*, whose narrator constantly attempts to make the connections his characters cannot make, Mailer's enormous book is made of small sections typographically separated from one another by spaces. In this it *enacts* a kind of intertextuality, even going so far as having some chapters virtually composed of juxtaposed texts: newspaper accounts, Gilmore's letters, interview transcripts (see Anderson 1987:121). In the same way that Dreiser uses his chapters to offer summarizing global understandings of the overwhelming activity of American life, so Mailer uses spaces to offer the innumerable *asserted* interpretations that constitute his vision of America. Every paragraph in *The Executioner's Song* offers a sign by which to read the life of Gary Gilmore: a can of beer, a senseless murder, an apple tree, all are "readings" of his life.

But they are signs to be read in "voices," in the indirect discourse of the characters who inhabit *The Executioner's Song*. Here Mailer follows Dr. Joyce's prescription of silence. But it is a noisy and cacophonous silence of many voices speaking simultaneously, comparable to the constant din of background noise Gilmore complains about in prison. As McCord notes, "there is no such omniscient narrator in Mailer's masterpiece; all the news come through an intervening consciousness or viewpoint, and the text thus enacts through its form the idea that there is no unmediated experience, no world except that created by consciousness and language" (1986:71). The text thus *enacts* its own intertextuality, what McCord later describes as the "competing discourses" (1986:78) of Mailer's internal intertextuality in the formality of what I am calling analogical thinking. What competes, moreover, are different interpretations of experience, different "moments," as dialectical philosophy describes it, of understanding. These philosophical moments attempt to do what Dreiser attempts, to capture and comprehend the frenzied moments of American life in "strategies" of intelligent action. Mailer said that he had planned to call his book "American Virtue" because, as John Hellmann summarizes his explanation, "he discovered in writing it that a concern with doing 'the right thing,' however varying the concept of what that might entail, was the trait most characteristic of Americans" (1981:59). Hellmann goes on to note that Mailer gave up this title because he was convinced that it would be misinterpreted as "sardonic." But what is most striking about this explanation is that it focuses on cliché—"the right thing" (like "the right stuff")—just the kind of "received ideas" that Flaubert suggests constitute nothing. That is, while Dreiser uses—often quite unconsciously—the necromancy of received ideas to make sense out of experience, Mailer presents a "true life novel" that represents that semiotic process on every page, in every paragraph—in various moments—indirectly, in its class-determined characters' "manners" of understanding. This representation is still semiotically conceived, but it is situated in the very commodification of junk that Dreiser articulates, situated in the *difference*—the analogical interplay—between human energies and desires and "junk" meanings.

The Executioner's Song presents a structure of texts defining the right thing, yet those things themselves are arbitrary to the extent of inviting without *authorizing* their intertextual reading. Take, for instance, the *apple tree* of the book's first sentences. "Brenda was six when she fell out of the apple tree. She climbed to the top and the limb with the good apples broke off. Gary caught her as the branch came scraping down. They were scared" (1979:5). This beginning seems to resonate with other texts—the Bible, Faulkner perhaps, even the ambiguous apple tree in the backyard of Joyce's "Araby." It does so precisely because of its *textual* situation at the beginning of the book. But the style, like that of Joyce, simply does not authorize any particular connection between this text and other texts. Here an absolute paratactic discourse creates no hierarchies of meaning, calls attention to none of its elements. It is as if the tree is simply a tree, and the great anxiety of this beginning is to make sense out of it. But *The Executioner's*

Song never authorizes a way of understanding its indirect discourse. Moreover, as Chris Anderson notes,

> the language continues in this vein for over a thousand pages, rarely varying in tone or emphasis, and this is the key to its effect. With a minimum organization and intervention, Mailer takes us from one point in Gilmore's life up to the end, relentlessly recording all the trivia, all the meaningless details of his experience, reproducing the texture of his life without making it meaningful or giving it a literary shape. . . . The obvious flatness of the language mirrors the randomness of detail. (1987:119)

The momentary quality of the indirect discourse of *The Executioner's Song* is most unnerving in its randomness. Gossip and voyeurism carry the text along, and it is, I suspect, the nonfictional status of this "true life story," as Mailer calls it in the afterword (1979:1053), that sustains it in the face of its own trivia. Mailer hears America singing in *The Executioner's Song,* but the varied carols of the momentary indirect discourses he hears never quite achieve melody beyond its individual voices, its indirect moments.

The Discourse of Event

> The siren song turns into the maddening noise of promotional
> culture: all emotional primitivism on the one hand, and the
> artificial intelligence of a serial culture under the sign of the
> quantum technology on the other.
> —Kroker and Cook, *The Postmodern Scene*

In *Executioner's Song* Mailer hears America singing, but it is as if the songs he hears are the programed clichés of television jingles, as if, as Kroker and Cook say, the siren song of America singing has turned promotional. For *The Executioner's Song* is a novel about "promotion" in a very different sense from Clyde's quest for promotions in his work and life. Schiller and Gilmore, Boaz and Farrell, even Mailer himself—author of *Advertisements for Myself*—are all engaged in self-promotion. Moreover, the book itself grows out of television and its own maddening promotional noise: Schiller pursues the story, which he finally sells to Mailer, as a possible TV mini-series, one that was eventually aired. In narrating the very self-promotion of Schiller within its larger narrative of Gilmore, the book presents intertextuality with a vengeance, what Kroker calls the "hysterical semiology" of the postmodern scene (1986:79). Such postmodern semiology "functions," as Kroker says, "on the basis of a transformation of the *real* into an empty 'sign system' " (1986:100); it is "a technology of hyper-symbolization . . . which functions by processing culture and economy into a sign-system (a *radical* structuralism) endlessly deployable in its rhetoric and always circular in its movement" (1986:75), a sign system that "refracts its 'fictitious' *terms* in a ceaseless process of lateral referentiality" (1986:108). As such, hysterical semiology is "a pure sign-system: it cannot be embedded in a chain of finalities because . . . [it] signifies the cancellation of vertical being" (1986:79).

Here is an intertextuality that is all surface, no depth—the opposite of Yeats's Symboliste depths—the discourse of event. The interplay among its voices is like the ceaseless changing of channels on a television set, the ceaseless interchangeability of its elements, the *temporal* arbitrariness of its signs. In this way, as Kroker says,

> the new information of the electronic mass media is directly destructive of meaning and signification, or neutralizes it. Information, far from producing an "accelerated circulation" of meaning, a plus-value of meaning homologous to the economic plus-value which results from the accelerated rotation of capital, implies the destruction of *any* coherent meaning-system. (1986:176–77)

Such "hysterical semiology"—Kroker might have called it "panic semiosis"—is what he calls "the death of the social and the triumph of signifying culture, . . . the indefinite reversibility and self-liquidation of all the foundational *recits* of contemporary culture" (1986:26). It is a semiological *overload* that destroys the *social* basis of sign systems by multiplying the *moments* of discourse—the varied voices—beyond coherence.

Thus, if the characters' indirect voices of *The Executioner's Song* ape the sensitivity of Wharton in her attempt to read signs of social life everywhere, they also ape Dreiser's interpretive strategies, his attempt to control the uncontrollable energy of American ambition. The plenitude of signs overwhelms the reader of *The Executioner's Song* very much like the plenitude of power overwhelms the reader of *An American Tragedy* until semiosis itself—that great Enlightenment science—explodes under its own fullness: as Dreiser says in the passage I have quoted, "the will and the courage . . . recede in precipitate flight, leaving only panic and temporary unreason in its wake" (1964:463). Gilmore, in willing his own death and *using* it as a media event, is the very *signifier* of such semiotic explosion.

Here Mailer is attempting to counter the genteel semiotic tradition not with positive tragic events but with overload, panic semiosis, the negativity of analogy gone wild in the proliferation of zero signs.

This panic controls not only Dreiser—in his rush to make sense, to make tragedy out of the accidental experience of Clyde Griffith—but also Mailer's commentators. Thus, Chris Anderson immediately transforms the experience of *The Executioner's Song* into a significatory system. In this understanding Gary Gilmore himself is a kind of zero sign, since, as Anderson amply demonstrates, Gilmore himself resists any kind of explanation of his behavior: " 'What I do,' he says, 'is the absence of thought' void of content, motive" (1987:800). Anderson goes on to cite Gilmore's description of himself as "slightly less than bland" and notes that, "as he struggles to understand Gilmore's personality and feeling, Schiller comes to realize that the murders express a deep and even terrifying void" (1987:126). This leads Anderson to the conclusion that there is an important *figurative* signification here: "textuality figures superficiality," he asserts (1987:127). That is,

> on a second reading stylistic traces of Mailer's earlier voice begin to emerge, examples of a language that could only come from Mailer himself as author behind the silent poses, and these serve to direct the flow and meaning of the text, rendering its very flatness and superficiality figurative. A voice emerges which gives us the key to reading the voice of the recorder as ironic, a way of disclosing Mailer's sense that the Gilmore story is fundamentally meaningless, representative of a void. (1987:122)

Here is semiosis with a vengeance, the discovery of a "figurative" sign in the absence of signs, transforming nothing into something. Such a figurative sign functions by means of the premature closure of transforming similitude to identity, of making a pattern of moments, an attempt to understand Gilmore's story in ways that Mailer, posing questions that cannot be answered, never attempts.

In other words, this is an example of the broadest sense of intertextuality imaginable: the *textualization* of experience so that one can make sense, *any* kind of sense. If meaning is textual and intertextual, if it depends upon the analogical play between elements, phonemes, lexemes, different texts themselves—then "making sense" of experience, transforming accident into tragedy, pain into a motive for action (murder), is a kind of unavoidable neocromancy, a hysterical semiosis. Jacques Derrida addresses this very procedure of *textualization* throughout his work. Textualization—

including the appropriations of the *intertextual*—is always violent in a violence that Jacques Lacan figures as "murder" (1977a:104). Yet such violence, Derrida argues, responds to an even greater violence in a kind of "panic," a hysterical rush to meaning. "Discourse," Derrida writes,

> if it is originally violent, can only *do itself violence,* can only negate itself in order to affirm itself, make war upon the war which institutes it without ever *being able* to reappropriate this negativity, to the extent that it is discourse. *Necessarily* without reappropriating it, for if it did so, the horizon of peace would disappear into the night (worst violence as previolence). This secondary war, as the avowal of violence, is the least possible violence, the only way to repress the worst violence, the violence of primitive and prelogical silence, of an unimaginable night which would not even be the opposite of day, an absolute violence which would not even be the opposite of nonviolence: nothingness or pure non-sense. Thus discourse chooses itself violently in opposition to nothingness or pure non-sense. (1978:130)

Here Derrida is describing the "choice" of intertextuality over discourse without discursive (that is to say, "meaningful") contexts, a discourse of event conceived as random moment. The energy of this choice is what distinguishes Dreiser from Wharton for Mailer. For Dreiser *not* to see Clyde Griffith's life as a tragedy, *not* to articulate his motives as a kind of rational dialogue, *not* to discover in the accident of his life an analogy for America itself, would plunge the world into panic and horror worse than the unintelligibility of his explanations. This is another intertextuality, a *radical* intertextuality that apprehends and constellates an analogical relationship between random, momentary events and the order of discourse.

It is not the same for Wharton. The motive behind Newland Archer's refusal to act is solely tactical: he never acknowledges, as Wharton herself never acknowledges, the possibility that the sensibility that has governed his life might be a strategic act of violence; that the semiotic forms that situate him in a privileged position in his world might articulate a violence against the world responding to the greater violence of accident and nothingness. Because such motivation remains only possible, I cannot say once and for all, as Archer can and Anderson can and Capote can, what the "experience" of *The Executioner's Song* figures, what *beer* in that book, for instance, signifies, or whether the fall from the apple tree at the beginning is a meaningful sign existing in an intertextual network that constitutes it as a sign insofar as it refers to "the equivalent content of a signifying element" in another semiotic system (Greimas and Courtés 1982:159) or whether it is a random and momentary event. Instead, the book offers such events as momentary and repeated analogies to be taken up and put down, configured and coalesced in patterns of meaning amid the simultaneous struggle between semiosis and silence (that Wharton engages in) and semiosis and noise (that Dreiser engages in), the prescriptions of Dr. Joyce and Dr. Mailer. Instead, I suspect, the book attempts to articulate the energy of America as a kind of virtue.

Mailer does this in an intertextual discourse—a postmodern American discourse—that, engaging, analogically, both external texts and genres and the internal interplay of textuality itself, also engages in its quiet hysteria the absolute violence behind its text and behind Griffith, Gilmore, and the cacophony of America's random and momentary voices. *The Executioner's Song* offers a figure for this *radical* intertextuality in its description of Pete Falovan's prayer:

> He prayed that the Lord have mercy on Nicole and Gary, and bless them, and that Gary get some control of himself. Pete didn't remember all the things he said in the prayer, or even if he held her hand while he prayed. One was not supposed to remember what was said in prayers. It was a sacred moment, and not really to be repeated. (1979:133)

Prayer, in this passage, can stand for the trivia and tedium of Gary's life and Mailer's narrative of his life. But more important, I think, it describes the discourse of the moment, the discourse of event. Prayer here addresses God at a particular moment in particular circumstances. It cannot be repeated because it is a response to the world rather than an understanding of it; it does not lend itself to logic or even analogic. Such an act can be understood as a figure of a situation in the semiosis of synecdoche. But, more important, it is an unrepeatable event, essentially random, violent, without the possibility of semiotic assimilation, paraphrase, or positive analogy, without any intertextual status. This prayer, like television, implies the destruction of any coherent meaning-system.

Here is a discourse *radically* about nothing, about inconsequential and random events, including language events. In this, event is conceived, as Kroker and Cook describe the "panic philosophy" of postmodern culture, as meaningless and contextless, America singing a Coke commercial: "The postmodern scene," they write, "is a panic site, just for the fun of it" (1986:27). Paul de Man, in what I take to be his most nihilistic statement, articulates such a panicked vision of the interplay between event and discourse. Such interplay, as I have suggested, can lead to the reduction of event to semiosis or to the reductive commodification of language. But de Man describes it as simply random interplay. "*The Triumph of Life*," he writes,

> warns us that nothing, whether deed, word, thought or text, ever happens in relation, positive or negative, to anything that precedes, follows or exists elsewhere, but only as a random event whose power, like the power of death, is due to the randomness of its occurrence. (1979a:69; see Schleifer 1985a:222)

De Man, as many have suggested since the revelation of his wartime anti-Semitic writings and his subsequent silence, may have had a personal stake in understanding events to be radically unconnected to any larger historical sequence, but his sense of the "randomness" of events finds echo in Dreiser and Mailer. (In the postscript I will try to show how analogical thinking, in the example of Michel Foucault, might well—or at least momentarily— "redeem," as Benjamin says, such events.) Dreiser and Mailer present two kinds of randomness in *An American Tragedy* and *Executioner's Song*. Both are in opposition to the world of Wharton—and the world of Sondra Finchley—in which only tactics are necessary because the social order makes sense. Dreiser's is the randomness of unconscious motivation; Mailer's is the randomness of the arbitrary nature of the sign taken as event. But the sign for both is murder and violence beyond intelligence, and for both the signs are only achieved through the play of texts and the suggestions of analogy.

Mailer, as he says, achieves what Dreiser cannot achieve, a sense of America living for the moment. Such a sense destroys the possibility of discourse by destroying intertextual spaces and voices. The moment— "Miller Time," as the commercials say, or the speed with which headaches go away—commodify experience and commodify discourse. *The Executioner's Song*, however, uses such commodified discourse as an element of play in its own intertextual strategies, both internally, in the play of voices throughout the book, and externally, in relation to Dreiser's book (and Capote's as well) and in relation to the violence of random and meaningless American language. Doing so, Mailer achieves a book that is simultaneously about nothing and something, babel and a song—a book that can clarify the nation's vision of itself, including the vision of earlier texts.

Postscript

Enlightenment after Foucault
Cartesian Economics and
Post-Enlightenment Analogy

The Executioner's Song, I think, can help focus what I have attempted to examine and present—to constellate—throughout *Analogical Thinking,* the strategies and tactics of nonhierarchical analogies that govern post-Enlightenment conceptions of meaning in semiotics and structural linguistics, pluralized subjects of experience and knowledge in the science and art forms of the twentieth century, and modes of interpretation that use both of these things to apprehend meaning in contemporary literary studies. In part 3 of this book I have tried to gather together what I take to be the great project of post-Enlightenment thinking, the attempt to find a place for the sacred in the secular world we have inherited from the Enlightenment. Yeats's bardic lyrics, contemporary attempts to recover the Bible for our time, and even Mailer's valorization of bombast within a radically postmodern culture—as well as Foucault's historicizing, Saussure's science, Derrida's philosophizing, and Benjamin's storytelling—are all attempts to find a place for the sacred within the secular simplicities of Enlightenment value.

The Enlightenment itself, of course, was and is not monolithic; it too jumbled together new and received notions and institutions, like the aristocratic politics and the bourgeois economics that exist together, uneasily, in the early twentieth century or the anxiety with which Kant or Smith asserts the necessity of harmony and natural goodness in the world. But the uneasiness of such assertions reside in the fact that analogies between nature and culture, between values established by land and those established by the constantly changing semiotics of money, between the empiricism of science and the evaluations of the humanities, themselves do not fit within the parsimonies of the necessary and sufficient truths of Enlightenment logic. An alternative to such truths, I have been arguing, is the very analogical thinking that can be discerned, constellated within the science, philosophy, and interpretations of early-twentieth-century culture. Such thinking, I believe, is one feature of what many have recently described, quite vaguely, under the term *post-modern*. I prefer *post-Enlightenment* because it more fully relates the strategies and tactics of understanding I have surveyed under the figure of analogy to the received "early modern" tactics of Enlightenment secularization, and it suggests, I hope, that the pluralities of analogy do not replace the simplicities, accuracies, and generalizations of Enlightenment thinking but supplement them and alternate with them in our world, which is more crowded with people, metonymic information, and complicated knowledges.

A final constellation, then—one that focuses, as the introduction does, on the work of historicism in the analogical thinking of Michel Foucault— might gather together the spacious semantics of analogical thinking and the precisions of Enlightenment formalisms as *levels* of understanding that play together, sometimes harmoniously and sometimes dissonantly, in the similarities and differences of analogy, constellation, and timeliness. The over-determined term *economy* examined here, in its senses of the organized interplay of elements, a system of value, and humble economizing, gathers together, but does not quite harmonize, accuracies, generalities, and simplicities in the superimposition I pursue between René Descartes and Foucault. Descartes pursues an economy of clear and distinct ideas that conditions the mechanical conception of phenomena, atemporal truths, and autonomous subjects of the Enlightenment, while Foucault, as I suggested in the introduction, presents heterogeneous phenomena and disciplinary power under the comprehensive conception of *event,* which might well allow us to see—and perhaps "redeem"—understanding and experience in conjunction with the category of analogy.

Identity and Similarity, Things and Events

In 1976 Michel Foucault asserted that "what has emerged in the course of the last ten or fifteen years is a sense of the increasing vulnerability to criticism of things, institutions, practices, discourses" (1980:80). This list of "things, institutions, practices, discourses," like the famous list he cites from Borges at the beginning of *The Order of Things,* has a peculiar incoherence, a failure to achieve continuity, coherence, and conclusion, that, in this 1976 lecture, Foucault worries characterizes his own work (1980:78) in terms of its comprehension of different strands and levels that are both "superimposed" upon and "discontinuous" with one another (1980:85). One way to focus on the economy of such a list, such a gathering, such a comprehension, is to read Foucault analogically in relation to his great predecessor and teacher René Descartes. Such a focus comprehends Fou-

cault's economy of values, strategies, and events in an analogical relationship with the received Cartesian economics of a secular and mechanistic
universe that is comprised, simply, of things in the world.

That is, in this postscript I am figuring our inheritance of Enlightenment values in terms of the intellectual economics of Descartes in relation to
the work of Foucault in order to show that Foucault's project is an
instance—and also more than an instance—of what, throughout *Analogical Thinking,* I have been trying to describe as our post-Enlightenment
ethos. (I have chosen to end this book with a "postscript" rather than a
conclusion because, as I hope to have demonstrated, an important aspect of
analogical thinking is that it does not come to rest, once and for all, in
conclusions.) I am focusing on the economy of "things" in the world because a significant part of our Cartesian/Enlightenment inheritance assumes
that both knowledge and events are phenomena that function, mechani-
cally, like worldly objects that can be embodied and accumulated and that
such an assumption allows for the easy dismissal of analogical comprehensions as random and arbitrary. In response to this tradition Foucault says in
"What Is Enlightenment?" that "the critical ontology of ourselves has to be
considered not, certainly, as a theory, a doctrine, nor even as a permanent
body of knowledge that is accumulating; it has to be conceived as an
attitude, an ethos, a philosophical life in which the critique of what we are is
at one and the same time the historical analysis of the limits that are
imposed on us and an experiment with the possibility of going beyond
them" (1984:50). Such going beyond, as Eve Tavor Bannet has said of
Wittgenstein, is a function of analogical thinking: "Analogical reasoning
has everything to do with how we 'go on' because both in our disciplines
and in our everyday uses of language, we are always using analogies to
translate familiar terms, concepts, and images from one place to another
place" (1997:656).

The mechanical and mathematical comprehension of the world that
Descartes articulates, and to a significant degree initiated in the West, precisely comprehends knowledge in terms of things that, as Foucault says
here, are bodied forth and capable of accumulation in a manner that valo-
rizes *atemporal* knowledge over *historical* power, identity over similarity,
by conceiving phenomena as existing within a timeless economy of things.[1]

***

1. In *What Is a Thing?* Martin Heidegger describes this economy in terms of
"what should be uniformly determinative of each body as such, that is, for being
bodily. All bodies are alike. No motion is special. Every place is like every other,
each moment like any other. Every force becomes determinable only by the
change of motion which it causes—this change in motion being understood as a

Descartes's central doctrine of "clear and distinct ideas" is wholly dependent on the mechanical atemporality of the "self-evidence" of things. Such self-evidence is closely connected to Descartes's conception of "intuition." "Intuition," Stephen Gaukroger writes in his masterful intellectual biography of Descartes, "has two distinctive features: it is an instantaneous act, and it consists in a clear and distinct grasp of an idea" (1995:118; see also 342 in relation to the *cogito*). Moreover, within the mechanical sense of the world Descartes subscribes to—a world in which all forces are reduced to momentary collisions that specifically exclude actions at a distance—event is always secondary to existence: the "duration" of a thing, Descartes asserts, "always remains unmodified," so that, like numbers, it is best conceived as what he calls a "universal" of knowledge and thinking (Descartes 1985:211, 212). The elimination of temporality as possibly modifying material objects, like Descartes's elimination of the traditions of culture in favor of the individual reasoning subject that Ernest Gellner describes in his history of reason (1992) and the more general "decontextualization" of knowledge that Stephen Toulmin describes in relation to the great religious wars of Descartes's lifetime (1992:21), results in the parsimonious reason of Descartes's mechanistic world, the easy transformation of similarity to identity.

Gellner argues that reason has a history and it arises with Descartes's assertion of "the sovereignty of Reason" (1992:1). The opposite of reason for Descartes, Gellner argues, is culture, and "liberation from error requires liberation from culture, from 'example and custom' as [Descartes] calls it" (1992:2). Toulmin pursues this argument from the vantage of history rather than philosophy and demonstrates that the political and social turmoil of the Thirty Years' War led Descartes and many of his contemporaries to eschew historical and cultural explanations of phenomena for the abstractions of mathematics and natural philosophy (1992). Together, Gellner and Toulmin offer what Horkheimer and Adorno describe as a "historico-cultural (*geistesgeschichtlich*)" (1972) understanding of what has be taken as the timeless and abstract notion—the ordinary and general case—of

---

change of place. All determinations of bodies have one basic blueprint (*Grundriss*), according to which the natural process is nothing but the space-time determination of the motion of points of mass. This fundamental design of nature at the same time circumscribes its realm as everywhere uniform" (1967:91). Descartes's mechanics of things, I should say, was significantly modified in later Enlightenment dynamics. For a discussion that brings together ideas of "things" in relation to post-Enlightenment apprehensions in music, poetry, Heidegger, Freud, Lacan, and others, see my essay " 'What Is This Thing Called Love?' Cole Porter and the Rhythms of Desire" (1999).

Enlightenment reason. Moreover, Descartes's definition of understanding outside cultural and historical modes of apprehension is clear in the transformation of analogy into identity in the Enlightenment that Bannet describes. Using Newton as a chief example, Bannet argues that "stressing resemblance over difference to make different entities more or less alike transformed analogy into an equivalence. . . . And a slippage between 'might be' and 'is' was introduced to convert the moment of analogical reasoning or projection . . . into an unequivocal affirmation" (1997:658). Descartes's description of such "unequivocal affirmation" is the "clear and distinct ideas" he learned from mathematics.

Such parsimonious reason structures the sense of economy that arises in the Cartesian Enlightenment. In an interview entitled "Truth and Power" Foucault offers the following description of the "economy of power" that can stand not only for his own comprehension of what he calls elsewhere in that interview "the mechanics of power" (1980:116) and "the 'political economy' of truth" (1980:131) but also for the mechanistic economy of Descartes in relation to which Foucault's work is both superimposed and discontinuous.

> Not only did the monarchies of the Classical period develop great state apparatuses (the army, the police and fiscal administration), but above all there was established at this period what one might call a new "economy" of power, that is to say procedures which allowed the effects of power to circulate in a manner at once continuous, uninterrupted, adapted and "individualised" throughout the entire social body. These new techniques are both much more efficient and much less wasteful (less costly economically, less risky in their results, less open to loopholes and resistances) than the techniques previously employed which were based on a mixture of more or less forced tolerances (from recognised privileges to endemic criminality) and costly ostentation (spectacular and discontinuous interventions of power, the most violent form of which was the "exemplary," because exceptional, punishment). (1980:119)

This "economism," as he describes it elsewhere, which both liberalism and Marxism share as part, I believe, of their Enlightenment inheritance, above all apprehends power as a thing in the world that, as Foucault says, "one is able to possess like a commodity, and which one can in consequence transfer or alienate, either wholly or partially, through a legal act or through some act that establishes a right, such as takes place through cession or contract." This theoretical construction, Foucault continues, is essentially based on "the clear analogy ... between power and commodities, power and wealth" (1980:88). As opposed to the exemplary and exceptional case in pre-Enlightenment "interventions of power," the Enlightenment economy Foucault describes, and to some extent participates in, is based upon the ordinary and general case in an economy of generalized and interchangeable *things*. Still, unlike the Cartesian economy of Enlightenment understanding that depends, to large degree, on prohibition, limit, and above all on a reductive simplicity that allows all sorts of relationships to be apprehended as simple and self-evident things in the world (see Foucault 1990:83), the economy of understanding, social organization, and ordinary experience that Foucault describes depends on the positive nature of comprehension, power, and information, phenomena apprehended as *events*.

Cartesian Economics: Force and Language

For this reason I am arguing that Foucault participates in the analogical thinking that became important in our century as a mode of comprehension supplementing received Enlightenment ideas concerning the nature of understanding and explanation. (I'll even go so far in supporting this argument as to demonstrate Foucault's congruence with Bertrand Russell.) Those received ideas revolved around Descartes's conception of clear and distinct ideas and the global assumption, central to Enlightenment science from Newton to Einstein, that the criteria for scientific explanation entailed three concerns I have repeatedly mentioned: accuracy, simplicity, and generalizability. The criterion of generalizability, as Thomas Kuhn has argued, includes the possibility of scientific prediction (1977:322); it does so, I believe, precisely because its generalizations are atemporal and nonhistorical, its truths are once and for all. In any case, all three of these criteria are closely tied to a particular secular and mechanistic conception of "things," what Horkheimer and Adorno describe as the "conversion of enlightenment into positivism, the myth of things as they actually are" (1972:x), and Toulmin describes as the transformation in the West of "anthropomorphic" to "mechanomorphic" mythologizing (1982:24). Moreover, these intellectual matters were and are closely tied to the politics of the Enlightenment, which, as I mentioned in the introduction, entailed a curious combination of liberation and domination. Latour describes this combination as the "double task of domination and emancipation" (1993:10); and Foucault describes it, more generally, as "a modification of the preexisiting relation linking will, authority, and the use of reason" (1984:35). (These three categories correspond to the experience, social organization, and understanding I have mentioned already.)

Both the intellectual and political assumptions governing Enlightenment values are founded upon modes of representation of hierarchy and reduction, which Foucault calls "models of functional subordination or formal isomorphism" (1980:89) and I have called the general semiotics and subjective idealism of the Enlightenment (chap. 3; see also 2000: chap. 1). As I noted in the introduction, systematic mathematical formalism was Descartes's achievement in philosophy and natural philosophy at the beginning of Enlightenment modernity, and it is governed by parsimonious hierarchies of synecdoche, in which parts are taken to stand for the whole or, less usually, wholes are taken to stand for parts. It is precisely this "standing for"—the economy of invariables and variables and the elevation of identity over similarity—that analogy eschews.

At the heart of the reductive synecdochical hierarchies is the mechanistic world order that Descartes formulated during the turbulence of the Thirty Years' War in the first half of the seventeenth century, a mechanical science and mechanical worldview, which, in his lifetime, superseded to a significant extent the vitalism and organicism of received Aristotelian conceptions of the world and experience and transformed rhetoric, experience, and understanding. Such a mechanistic worldview, above all, makes parsimony its guiding principle so that what Descartes calls clear and distinct ideas and Leibniz calls necessary and sufficient truth govern understanding and entail the parsimonious criteria of Enlightenment science and reason: simplicity, accuracy, and generalizability. These three criteria govern the combination of empiricism and system that Ernst Cassirer describes in *The Philosophy of the Enlightenment* as a wider sense of "calculus," which "thus loses its exclusively mathematical meaning" (1951:23). Such a calculus creates "a general science of the forms of thought" (1951:28), the simplicity and generalizability I mentioned earlier. The mechanical worldview is based upon such a combination of simple (and interchangeable) elements and general system, but it is also based upon an emerging empiricism, what Cassirer calls the "analytical" as well as synthetic aspect of science (1951:10). Toulmin describes all three of these criteria in the double goal of Descartes's work. "The method of basing theories on 'clear and distinct' concepts thus appealed to Descartes for two distinct kinds of reasons," he writes; "*instrumental*, as solving problems in the empirical sciences, and *intrinsic*, as a source of 'certainty' in a world where skepticism was unchecked" (1992:73). "Given the *Meditations* alone," Toulmin concludes, "we may read Descartes as a pure 'foundationalist'; but, in the

Principles [*of Philosophy*], he is clearly working more as a code breaker, or 'cryptanalyst' . . . . [in an attempt] to decipher natural phenomena in terms that apply generally to phenomena he has not yet had the chance to consider" (1992:73–74).

Descartes's conception of clear and distinct ideas is central to a mechanical and mathematical conception of the world. This formulation, in fact, corresponds to the clear simplicity, the distinct accuracy, and the general ideas of Enlightenment science. Descartes assumes, as Gaukroger argues, that "the corporeal world can be characterized exhaustively in geometrical terms, and that such a characterization provides one with a clear and distinct grasp of its constituents and their behaviour." The key to this undertaking, Gaukroger continues, "is the doctrine of clear and distinct ideas, and the general aim is to use the criterion to generate indubitable veridical notions of God and the mind, and then to show that the same criterion, when applied to the corporeal world, yields a mechanist model of the corporeal world" (1995:338). At the heart of this description is the parsimony of applying "the same criterion"—that of clear and distinct ideas—to spirit and matter. In the *Meditations*, while Descartes concedes that "corporeal things exist," he adds that "they may not all exist in a way that exactly corresponds with my sensory grasp of them, for in many cases the grasp of the senses is very obscure and confused. But at least they possess all the properties which I clearly and distinctly understand, that is, all those which, viewed in general terms, are comprised within the subject-matter of pure mathematics" (1984:55). Descartes's reconception of mathematics at a level of abstraction that allowed him to equate algebra and geometry forms the basis of mathematical physics. Cassirer describes this project toward the end of *The Philosophy of the Enlightenment:* "Descartes' outline of physics, as he sketches it in his treatise *The World,* illustrates the motto: 'Give me matter, and I will build you a world.' The physicist and natural philosopher can risk such a construction, for the plan of the universe lies clearly before him in the general laws of motion. He does not have to take these laws from experience; they are of a mathematical nature and, accordingly, are contained in the fundamental rules of 'universal knowledge' (*mathesis universalis*) whose necessary truth the mind recognizes within itself" (1951:335).

In the early twentieth century Oswald Spengler argued that Cartesian mathematics is a defining feature of the Western culture (1926:74). This is important for my argument here because part of my "method" is the attempt to analogically define the mechanisms of Cartesian economics against the post-Enlightenment economics of semiotics, collaboration, and interpretation gathered together in the figure of Foucault. I should say that I

come to my readings of Descartes as a student of twentieth-century literature, culture, and experience. In fact, what has brought me to him is my
sense that an important way to understand the remarkable transformations
in Western culture that began in the second Industrial Revolution of the late
nineteenth century is to understand those transformations (that often go
under the name of twentieth-century modernism) in relation to the fulfill-
ment and exhaustion of the mechanistic worldview beginning in the mid-
seventeenth century. That fulfilment is often described, in the terms of
Descartes's eighteenth-century followers, as the "Enlightenment": like Descartes himself, his followers recurrently speak of "the light of reason." It is
my contention that both twentieth-century modernism and especially the
postmodernism I have described in Yeats, collective Bible studies, and
Mailer are better characterized in terms of "post-Enlightenment" analogical thinking, including the analogical relationships between modernism and
postmodernism examined in part 3, knowledge and disciplinarity in part 2,
and neutralization and deconstruction in part 1.

Post-Enlightenment culture supplements rather than supersedes Enlightenment modernity: it adds to the reductions of its clear and distinct
ideas and to the generalizations of its "necessary and sufficient truths" the
supplement of information and interpretation, semiotics and phenomenology. Thus, in his articulation of information theory I examine in chapter 3,
Norbert Wiener writes in the mid-twentieth century that "information is
information, not matter or energy. No materialism which does not admit
this can survive at the present day" (1961:132). Similarly, Gaukroger writes
in his study of Descartes that

> in the twentieth century, two developments have occurred which . . .
> have resulted in the two areas that Descartes had begun to abandon in
> the 1630s being pursued with a new vigour. First the question of inter-
> pretation received a new lease of life with the work of Frege, and then
> Wittgenstein and Husserl, to the extent that questions of meaning and
> interpretation came to usurp epistemology in attempts to understand
> our cognitive relation to the world. Secondly, advances in understanding
> brain functions, "artificial intelligence". . . , and the area of cognitive
> science generally revealed . . . avenues [of inquiry] that would have
> seemed a dead end to seventeenth-century thinkers . . . [governed as
> they were by] a traditional sceptically driven epistemology. (1995:7, 8)

Descartes marks this abandonment, in opposite ways, in his treatment of
force and his treatment of language, what Foucault might describe as the
power and knowledge of disciplines and semiotics examined in part 2 and

part 1 of this book.[2] In Descartes force remains a theological concept because it is difficult to distinguish in his account of force the line separating
the physical and the divine: it is precisely in his treatment of the mechanics
of force that the "mechanistic mathematical physics" of his natural philosophy and the faithfulness of his metaphysics are identified with one another
(Gaukroger 1995:269, 245). In the definition of force the double focus on
physics and metaphysics in Descartes achieves its clearest articulation: in
the concept of force, the parsimonious "atemporality" of his universalist
science and the spacious "eternity" of his religious faith seem to approach
identity. In the pre-Enlightenment understanding of medieval historiography and narrative, as Elizabeth Ermarth has argued, the meaningful distinctions in comprehending time "depend upon the contrast between time and
eternity" (1983:25). Enlightenment definitions, such as those of the followers of Descartes and Newton, homogenize time so that the opposite of time
is not another *analogical* manifestation of time—eternity—but the *logical*
absence of time, an "atemporal" essence.

   That is, when time is conceived as a logical category—Cassirer's "form
of thought" (1951:28)—to which, parsimoniously, forms of (empirical)
timeliness can be reduced, transcendental essences can be discovered, empirically, in immanent phenomena. "When time and space are conceived as
homogeneous," Ermarth argues, "—that is, the same universally—then it
becomes possible to chart both the differences and similarities in nature
which give rise to those generalizations in science and art that we call laws.
In formulating such laws no attempt is made to save the appearances. In
fact, we might say that in reducing the welter of particulars to some abstract
regularity, scientific and realistic generalizations represent an attempt to
save the essences" (1983:17–18). Atemporal "essences" replace sacred
"eternity" as the opposite to time. This reduction, I am arguing, is the

---

   2. That the comprehension of meaning in terms of both disciplinary institutions and semiotics corresponds to the descriptions of power and knowledge in
the work of Foucault—and, indeed, in much of twentieth-century modernism
(e.g., Yeats's question "Did she put on his knowledge with his power / Before
the indifferent beak could let her drop?")—is fascinating in light of Gaukroger's
argument that Descartes abandoned the exploration of both a materialist physi-
ology of brain functioning and the methodical (scientific) study of meaning in
favor of a skeptically driven epistemology. The combination of physics and
metaphysics in Descartes avoids both of these avenues of inquiry in favor of
what Michael Harrington has described (in reference to Engels) as a "mystical"
materialism that attributes "divine and providential qualities to matter itself"
(1983:80). Thus, the force and meaning I examine in relation to Foucault's
"economics" is governed by the post-Enlightenment project of rethinking the
relationships between power and knowledge.

source of the combination of physics and metaphysics in Descartes that both Gaukroger and Toulmin mention, the apprehension of analogy as identity. And, as I said, the clearest example of this combination is in Descartes's concept of force.

If Descartes's treatment of force allowed him to close the gap between the physical and the divine, then his treatment of language had the opposite effect. In Descartes language more fully than force delineates the problem that gives rise to the parsimonies of his mechanistic worldview insofar as language calls attention to the problem a mechanical worldview attempts to solve, the presence of spirit in a world wracked by enormous uncertainty, chaos, and seemingly meaningless destruction.[3] This is because such a mechanical worldview cannot accommodate the feedback and seeming "action at a distance" of communication as readily as it can accommodate physical forces even when they are conceived to originate supernaturally. Thus, in the *Discourse on Method* Descartes presents a mechanistic description of somatic life in which there is no room for the feedback of information theory: "we can certainly conceive," he writes, "of a machine so constructed that it utters words, and even utters words which correspond to bodily actions causing a change in its organs (e.g., if you touch it in one spot it asks what you want of it, if you touch it in another it cries out that you are hurting it, and so on). But it is not conceivable that such a machine should produce different arrangements of words so as to give an appropriately meaningful answer to whatever is said in its presence, as the dullest of men can do" (1985:140).

For Descartes language seems to traffic in a peculiar kind of immateriality that is very different from the materials upon which force acts. In this regard Descartes's description of language is particularly interesting. In *The World* (*Le Monde*) he writes:

> Words, as you well know, bear no resemblance to the things they signify, and yet they make us think of these things, frequently even without our paying attention to the sound of the words or to their syllables. Thus it may happen that we hear an utterance whose meaning we understand

3. As I have suggested, Toulmin makes this the center of his argument about "the hidden agenda of modernity" in *Cosmopolis*. His central argument is that Descartes's search for certainty is a powerful response to the enormous uncertainties associated with the Thirty Years' War. Gaukroger, as we will see in a moment, situates this problem in terms of the heresy of naturalism. In a very different vein Walter Benjamin describes the response in Germany to the enormous disruptions of the Thirty Years' War in *The Origin of German Tragic Drama*.

perfectly well, but afterwards we cannot say in what language it was spoken. Now if words, which signify nothing except by human convention, suffice to make us think of things to which they bear no resemblance, then why should nature not also have established some sign which would make us have the sensation of light, even if the sign contained nothing in itself which is similar to this sensation? Is it not thus that nature has established laughter and tears, to make us read joy and sadness on the faces of men? (1985:81)

The World is not an examination of discourse but a "Treatise on Light," and here, in figuring the mechanisms and apprehensions of light in terms of the functioning of discourse, Descartes is presenting an apprehension of language very different from the mechanical language he suggests in the *Discourse on Method;* and, for that matter, he is presenting an apprehension of force very different from the "microscopic mechanical processes" (Gaukroger 1995:70) of his physics. This is clear from the way Descartes continues in *The World* to describe the physical sound of words "without attending to their meaning" (1985:82) in a manner that approaches the hurtful cries of the automaton described in the *Discourse*.[4]

In the work of semiotics—the work described in part 1 of this book—the very "primal cry" of pain Descartes claims possible for an automaton has been the object of study in the context of meaning and interpretation Gaukroger mentions. Information, as we have seen, functions by means of redundancy rather than mechanical reduction, and if, as Wiener says, it *supplements* matter and energy, it does so, as Descartes suggests, with meanings and meaning-effects that are of another order of comprehension than the necessary and sufficient truths and the clear and distinct ideas of a mechanistic order. Thus, A. J. Greimas notes that "at the moment of perception" a listener "eliminates about 40 percent of the redundancies" of a message.

---

4. Wiener touches on the relationship between optics and mechanics in describing the opposition between the mechanics of Newton and the optics of Leibniz. Leibniz's interest in optics, Wiener argues, was part of his larger concern for "ideas of communication": "Leibniz's computing machines were only an offshoot of his interest in a computing language, a reasoning calculus which again was in his mind merely an extension of his idea of a complete artificial language" (1967:28). Thus, Leibniz is closer to Einstein than Newton is. "For our purposes," Wiener concludes, "the important thing is that in Einstein's work, light and matter are on an equal basis, as they had been in the writings before Newton; without the Newtonian subordination of everything else to matter and mechanics" (1967:30). In *Cybernetics* he examines the relationship between "Gestalt and Universals" (chap. 6) by focusing on the informational feedback of the sense of sight.

"Inversely," he argues, "the reception of the poetic message can be inter-preted as the valorisation of redundancies" (cited in Schleifer 1987:152) so that redundancies of sound or grammar or even semantics become meaning-ful rather than discarded. "What is common to all [poetic] phenomena," he says elsewhere,

> is the shortening of the distance between the signifier and the signified: one could say that poetic language, while remaining part of language, seeks to reachieve the "primal cry," and thus is situated midway be-tween simple articulation and a linguistic double articulation. It results in . . . [an] illusory signification of a "deep meaning," hidden and in-herent in the plane of expression. (Cited in Schleifer 1987:152–53)

In this technical linguistic description Greimas is describing the *effects* po-etry creates in terms of the economy of analogical abundance inscribed within semiotics, its assumption that language can use *anything* for its meanings and can repeatedly alternate and reconfigure its procedures. Charles Taylor calls this the "successive renewals" of language (1991), and Saussure describes this, more technically, as the arbitrary nature of the sign. I am arguing that the concept and procedures of analogical thinking best capture the sense of the repeated alternations and reconfigurations of mean-ing that semiotics studies, collaborations enact, and criticism interprets. (Pete Falovan's definition of prayer, which Mailer encounters in *The Execu-tioner's Song*, offers another version of this primal cry, as does Yeats's apostrophe and, in a different way, Jesus' parables [see Miller 1991].)

Descartes initiated a different order of understanding from semiotics and information theory, a mechanistic realm of clear and distinct ideas that are essentially atemporal and repeat themselves simply, without alteration—an order, as we have seen, that assumes the metaphysics of "self-evidence" and "intuition." By analyzing poetry in terms of its primal cry—its illusory approach to an articulation in which the opposition between meaning and matter is erased—Greimas is offering a nonmechanistic and a nonintuitive model of understanding. Such a semiotic model emphasizes, in its assump-tion of the arbitrary nature of the sign, the always-present possibilities of different, *analogical* interpretations of the "same" phenomena. In place of the reductions and simplicities of mechanistic accounts of the world, Grei-massian semiotics is presenting the overdeterminations and complexities of information theory. In this instance the primal cry of poetry—as opposed to the painful cry of Descartes's automaton—bears with it the *intelligence* of signification, even if within the overdeterminations and complexities of information theory such intelligence cannot be reduced to simple matter or force (or even force conceived as spirit), nor can it be reduced to a single meaning, atemporally true, once and for all.

Descartes does not pursue questions of meaning and interpretation in his examination of force—he does not extend ideas of force to historical, social, and institutional relations of power—but instead reiterates the great assumption governing the economy of his philosophy: the absolute separation of inert matter and spirit. (This assumption of the absolute separation of matter and spirit conditions Descartes's quasi-divine definition of the force that acts on inert matter and his wholly spiritual definition of language.)[5] In the early seventeenth century Descartes, on the Continent, was working in the context of the Continental wars of religion and politics as well as the heresy of naturalism that seemed to arise in the midst of the destructiveness of those war. Naturalism suggested that a truly supernatural deity is not necessary in explaining a whole range of events that traditionally had been explained by God (see Gaukroger 1995:148). At one extreme naturalism leads to a kind of pagan pantheism and magic, the very analogical thinking that Stanley Tambiah argues inhabits magic (1985:69–73); at the other, it suggests that traditionally supernatural events all have naturalistic explanations. Descartes opposes such naturalisms with his stark mechanistic comprehension of the world: nature is reduced to "matter," which is inert and dead, and only God can endow matter with life, spirit, and force. For Descartes such matter is simple, essentially atemporal, and self-evidently self-same and unchanging. As Gaukroger notes, for Descartes one simple "eternal truth" is "the unalterability of the past" (1995:

5. Walter Benjamin's definition of allegory, growing out of his analysis of the seventeenth-century German *Trauerspiel,* which also arose in the context of the Thirty Years' War, also marks, negatively, a species of the mechanistic materialism that Descartes is articulating in his philosophy. "Where in the symbol," Benjamin notes, "destruction is idealized and the transfigured face of nature is fleetingly revealed in the light of redemption, in allegory the observer is confronted with the *facies hippocratica* of history as a petrified, primordial landscape. Everything about history that, from the very beginning, has been untimely, sorrowful, unsuccessful, is expressed in a face—or rather in a death's head. . . . This is the heart of the allegorical way of seeing. . . . The greater the significance, the greater the subjection to death, because death digs most deeply the jagged line of demarcation between physical nature and significance" (1977:166). In a sense Descartes articulates a positive sense of this "allegory" in his equation of physical and metaphysical force in a mechanistic world in which physical nature and significance are absolutely separate. He replaces Benjamin's "face—or . . . death's head" with the "light of reason" of Enlightenment knowledge, which creates the possibility of reading "joy and sadness on the faces of men" (1985:81).

366). Modern semiotics offers an alternative to this worldview, a non-mechanistic model of understanding that emphasizes, in its assumption of the arbitrary nature of the sign, the always-present possibilities of different interpretations of the same phenomena, phenomena conceived not as *things* but as *events*. In place of the reductions and simplicities of mechanistic accounts of the world, semiotics presents the overdeterminations and complexities of information theory and of social life more generally. It offers the possibilities of *post*structuralism, *post*modernism, *post*-Enlightenment, in which present and past reconfigure and alter each other. Along with the simplicities of equations of identity it presents the complexities of assertions of similarity.

Foucauldian Economics: Semiotics and Disciplinarity

The key in Descartes's embracing the mechanics of force over the social (e.g., "historico-cultural") conventions and semiotics of language is the "matter" that Cassirer claims as the foundation of the economies of knowledge, physics, and social organization within the ethos Descartes has left us. It is precisely in terms of the matter of mechanics that our "post-Enlightenment" culture supplements rather than supersedes Enlightenment modernity: it adds to the reductions of its clear and distinct ideas and to the generalizations of its necessary and sufficient truths the supplement of information and interpretation, semiotics and disciplinarity. Thus, when Wiener asserts in the mid-twentieth century that "information is information, not matter or energy" (1961:132), he is not arguing for a kind of spiritualized information, super-added to the received materialisms of Enlightenment science in the way that spirit is added inert matter in Cartesian metaphysics; nor is he suggesting that the complications of information are to be contrasted with the (reductive) simplicities of matter and energy. Rather, he is arguing that the complications of information help us to apprehend matter and energy as *complicated* phenomena themselves. "The mechanical brain," he writes, "does not secrete thought 'as the liver does bile,' as the earlier materialists claimed, nor does it put it out in the form of energy, as the muscle puts out its activity" (1961:132). For Wiener information is not of the order of material bodies, but at the same time it is not simply immaterial either. Instead, it is on the order of an event in time that cannot be "liberated" once and for all, as Descartes had hoped, from the arbitrary errors of custom and example. (Wiener does argue, however, that it can be momentarily liberated from such historico-cultural considerations.)

Foucault's signal contribution to this conceptual transformation of post-Enlightenment thought is to assert the essentially *political* (and there-fore *historical* and *disciplinary*) nature of information, the analogy that can be apprehended between power and knowledge. Others in our century have superimposed upon information other schemas such as the "overdetermina-tions" of psychological life Freud described and Picasso depicted, the "retro-spective" analyses of quantum physics Niels Bohr and Werner Heisenberg articulated, and the "constellations" of understanding that Walter Benja-min and Ludwig Wittgenstein discussed. But, more explicitly than these others, Foucault replaces the Cartesian economy of identifiable things with a post-Enlightenment economy of similar events. Thus, as I note in the introduction, in "The Order of Discourse" Foucault attempts to define "the notion of event" that is "rarely taken into consideration by philosophers" (1981:69). He defines the event in fully anti-Cartesian ways. "Naturally," he writes,

> the event is neither substance nor accident, neither quality nor process; the event is not of the order of bodies. And yet it is not something immaterial either; it is always at the level of materiality that it takes effect, that it is effect; it has its locus and it consists in the relation, the coexistence, the dispersion, the overlapping, the accumulation, and the selection of material elements. It is not the act or the property of a body; it is produced as an effect of, and within, a dispersion of matter. Let us say that the philosophy of the event should move in the at first sight paradoxical direction of a materialism of the incorporeal. (1981:69)

If Descartes's aim were to create a spiritualism of the corporeal—to compre-hend the mechanics of the endowment of inert matter with force—then Foucault's aim is the opposite: to comprehend an economy that material-izes power.

The locus of such a economy is the event conceived, as it is conceived here, as something other than matter or energy. That something "other" is the information that Wiener describes, which, like the event in Foucault's abstract description, is neither matter nor energy. Instead, information is a mode of interacting with the world, "a name," Wiener writes, "for the content of what is exchanged with the outer world as we adjust to it, and make our adjustment felt upon it. The process of receiving and of using information is the process of our adjusting to the contingencies of the outer environment, and our living effectively within that environment" (1967:26–27). Such naming, as I suggested in the introduction following Burrell, is the activity of analogical thinking, its semanticization of logical relationships, which apprehends a whole that is greater than the (mechanical) sum of its parts. Such wholes are nominal and analogical but enact a nominalism that has purchase on the real. Thus, Wiener's name, "information," is analogous to Foucault's description of event as an "effect," a mode of "selection of material elements," a mode of apprehension that transforms a *series* of "things" and thinglike properties into a *sequence* of meaning (see Eco 1983:213; and Ricoeur 1984:x), which, I have argued, is the work of analogical thinking. Foucault makes the economy of power essentially temporal—the temporality of historical events—rather than situating power within the Enlightenment economy of knowledge that traffics in the exchange of essentially atemporal things.

It is in just such terms that Foucault defines *disciplinarity* as "nonsovereign power" (1980:105), a kind of power that is "both intentional and nonsubjective" (1990:94). In the understanding and exercise of power, Foucault describes two economies: one based upon the "Sovereign" of the monarchies of the classical period that I have already quoted at length—a version of the sovereign power of God's spiritual force in the world Descartes describes—and a second, what he describes as "a genuinely new economy of power" and "one of the great inventions of bourgeois society" that is based upon "disciplinary power" (1980:104, 105). "This [second] type of power," he writes,

> is in every aspect the antithesis of that mechanism of power which the theory of sovereignty described or sought to transcribe. The latter is linked to a form of power that is exercised over the Earth and its products, much more than over human bodies and their operations. The theory of sovereignty is something which refers to the displacement and appropriation on the part of power, not of time and labour, but of goods and wealth. . . . It enables power to be founded in the physical existence of the sovereign, but not in continuous and permanent systems of surveillance. The theory of sovereignty permits the foundation of an absolute power in the absolute expenditure of power. It does not allow for a calculation of power in terms of the minimum expenditure for the maximum return. (1980:104–5)

Sovereign power, like aristocratic sovereignty, is based upon the earth and its products; it is based upon "real estate," mercantilist wealth embodied in an economy of things. Disciplinary power, like the regime of the bourgeoisie, is based upon an economy of discourse and the "things, institutions, practices" that discourses condition and that at the same time constitute those discourses. Disciplinary dominion of the bourgeoisie is based upon events, not things, and these two orders of power—that of the sovereign and that of disciplinarity—are, as Foucault says, "so heterogeneous that they cannot possibly be reduced to each other" (1980:106).

Moreover, in the economy of disciplinarity the very sovereign subject, the *Cartesian* subject par excellence existing as an atemporal entity—Kant's "*thing* in itself"—is almost unrecognizable. "The individual," Foucault writes using the language of Descartes's mechanical universe,

> is not conceived as a sort of elementary nucleus, a primitive atom, a multiple and inert material on which power comes to fasten or against which it happens to strike, and in so doing subdues or crushes individuals. In fact, it is already one of the prime effects of power that certain bodies, certain gestures, certain discourses, certain desires, come to be identified and constituted as individuals. The individual, that is, is not the *vis-à-vis* of power; it is, I believe, one of its prime effects. The individual is an effect of power, and at the same time, or precisely to the extent to which it is that effect, it is the element of its articulation. (1980:98)

Such an effect—like the very effects we call events and meaning (meaning-effects)—is closely tied to what Foucault calls "discourse" and what I have been calling "analogies of information." Information is an effect of power, and it is precisely not reducible to an economy of *things*—an economy of matter and energy—insofar as the *timeliness* of its articulation matters.

Even a mathematician as traditional as Bertrand Russell, who pursued so vigorously the sovereign science of mathematics as the very "logic of thought" (as opposed to the discursive "rhetoric" of thought)—even Bertrand Russell finds it necessary to rethink the material *thingness* of phenomena in relation to the new science of the twentieth century. "In the old view," Russell writes in the *ABC of Relativity,*

> a piece of matter was something which survived all through time, while never being at more than one place at a given time. This way of looking at things is obviously connected with the complete separation of space and time in which people formerly believed. When we substitute space-time for space and time, we shall naturally expect to derive the physical world from constituents which are as limited in time as in space. Such constituents are what we call "events." An event does not persist and move, like the traditional piece of matter; it merely exists for its little

moment and then ceases. A piece of matter will thus be resolved into a series of events.... The whole series of these events makes up the whole history of the particle, and the particle is regarded as *being* its history, not some metaphysical entity to which the events happen. (1925:208–9)

The economy Russell is describing, like that of Foucault, is one of events and power rather than things and knowledge.

Post-Enlightenment Analogy

What is striking about this economy is the fact that, although it is unreconcil-able to the economy of sovereign things—although it is "discontinuous" with secular materiality of Enlightenment/Cartesian mechanics—it is also, at the same time, "superimposed" upon that received system (just as Cartesian mechanics is superimposed upon pre-Enlightenment sovereignty), analogous to it insofar as it "marks both the likeness and the difference in our applica-tion of words from case to case" (Bannet 1967:656). The post-Newtonian science Russell describes does not supersede Newtonian mechanics; it supple-ments it. And the economy of disciplinary events Foucault describes does not supersede the sovereignty of "real" wealth, of spectacle rather than surveil-lance, of the spiritualism of the corporeal; it superimposes itself on each of these in a gathering that, as Foucault says of Borges's list, continues "to disturb and threaten with collapse our age-old distinction between the Same and the Other" (1970:xv). What disturbs this distinction most of all, I think, is what lies at the very heart of both information and analogical thinking—namely, redundancy. Redundancy is the motor of analogy and its restless ability to always spin new refinements and never come to rest in identity, just as it is for Foucault, I believe, the motor of power and its *timely* economics.

The multiplicities of power is a central theme in Foucault, and what he says of power can be said as well of analogy's "application" of words from place to place. Thus, in *The History of Sexuality* he writes that

the analysis, made in terms of power, must not assume that the sover-eignty of the state, the form of the law, or the over-all unity of a domina-tion are given at the outset; rather, these are only the terminal forms power takes. It seems to me that power must be understood in the first instance as the multiplicity of force relations immanent in the sphere in which they operate and which constitute their own organization; as the process which, through ceaseless struggles and confrontations, transforms, strengthens, or reverses them; as the support which these force relations find in one another . . . ; and lastly, as the strategies in which they take effect. . . . The omnipresence of power: not because it has the privilege of consolidating everything under its invincible unity, but because it is produced from one moment to the next, at every point, or rather in every relation from one point to another. Power is everywhere; not because it embraces everything, but because it comes from everywhere. And "Power," insofar as it is permanent, repetitious, inert, and self-reproducing, is simply the over-all effect that emerges from all these mobilities. (1990:92–93)

In this passage Foucault is narrating the effect of the simplicity, atemporality, and positivism of a self-same "Power" (with a capital *P*), conceived as permanent, self-identical, and inert. Such a conception of Power—the very Power of Descartes's mechanistic economy of simple, timeless, positive *things*—comprehends Power as the effect of temporal events just as, in Russell, the seeming "metaphysical entity" of a particle to which events seem to happen (1925:209) is simply an effect of momentary and multiple events. Such a comprehension apprehends the abstract formalism of reductive mechanics as the semantic formalism of timely semiotics and the self-same as the postformalist recognition of similarities over time.

Just as, in Toulmin's and Gaukroger's discussions, Descartes's thinking is imbricated in the turmoil and chaos of the Thirty Years' War, so the economy of disciplinarity, of event, of timeliness altogether—the economy of analogy as I have pursued it throughout this book—responds to the remarkable abundances, goods, populations, and knowledges of the second Industrial Revolution, the transformation of industrial to finance capital at the end of the nineteenth century. The economy Foucault describes, as I argue in *Modernism and Time*, forms a "logic of abundance" that responds to overdetermined rather than necessary and sufficient truth, which semiotics teaches us to see; to the timeliness of emergent power rather than atemporal things, which the historical collaborations of knowledge and disciplines enact; and to the analysis rather than the self-evidence of event, which is the work of the analogical interpretations of criticism. Redundancies—in information, social relations, and meaning—disturb the distinction between the same and the other by making timeliness a factor in their identities so that both the same and the other can be apprehended as events as well as things. As events, they are unique but also susceptible to being gathered with and superimposed upon other events so that they only momentarily rest as self-same: an event, such as the Battle of New Orleans, can always be comprehended and constellated as an element of "another" event, the War of 1812. It is the *responsiveness* to events in time that distinguishes Saussure's linguistics of perception from the linguistics of expression in the nineteenth century and Wiener's understanding of information from the received understandings of matter and energy—understandings "received" via the mechanical materialism of the seventeenth-century Enlightenment that Descartes helped to articulate. It is *this* responsiveness that characterizes the analogical thinking of semiotic levels, institutional disciplines, and postmodern interpretation.

Foucault is responding to such abundances in the understanding, social organization, and ordinary experience of our time. Thus, he wrote in 1980, "I do not believe in the old dirges about decadence, the lack of good writers, the sterility of thought, the bleak and foreboding horizons ahead of us. I believe, on the contrary, that our problem is one of overabundance; not that we are suffering from an emptiness, but that we lack adequate means to think all this is happening" (cited in Gordon 1993:31). He articulates this response by focusing repeatedly, as he says, on "certain moments" that exist within a plethora of moments that go on and on and on. Such a response—such multiple responses—supplement Enlightenment truth so that abstract and semantic formalism, sovereign and disciplinary power, modern and postmodern apprehensions, exist, impossibly, Borgesianly, side by side. This, then, is the economy that Foucault articulates for us, the discourse of *our* Enlightenment. "We are not talking about a gesture of rejection," Foucault writes in "What Is Enlightenment?"

> We have to move beyond the outside-inside alternative; we have to be at the frontiers. Criticism indeed consists of analyzing and reflecting upon limits. But if the Kantian question was that of knowing what limits knowledge has to renounce transgressing, it seem to me that the critical question today has to be turned back into a positive one: in what is given to us as universal, necessary, obligatory, what place is occupied by whatever is singular, contingent, and the product of arbitrary constraints? (1984:45)

Such arbitrary constraints is the work of analogy, the nominalism of discourse that engages the world. And in the redundancies of meaning, disciplines, and interpretations—in language, collaboration, and interpretation—that work enacts a post-Enlightenment economy of events in analogical apprehensions of significance and value.

Bibliography

Adorno, Theodor. 1992. "Introduction to Benjamin's *Schriften.*" In *Notes to Literature,* vol. 2, trans. Shierry Weber Nicholsen, 220–32. New York: Columbia University Press.

Albright, Daniel. 1997. *Quantum Poetics: Yeats, Pound, Eliot, and the Science of Modernism.* Cambridge: Cambridge University Press.

Anderson, Chris. 1987. *Style as Argument.* Carbondale and Edwardsville: Southern Illinois University Press.

Anderson, James F. 1967. *Reflections on Analogy of Being.* The Hague: Martius Mijhoff.

Arac, Jonathan. 1989. *Critical Genealogies: Historical Situations for Postmodern Literary Study.* New York: Columbia University Press.

Attridge, Derek. 1988. *Peculiar Language.* Ithaca: Cornell University Press.

Auden, W. H. 1950. "Yeats as an Example." In *The Permanence of Yeats,* ed. James Hall and Martin Steinmann, 308–14. New York: Collier Books.

Bakhtin, M. M. 1986. *Speech Genres and Other Late Essays,* trans. Vern McGee. Austin: University of Texas Press.

[Bakhtin] / Volosinov, V. N. 1986. *Marxism and the Philosophy of Language,* trans. Ladislav Matejka and I. R. Titunik. Cambridge: Harvard University Press.

Bambach, Charles R. 1995. *Heidegger, Dilthey, and the Crisis of Historicism.* Ithaca: Cornell University Press.

Bannet, Eve Tabor. 1997. "Analogy as Translation: Wittgenstein, Derrida, and the Law of Language." *New Literary History* 28:655–72.

Barber, William. 1967. *A History of Economic Thought.* New York: Praeger.

Barthes, Roland. 1967. *Elements of Semiology,* trans. Annette Lavers and Colin Smith. Boston: Beacon Press.

———. 1973. *Mythologies,* trans. Annette Lavers. London: Granada.

———. 1977. *Image-Music-Text,* trans. Stephen Heath. London: Fontana.

Baudrillard, Jean. 1975. *The Mirror of Production,* trans. Mark Poster. St. Louis: Telos Press.

———. 1981. *For a Critique of the Political Economy of the Sign,* trans. Charles Levin. St. Louis: Telos Press.

———. 1983. *Simulations,* trans. Paul Foss, Paul Patton, and Philip Beitchman. New York: Semiotext(e).

Benjamin, Walter. 1969. *Illuminations,* trans. Harry Zohn. New York: Schocken.

———. 1977. *The Origin of German Tragic Drama*, trans. John Osborne. New York: Verso.

———. 1978. *Reflections: Essays, Aphorisms, Autobiographical Writing*, trans. Edmund Jephcott. New York: Schocken Books.

———. 1979. *One-Way Street and Other Writings*, trans. Edmund Jephcott and Kingley Shorter. London: New Left Books.

———. 1989. "N [Re the Theory of Knowledge, Theory of Progress]," trans. Leigh Hafrey and Richard Sieburth. In *Benjamin: Philosophy, Aesthetics, History*, ed. Gary Smith, 43–83. Chicago: University of Chicago Press.

Benveniste, Emile. 1977. *Problems in General Linguistics*, trans. Mary E. Meek. Coral Gables: University of Miami Press.

Bernstein, Richard J. 1983. *Beyond Objectivism and Relativism: Science, Hermeneutics, and Praxis*. Philadelphia: University of Pennsylvania Press.

Bettelheim, Bruno. 1984. *Freud and Man's Soul*. New York: Vintage Books.

Bible and Culture Collective [George Aichele, Fred Burnett, Elizabeth Castelli, Robert Fowler, David Jobling, Stephen Moore, Gary Phillips, Tina Pippin, Regina Schwartz, and Wilhelm Wuellner]. 1995. *The Postmodern Bible*. New Haven: Yale University Press.

Blaug, Mark. 1985. *Economic Theory in Retrospect*. 4th ed. Cambridge: Cambridge University Press.

Blonsky, Marshall. 1985. "Introduction: The Agony of Semiotics: Reassessing the Discipline." In *On Signs*, ed. Marshall Blonsky, xiii–lv. Baltimore: Johns Hopkins University Press.

Bohr, Niels. 1958. *Atomic Physics and Human Knowledge*. New York: John Wiley and Sons.

Brooks, Cleanth. 1947. *The Well Wrought Urn*. New York: Harvest Books.

Buck-Morss, Susan. 1977. *The Origin of Negative Dialectics: Theodor W. Adorno, Walter Benjamin, and the Frankfurt Institute*. Hassocks, Sussex: Harvester Press.

Burrell, David. 1973. *Analogy and Philosophic Language*. New Haven: Yale University Press.

Campbell, Jeremy. 1982. *Grammatical Man*. New York: Touchstone Books.

Cassirer, Ernst. 1951. *The Philosophy of the Enlightenment*, trans. Fritz Koelln and James Pettegrove. Princeton: Princeton University Press.

Cottom, Daniel. 1991. *The Abyss of Reason: Cultural Movements, Revelations, and Betrayals*. New York: Oxford University Press.

Culler, Jonathan. 1976. *Saussure*. Glasgow: Fontana.

———. 1981. *The Pursuit of Signs*. Ithaca: Cornell University Press.

Darrow, Clarence. 1971. "Touching a Terrible Tragedy." In *Studies in "An American Tragedy,"* ed. Jack Salzman, 5–9. Columbus, OH: Charles E. Merrill.

Davidson, Donald. 1974. "On the Very Idea of a Conceptual Scheme." *Proceedings of the American Philosophical Association* 47:5–20.

———. 1980. *Essays on Actions and Events*. Clarendon: Oxford University Press.

Davis, Robert Con, and Ronald Schleifer. 1991. *Criticism and Culture: The Role of Critique in Modern Literary Theory*. Essex: Longman.

Deleuze, Gilles. 1984. *Kant's Critical Philosophy,* trans. Hugh Tomlinson and Barbara Habberjam. Minneapolis: University of Minnesota Press.

De Man, Paul. 1969. "The Rhetoric of Temporality." In *Interpretation: Theory and Practice,* ed. Charles Singleton, 173–210. Baltimore: Johns Hopkins University Press.

———. 1979a. *Allegories of Reading: Figural Language in Rousseau, Nietzsche, Rilke, and Proust.* New Haven: Yale University Press.

———. 1979b. "Shelley Disfigured." In *Deconstruction and Criticism,* ed. Harold Bloom et al., 39–74. New York: Continuum.

———. 1984. "Image and Emblem in Yeats." In *The Rhetoric of Romanticism,* 145–238. New York: Columbia University Press.

———. 1986. *The Resistance to Theory.* Minneapolis: University of Minnesota Press.

Derrida, Jacques. 1976. *Of Grammatology,* trans. Gayatri Spivak. Baltimore: Johns Hopkins University Press.

———. 1978. *Writing and Difference,* trans. Alan Bass. Chicago: University of Chicago Press.

———. 1979. "Living On / Border Lines," trans. James Hulbert. In *Deconstruction and Criticism,* ed. Harold Bloom et al., 75–176. New York: Continuum Press.

———. 1981a. *Positions,* trans. Alan Bass. Chicago: University of Chicago Press.

———. 1981b. *Dissemination,* trans. Barbara Johnson. Chicago: University of Chicago Press.

———. 1982. *Margins of Philosophy,* trans. Alan Bass. Chicago: University of Chicago Press.

———. 1986. *Memoirs for Paul de Man,* trans. Cecile Lindsay, Jonathan Culler, and Eduardo Cadava. New York: Columbia University Press.

———. 1994. "The Principle of Reason: The University in the Eyes of Its Pupils," trans. Catherine Porter and Edward Morris. In *Contemporary Literary Criticism,* ed. Robert Con Davis and Ronald Schleifer, 320–40. New York: Longman.

Descartes, René. 1984 and 1985. *The Philosophical Writings,* vols. 2 and 1, trans. John Cottingham, Robert Stoothoff, and Dugald Murdoch. Cambridge: Cambridge University Press.

Dinesen, Isak. 1961. *Winter's Tales.* New York: Vintage Books.

Dreiser, Theodore. 1964. *An American Tragedy.* New York: Signet.

Eagleton, Terry. 1990. *The Ideology of the Aesthetic.* Cambridge: Blackwell.

Eco, Umberto. 1976. *A Theory of Semiotics.* Bloomington: Indiana University Press.

———. 1983. "Horns, Hooves, Insteps: Some Hypotheses on Three Types of Abduction." In *The Sign of Three: Dupin, Holmes, Peirce,* ed. Umberto Eco and Thomas Sebeok, 198–220. Bloomington: Indiana University Press.

Elam, Diane. 1994. *Deconstruction and Feminism: Ms. en Abyme.* New York: Routledge.

Eliot, T. S. 1961. *On Poetry and Poets.* New York: Noonday Press.

———. 1975. *Selected Essays,* ed. Frank Kermode. New York: Harcourt.

Ellmann, Richard. 1954. *The Identity of Yeats.* New York: Oxford University Press.

Ermarth, Elizabeth Deeds. 1983. *Realism and Consensus in the English Novel.* Princeton: Princeton University Press.

Felman, Shoshana. 1983. *The Literary Speech Act: Don Juan with J. L. Austin, or Seduction in Two Languages,* trans. Catherine Porter. Ithaca: Cornell University Press.

Feuer, Lewis. 1974. *Einstein and the Generations of Science.* New York: Basic Books.

Fish, Stanley. 1989. "Being Interdisciplinary Is So Very Hard to Do." In *Profession 89,* ed. Phyllis Frankin, 15–22. New York: Modern Language Association, 1989.

Flaubert, Gustave. 1980. *The Letters of Gustave Flaubert: 1830–1857,* ed. and trans. Francis Steegmuller. Cambridge: Harvard University Press.

Foster, Hal, ed. 1983. *The Anti-Aesthetic: Essays on Postmodern Culture.* Port Towsend, WA: Bay Press.

Foucault, Michel. 1970. *The Order of Things.* New York: Pantheon Books.

———. 1972. *The Archaeology of Knowledge,* trans. A. M. Sheridan Smith. New York: Harper.

———. 1977. "Nietzsche, Genealogy, History." In *Language, Counter-Memory, Practice,* trans. Donald Bouchard and Sherry Simon, 139–64. Ithaca: Cornell University Press.

———. 1980. *Power/Knowledge: Selected Interviews and Other Writings, 1972–1977,* ed. Colin Gordon. New York: Pantheon Books.

———. 1981. "The Order of Discourse," trans. Ian McLeod. In *Untying the Text: A Post-Structuralist Reader,* ed. Robert Young, 48–78. London: Routledge and Kegan Paul.

———. 1984. "What Is Enlightenment?" trans. Catherine Porter. In *The Foucault Reader,* ed. Paul Rainbow, 32–50. New York: Pantheon Books.

———. 1990. *The History of Sexuality,* vol. 1, trans. Robert Hurley. New York: Vintage.

———. 1994. "What Is an Author?" trans. Josué Harari. In *Contemporary Literary Criticism,* ed. Robert Con Davis and Ronald Schleifer, 342–53. New York: Longman.

Fowler, Alastair. 1982. *Kinds of Literature.* Cambridge: Harvard University Press.

Freud, Sigmund. 1963. "The Wolf Man." In *Three Case Histories.* New York: Collier Books.

Frow, John. 1986. *Marxism and Literary History.* Cambridge: Harvard University Press.

Frye, Northrop. 1994. "The Function of Criticism at the Present Time." In *Contemporary Literary Criticism,* ed. Robert Con Davis and Ronald Schleifer, 34–45. New York: Longman.

Galan, F. W. 1985. *Historic Structures: The Prague School Project, 1928–1946.* Austin: University of Texas Press.

Gardner, Howard. 1985. *The Mind's New Science: A History of the Cognitive Revolution.* New York: Basic Books.

Gaukroger, Stephen. 1995. *Descartes: An Intellectual Biography*. New York: Oxford University Press.

Geertz, Clifford. 1973. *The Interpretation of Cultures*. New York: Basic Books.

Gellner, Ernest. 1992. *Reason and Culture*. Cambridge: Blackwell.

Godzich, Wlad. 1986. "Foreword: The Tiger on the Paper Mat." In Paul de Man, *The Resistance to Theory*, ix–xviii. Minneapolis: University of Minnesota Press.

Gordon, Colin. 1993. "Question, Ethos, Event: Foucault on Kant and Enlightenment." In *Foucault's New Domains*, ed. Mike Gane and Terry Johnson, 19–35. London: Routledge.

Goux, Jean-Joseph. 1990. *Symbolic Economies: After Marx and Freud*, trans. Jennifer Curtiss Gage. Ithaca: Cornell University Press.

———. 1994. *The Coiners of Language*, trans. Jennifer Curtiss Gage. Norman: University of Oklahoma Press.

Graff, Gerald. 1987. *Professing Literature: An Institutional History*. Chicago: University of Chicago Press.

Greimas, A. J. 1983. *Structural Semantics*, trans. Daniele MacDowell, Ronald Schleifer, and Alan Velie. Lincoln: University of Nebraska Press.

———. 1989a. *On Meaning*, trans. Paul Perron and Frank Collins. Minneapolis: University of Minnesota Press.

———. 1989b. "On Meaning," trans. Paul Perron and Frank Collins. *New Literary History* 20:539–50.

Greimas, A. J., and François Rastier. 1968. "The Interaction of Semiotic Constraints." *Yale French Studies* 41:86–105.

Greimas, A. J., and J. Courtés. 1982. *Semiotics and Language: An Analytical Dictionary*, trans. Larry Crist, Daniel Patte, et al. Bloomington: Indiana University Press.

Hale, Oron. 1971. *The Great Illusion: 1900–1914*. New York: Harper Torchbooks.

Haraway, Donna. 1991. "Situated Knowledges: The Science Question in Feminism and the Privilege of Partial Perspective." In *Simians, Cyborgs, and Women*, 183–201. New York: Routledge.

Harrington, Michael. 1983. *The Politics of God's Funeral*. New York: Penguin.

Harvey, David. 1989. *The Condition of Postmodernity*. Cambridge: Blackwell.

Hayes, Carleton J. H. 1941. *A Generation of Materialism: 1871–1900*. New York: Harper Torchbooks.

Hayles, N. Katherine. 1991. "Constrained Constructivism: Locating Scientific Inquiry in the Theater of Representation." In *Interphysics: Postdisciplinary Approaches to Literature and Science*, ed. Robert Markley. *New Orleans Review* 18, no. 1: 76–85.

———. 1995. "Boundary Disputes: Homeostasis, Reflexivity, and the Foundations of Cybernetics." *Configurations* 2:441–67.

Heidegger, Martin. 1967. *What Is a Thing?* trans. W. B. Barton Jr. and Vera Deutsch. Chicago: Henry Regnery.

Heisenberg, Werner. 1952. *Philosophic Problems of Nuclear Science*, trans. F. C. Hayes. New York: Fawcett World Library.

———. 1958. *Physics and Philosophy*. New York: Harper.

Hellmann, John. 1981. *Fables of Fact: The New Journalism as New Fiction.* Urbana: University of Illinois Press.

Hirsch, E. D. 1985. "Back to History." In *Criticism in the University,* ed. Gerald Graff and Reginald Gibbons, 189–97. Evanston: Northwestern University Press.

Hjelmslev, Louis. 1961. *Prolegomena to a Theory of Language,* trans. Francis J. Whitfield. Madison: University of Wisconsin Press.

Holenstein, Elmar. 1976. *Roman Jakobson's Approach to Language,* trans. Catherine Schelbert and Tarcisius Schelbert. Bloomington: Indiana University Press.

Holyoak, Keith, and Paul Thagard. 1995. *Mental Leaps: Analogy in Creative Thought.* Cambridge: MIT Press.

Horkheimer, Max, and Theodor Adorno. 1972. *Dialectic of Enlightenment,* trans. John Cumming. New York: Seabury Press.

Howe, Irving. 1964. "Afterword." In Theodore Dreiser, *An American Tragedy,* 815–28. New York: Signet Books.

Hutcheon, Linda. 1988. *A Poetics of Postmodernism.* New York: Routledge.

———. 1989. *The Politics of Postmodernism.* New York: Routledge.

Huyssen, Andreas. 1986. *After the Great Divide: Modernism, Mass Culture, Postmodernism.* Bloomington: Indiana University Press.

Jakobson, Roman. 1962. *Selected Writings,* vol. 1. The Hague: Mouton.

———. 1971. *Selected Writings,* vol. 6. The Hague: Mouton.

———. 1987. *Language and Literature,* ed. Krystyna Pomorska and Stephen Rudy. Cambridge: Harvard University Press.

Jameson, Fredric. 1981. *The Political Unconscious.* Ithaca: Cornell University Press.

———. 1984. "Foreword." In Jean-Francois Lyotard, *The Postmodern Condition,* vii–xii. Minneapolis: University of Minnesota Press.

———. 1989. "Foreword." In A. J. Greimas, *On Meaning,* vii–xii. Minneapolis: University of Minnesota Press.

———. 1991. *Postmodernism; or, The Cultural Logic of Late Capitalism.* Durham: Duke University Press.

Jauss, Hans Robert. 1982. *Towards an Aesthetic of Reception,* trans. Timothy Bahti. Minneapolis: University of Minnesota Press.

Jay, Martin. 1993. *Downcast Eyes: The Denigration of Vision in Twentieth-Century French Thought.* Berkeley: University of California Press.

Johnson, Samuel. 1958. *Rasselas, Poems and Selected Prose,* ed. Bertrand Bronson. New York: Holt, Rinehart and Winston.

Kafka, Franz. 1974. *The Castle,* trans. Willa and Edmund Muir. New York: Schocken.

Kenner, Hugh. 1971. *The Pound Era.* Berkeley and Los Angeles: University of California Press.

———. 1973. *The Counterfeiters.* New York: Anchor Books.

Kermode, Frank. 1957. *Romantic Image.* New York: St. Martin's Press.

Kern, Stephen. 1983. *The Culture of Time and Space: 1880–1918.* Cambridge: Harvard University Press.

Kristeva, Julia. 1980. "Word, Dialogue, and Novel." In *Desire in Language,* trans. Thomas Gora, Alice Jardine, and Leon Roudiez, 64–91. New York: Columbia University Press.

———. 1984. *Revolution in Poetic Language,* trans. Margaret Waller. New York: Columbia University Press.

Kroker, Arthur, and David Cook. 1986. *The Postmodern Scene.* New York: St. Martin's Press.

Kuhn, Thomas S. 1970. *The Structure of Scientific Revolutions.* Chicago: University of Chicago Press.

———. 1977. *The Essential Tension: Selected Studies in Scientific Tradition and Change.* Chicago: University of Chicago Press.

Lacan, Jacques. 1977a. *The Four Fundamental Concepts of Psycho-Analysis,* trans. Alan Sheridan. Penguin: Hammonsworth.

———. 1977b. *Ecrits: A Selection,* trans. Alan Sheridan. New York: Norton.

Langbaum, Robert. 1975. *The Gaiety of Vision.* Chicago: University of Chicago Press.

———. 1977. *The Mysteries of Identity.* New York: Oxford University Press.

Latour, Bruno. 1986. "Visualization and Cognition: Thinking with Eyes and Hands." *Knowledge and Society: Studies in the Sociology of Culture Past and Present* 6:1–40.

———. 1987. *Science in Action.* Cambridge: Harvard University Press.

———. 1988. "A Relativistic Account of Einstein's Relativity." *Social Studies of Science* 18:3–44.

———. 1993. *We Have Never Been Modern,* trans. Catherine Porter. Cambridge: Harvard University Press.

Latour, Bruno, and Steve Woolgar. 1986. *Laboratory Life: The Construction of Scientific Facts.* Princeton: Princeton University Press.

Leatherdale, W. H. 1974. *The Role of Analogy, Model and Metaphor in Science.* New York: American Elsevier Publishing Co.

Lentriccia, Frank. 1985. "On Behalf of Theory." In *Criticism in the University,* ed. Gerald Graff and Reginald Gibbons, 105–10. Evanston: Northwestern University Press.

Lévi-Strauss, Claude. 1966. *The Savage Mind.* Chicago: University of Chicago Press.

———. 1975. *The Raw and the Cooked,* trans. John and Doreen Weightman. New York: Harper Torchbooks.

———. 1984. "Structure and Form: Reflections on a Work by Vladimir Propp," trans. Monique Layton, rev. Anatoly Liberman. In Vladimir Propp, *Theory and History of Folklore,* 167–89. Minneapolis: University of Minnesota Press.

Levitt, Norman, and Paul Gross. 1994. *Higher Superstition: The Academic Left and Its Quarrel with Science.* Baltimore: Johns Hopkins University Press.

Lyons, John. 1977. *Noam Chomsky.* New York: Penguin.

Lyotard, Jean-François. 1984. *The Postmodern Condition,* trans. Geoff Bennington and Brian Massumi. Minneapolis: University of Minnesota Press.

Mailer, Norman. 1966. *Cannibals and Christians.* New York: Dial Press.

———. 1979. *The Executioner's Song.* Boston: Little, Brown.

Markels, Julian. 1971. "Dreiser and the Plotting on Inarticulate Experience." In

Studies in "An American Tragedy," ed. Jack Salzman, 45–55. Columbus: Charles E. Merrill.

Markley, Robert. 1990. "The Rise of Nothing: Revisionist Historiography and the Narrative Structure of Eighteenth-Century Studies." *Genre* 23:77–101.

———. 1993. *Fallen Languages: Crises of Representation in Newtonian England, 1660–1740.* Ithaca: Cornell University Press.

———. 1994. "Money and Literature in the Age of Big Science." Unpublished paper presented at the annual meeting of the Society for Literature and Science, New Orleans, 47–70.

Martinet, André. 1962. *A Functional View of Language.* Oxford: Clarendon.

Marx, Karl. 1967. *Capital,* vol. 1, trans. Samuel Moore and Edward Aveling. New York: International Publishers.

McCord, Phyllis. 1986. "The Ideology of Form: The Nonfiction Novel." *Genre* 19:59–79.

McInerny, Ralph. 1996. *Aquinas and Analogy.* Washington, DC: Catholic University of America Press.

Melville, Stephen. 1986. *Philosophy beside Itself.* Minneapolis: University of Minnesota Press.

Mencken, H. L. 1971. "Dreiser in 840 Pages." In *Studies in "An American Tragedy,"* ed. Jack Salzman, 12–17. Columbus, OH: Charles E. Merrill.

Miller, J. Hillis. 1987. "Presidential Address 1986. The Triumph of Theory, the Resistance to Reading, and the Question of the Material Base." *PMLA* 102: 281–91.

———. 1991. "Parable and Performative in the Gospels and in Modern Literature." *Tropes, Parables, Performatives,* 135–50. Durham: Duke University Press.

Mink, Louis O. 1970. "History and Fiction as Modes of Comprehension." *New Literary History* 1:541–58.

Moore, Stephen. 1992. *Mark and Luke in Poststructuralist Perspectives: Jesus Begins to Write.* New Haven: Yale University Press.

Moretti, Franco. 1983. *Signs Taken for Wonders,* trans. Susan Fischer, David Forgacs, and David Miller. London: Verso Books.

Neal, Larry. 1990. *The Rise of Financial Capitalism.* Cambridge: Cambridge University Press.

Newman, Charles. 1985. *The Postmodern Aura.* Evanston: Northwestern University Press.

Nietzsche, Friedrich. 1957. *The Use and Abuse of History,* trans. Adrian Collins. Indianapolis: Bobbs-Merrill.

———. 1968. *The Will to Power,* trans. Walter Kaufmann and R. J. Hollingdale. London: Weidenfeld and Nicholson.

———. 1974. *The Gay Science,* trans. Walter Kaufmann. New York: Vintage Books.

O'Hara, Daniel. 1981. *Tragic Knowledge: Yeats's "Autobigraphy" and Hermenuetics.* New York: Columbia University Press.

———. 1987. "Yeats in Theory." In *Post-Structuralist Readings of English Poetry,* ed. Richard Machin and Christopher Norris, 349–68. Cambridge: Cambridge University Press.

Parkinson, Thomas. 1964. *W. B. Yeats: The Later Poetry.* Berkeley and Los Angeles: University of California Press.

Paulson, William. 1988. *The Noise of Culture.* Ithaca: Cornell University Press.

Peirce, Charles S. 1958. *Selected Writings.* New York: Dover Books.

Quine, Willard Van Orman. 1961. *From a Logical Point of View.* New York: Harper Torchbooks.

Readings, Bill. 1991. *Introducing Lyotard.* New York: Routledge.

Ricoeur, Paul. 1984. *Time and Narrative,* vol. 1, trans. Kathleen McLaughlin and David Pellauer. Chicago: University of Chicago Press.

———. 1985. *Time and Narrative,* vol. 2, trans. Kathleen McLaughlin and David Pellauer. Chicago: University of Chicago Press.

———. 1988. *Time and Narrative,* vol. 3, trans. Kathleen Blamey and David Pellauer. Chicago: University of Chicago Press.

Rorty, Richard. 1979. *Philosophy and the Mirror of Nature.* Princeton: Princeton University Press.

———. 1982. *Consequences of Pragmatism.* Minneapolis: University of Minnesota Press.

Ross, J. F. 1981. *Portraying Analogy.* Cambridge: Cambridge University Press.

Russell, Bertrand. 1925. *The ABC of Relativity.* New York: Harper and Brothers.

———. 1993. *Introduction to Mathematical Philosophy.* London: Routledge.

Said, Edward. 1994. "The Politics of Knowledge." In *Contemporary Literary Criticism,* ed. Robert Con Davis and Ronald Schleifer, 145–53. New York: Longman.

Saussure, Ferdinand de. 1959. *Course in General Linguistics,* trans. Wade Baskin. New York: McGraw Hill.

Schleifer, Ronald. 1985a. "The Anxiety of Allegory: De Man, Greimas, and the Problem of Referentiality." In *Rhetoric and Form: Deconstruction at Yale,* ed. Robert Con Davis and Ronald Schleifer, 215–37. Norman: University of Oklahoma Press.

———. 1985b. "The Pathway of *The Rose:* Yeats, the Lyric, and the Syntax of Symbolism." *Genre* 18:375–96.

———. 1987. *A. J. Greimas and the Nature of Meaning: Linguistics, Semiotics, and Discourse Theory.* Lincoln: University of Nebraska Press.

———. 1990. *Rhetoric and Death: The Language of Modernism and Postmodern Discourse Theory.* Urbana: University of Illinois Press.

———. 1999. " 'What Is This Thing Called Love?' Cole Porter and the Rhythms of Desire." *Criticism* 41:7–23.

———. 2000. *Modernism and Time: The Logic of Abundance in Literature, Science, and Culture, 1880–1930.* Cambridge: Cambridge University Press.

Schleifer, Ronald, Robert Con Davis, and Nancy Mergler. 1992. *Culture and Cognition: The Boundaries of Literary and Scientific Inquiry.* Ithaca: Cornell University Press.

Scott, Clive. 1976. "Symbolism, Decadence and Impressionism." In *Modernism: 1890–1930,* ed. Malcolm Bradbury and James McFarland, 206–27. Harmondsworth, UK: Penguin Books.

Sebeok, Thomas. 1986. "Review of John Poinsot, *Tractatus de Signis,* ed. and trans. John Deely." *New York Times Book Review* (30 March): 14–15.

Seidman, Steven, ed. 1994. *The Postmodern Turn: New Perspectives on Social Theory.* Cambridge: Cambridge University Press.

Sellars, Wilfrid. 1963. *Science, Perception and Reality.* London: Routledge and Kegan Paul.

Smith, Adam. 1937. *The Wealth of Nations.* New York: Modern Library.

Spengler, Oswald. 1926. *The Decline of the West,* vol. 1, trans. Charles Atkinson. New York: Alfred Knopf.

Steiner, George. 1971. *In Bluebeard's Castle.* New Haven: Yale University Press.

———. 1975. *After Babel.* New York: Oxford University Press.

———. 1989. *Real Presences.* Chicago: University of Chicago Press.

Stevens, Wallace. 1972. *The Palm at the End of the Mind,* ed. Holly Stevens. New York: Vintage.

Stocking, George. 1968. *Race, Culture, and Evolution.* New York: Free Press.

Stravinsky, Igor. 1982. *Themes and Conclusions.* Berkeley: University of California Press.

Symons, Arthur. 1958. *The Symbolist Movement in Literature.* New York: Dutton Books.

Tambiah, Stanley J. 1985. *Culture, Thought, and Social Action: An Anthropological Perspective.* Cambridge: Harvard University Press.

———. 1996. "Relations of Analogy and Identity: Toward Multiple Orientations to the World." In *Modes of Thought: Exploratons in Culture and Cognition,* ed. David Olson and Nancy Torrance, 34–52. Cambridge: Cambridge University Press.

Taylor, Charles, David Carr, and Paul Ricoeur. 1991. "Discussion: Ricoeur on Narrative." In *On Paul Ricoeur: Narrative and Interpretation,* ed. David Wood, 160–88. (Taylor's contribution appears on 174–79.) New York: Routledge.

Thomas, David Wayne. 1995. "Gödel's Theorem and Postmodern Theory." *PMLA* 110:248–61.

Tipton, Frank B., and Robert Aldrich. 1987. *An Economic and Social History of Europe, 1890–1939.* Baltimore: Johns Hopkins University Press.

Toulmin, Stephen. 1982. *Return to Cosmology: Postmodern Science and the Theology of Nature.* Berkeley: University of California Press.

———. 1992. *Cosmopolis: The Hidden Agenda of Modernity.* Chicago: University of Chicago Press.

Trubetzkoy, N. S. 1969. *Principles of Phonology,* trans. Christine Baltax. Berkeley: University of California Press.

Weber, Samuel. 1987. *Institution and Interpretation.* Minneapolis: University of Minnesota Press.

Wharton, Edith. 1968. *The Age of Innocence.* New York: Scribner's.

Whitehead, Alfred North. 1967. *Science and the Modern World.* New York: Free Press.

Wiener, Norbert. 1961. *Cybernetics.* Cambridge: MIT Press.

———. 1967. *The Human Use of Human Beings.* New York: Avon Books.

Williams, Raymond. 1958. *Culture and Society.* New York: Columbia University Press.

Wolin, Richard. 1989. "Experience and Materialism in Benjamin's *Passagen-*

werk." In *Benjamin: Philosophy, Aesthetics, History,* ed. Gary Smith, 210–27. Chicago: University of Chicago Press.

Woolgar, Steve. 1988. *Science: The Very Idea.* London and New York: Tavistock.

Yeats, W. B. 1955. *Letters,* ed. Allan Wade. New York: Macmillan.

———. 1957. *The Variorum Edition of the Poems of W. B. Yeats,* ed. Peter Allt and Russell K. Alspach. New York: Macmillan.

———. 1962. *Explorations.* New York: Macmillan.

———. 1965. *The Autobiography of W. B. Yeats.* New York: Macmillan.

———. 1968. *Essays and Introductions,* New York: Macmillan.

———. 1970. Yeats, *Uncollected Prose,* vol. 1: *First Articles and Reviews, 1886–1896,* ed. John Frayne. New York: Columbia University Press.

Index

Abundance, 93
Adorno, Theodor, 4, 182, 184
Albright, Daniel, 126n. 1, 128, 138
allegory, 149
analogy/analogical thinking, xii, 1–
  27, 34; and abundance, 90; and allegory, 154; beyond intelligence,
  155–78; and Cartesian Economics,
  179–99; and collaboration, 2–7,
  16, 24, 113, 121, 154; and comprehension, x; and conceptual schemes,
  16–24; and conjunction of semantics and syntax, 110; and constellations of wholeness, 4, 9–10, 26,
  195; and contradiction, 22, 23–24;
  and deconstruction, 64, 65–66, 69–
  70; and discourse, 16–24; and displacement, 62, 64; economy of,
  198; and equation, 2; and event,
  23; and experience, 121–22; formal
  mode of, ix–x; and Foucault, 100,
  184; and future, 121; and
  grammatology, 68–69; and history,
  121; and hypotactic discourse, 141;
  and identity, 183, 189; and
  imbrication, 113; and induction, 3;
  and information, 87, 89, 94, 194–
  95, 196; interpretative mode of, x,
  2–7, 8, 16, 24, 25–26, 155; and
  intertextuality, 155–56, 158; and
  knowledge, x, 7–16; and language,
  16; and language studies, 95; and
  law of excluded middle, 14; and levels, 24; linguistic nature of, 3, 128;
  and linguistic reciprocal presupposition, 42–43; and linguistics, 26, 69;
  and Mailer, 172, 177; and marking,
59–60; and meaning, x, 2–7; and
  metaphor, 16–17; and metonymy,
  2, 15; and modern, 128, 130, 140;
  momentary nature of, 73; motor of,
  197–98; movement of, 73, 95; and
  narrative, 11–15; and networking,
  113; and non-transcendental disembodiment, 92n. 4; operation of, 60–
  61; and parables, 141; and paradigms, 16–24; post-Enlightenment,
  179–99; postformalist mode of, ix,
  x, 25, 31, 96; and postmodern, 128,
  130–31; and postscript, 181; and
  power, 197–98; and pragmatism,
  131; and redemption of events,
  178; and redundancy, 87, 91, 197–
  98; and remembrance, 150; and responsiveness to events, 199; and
  rhetoric, 128–33; and second Industrial Revolution, 198; and semantic
  formalism, 25, 31, 59–61; and semiotics, 24, 50; and signification, 35;
  situated knowledge of, 15–16; and
  storytelling, 115–16, 150, 154; and
  Stravinsky, 137n. 2; and superimposition, 113; and Symbolism, 125–
  26; and theory, 100–101; three features of, 9–10; three modes of, x,
  2–7; and time, 25, 26; and work of
  the negative, x, 11, 16–24, 25, 73,
  175; and Yeats, 123, 133–39. *See
  also* deconstruction; information/
  information theory; interpretation;
  linguistics; meaning; post-
  Enlightenment; postmodernism;
  rhetoric; semantic formalism; semiotics; signification

theory (*continued*)
definition of, 100; Miller's definition of, 99; origin of term, 98. *See also* analogy/analogical thinking; semantics; syntax
Thirty Years' War, xi, 185, 189n. 3, 198
Thomas, David, 91–92n. 3
time/temporality, 182; and eternity, 141; and experience, 148; homogenized, 188; and information, 86; and knowledge, 116; as logical category, 188; and modernism, 142–43; Newtonian conceptions of, 3; and power, 195; problem of, 135; of semantics, 109. *See also* analogy/analogical thinking; information/information theory; knowledge; postmodernism; value
Tipton, Frank, 89–90n. 2
Todorov, Tzvetan, 38
Toulmin, Stephen, xi, 182, 184, 185, 189, 189n. 3, 198
Trubetzkoy, N. S., 43, 57, 62, 111
truth and value, 117–18

understanding, 182; Enlightenment, 184; parsimonious explanation of, 22; post-Enlightenment modes of, 122–23; postformalist, 118; Ricoeur's three modes of, 13–14; and semiotics, 193; and work of the negative, 16–17

Valéry, Paul, 116
value, x, 109, 110, 117–18; and meaning, 118; notation of, 108; and time, 118. *See also* Enlightenment

Ward, Samantha, xiii
Weber, Samuel, 100–101
West, Nancy, xiii
Wharton, Edith, 49, 156, 157, 159, 161–62, 163, 165, 166, 167, 169, 174, 176, 177, 178; *Age of Innocence,* 161, 169
Whitehead, Alfred North, 101, 102
Whitman, Walt, 167
Wiener, Norbert, 14, 22, 73, 75–76, 81, 87, 88, 89–90n. 2, 91, 92–93, 187, 190n. 4, 193, 194, 195, 199; *Cybernetics,* 14, 73, 190n. 4
Wilson, Charles, 79
Wimsatt, W. K., 97–98, 99
witnessing, x, xii, 6, 122; and seeing, 97–103
Wittgenstein, Ludwig, 2, 3–4, 11, 12, 24, 26, 60–61, 82, 181, 187, 194
Woolf, Virginia, 11, 14; *Mrs. Dalloway,* 14
Woolgar, Steve, 95, 112–14, 116
Wuellner, Wilhelm, 145

Yeats, William Butler, 6, 25, 27, 86, 121–40, 144, 155, 162, 174, 179, 187, 188n. 2; postmodern rhetoric of, 121–40